British Politics
People, Parties and Parliament

Anthony King

British Politics
People, Parties and Parliament

STUDIES IN HISTORY AND POLITICS
Under the editorial direction of Gerald E. Stearn

RUSSIA AND THE WEST FROM PETER TO KHRUSHCHEV
Edited by L. Jay Oliva, New York University

THE DEVELOPMENT OF THE COMMUNIST BLOC
Edited by Roger Pethybridge, University College, Swansea

CHURCH AND STATE IN AMERICAN HISTORY
Edited by John F. Wilson, Princeton University

BRITISH POLITICS
PEOPLE, PARTIES AND PARLIAMENT
Edited by Anthony King, University of Essex

SOLDIERS AND STATES
CIVIL-MILITARY RELATIONS IN MODERN EUROPE
Edited by David B. Ralston, Massachusetts Institute of Technology

Other volumes in preparation

STUDIES IN HISTORY AND POLITICS

British Politics
People, Parties and Parliament

Edited with an introduction by

Anthony King

University of Essex

D. C. HEATH AND COMPANY: BOSTON

Englewood · Chicago · Dallas · San Francisco · Atlanta

Table of Contents

Introduction

Political scientists in the United States have been fascinated by British politics at least since the time of Woodrow Wilson. They have studied Britain's politics more intensively than those of any other foreign nation. Equally, they have contributed more than the scholars of any other foreign country to Britain's understanding of her own politics. One need only cite the pioneering work of A. Lawrence Lowell at the beginning of this century, and the more recent studies of Samuel H. Beer, Harry Eckstein, Leon Epstein and Austin Ranney. Several of the most productive political scientists currently working in Britain are Americans.

A common language has undoubtedly helped foster this interest, and the sense of a common political heritage. Britain's status as a world power has also been a factor. But American scholars have quite clearly been attracted to the study of British politics in large part by the apparent dissimilarities between British politics and American. Whereas political life in the United States appears disorderly, fragmented, occasionally corrupt, and always in a state of rapid flux, British politics seem placid, orderly, disciplined, and responsible. Britain, by contrast with the United States, boasts a non-political civil service, tightly disciplined political parties, and a constitution which tends to promote unity in government instead of diversity. Britain moreover has managed to combine democracy with a continuing respect for civil liberties; there has never been a McCarthyite period in Britain.

Americans have reacted to the British system in ambivalent ways. Woodrow Wilson and E. E. Schattschneider wished the United States to adopt certain British institutions. Wilson admired the unity and authority which resulted from linking the executive with the legislature. Schattschneider and his colleagues on the American Political Science Association committee believed that only a British-type party system could offer an electoral choice that was both meaningful and effective. Others, like Clinton Rossiter, insist that small, relatively homogeneous Britain has little to teach America, with its continental land mass, ethnic diversity, and innumerable conflicting interests. They maintain that American institutions are uniquely adapted to American circumstances. Still others recognize the virtues of the British form of government but point out that the American system is much too well established to be changed.

This is not the place to argue the merits of these various interpretations. But it is worth noting that they all tend to take for granted what might be called the standard view of the British constitution. This view is repeated in essence in almost every textbook on the subject — British as well as American. It lays great stress on the role of the cabinet in making governmental decisions. It emphasizes the power of the government and minimizes that of backbench members of Parliament. It portrays the major political parties as monolithic entities dominated by national leaders. It draws attention to the elitist character of British society. It relegates pressure groups to a subsidiary role. This standard view certainly contains a large proportion of the truth, but the impression it leaves is of a political system curiously lacking in political life. British politics are made to seem cut-and-dried.

The reality is more complicated, and much more interesting. Indeed, the main purpose of this volume is to convey something of the color and complexity of British political life. Extracts from the writings and speeches of practicing politicians have been included, in addition to the observations of more detached political scientists and journalists. Most of the views expressed at least simplify those to be found in the standard textbooks; a few contradict them. In the "Grassroots" section, for example, it emerges that local party organizations and not the national party headquarters have almost complete control over the selection of parliamentary candidates. The section entitled "Followers and Leaders" enables the student to compare the views of Robert McKenzie, the leading British student of political parties, with those both of a prominent academic critic and of a Labour member of Parliament (at least by implication). The section on M.P.s emphasizes the influence of the backbencher.

Most of the selections deal with "politics" rather than "government." The distinction is, of course, quite arbitrary; the Oxford dictionary defines one in terms of the other. What has been attempted here is a rough division between the actual process of decision-making ("government") and the influences which shape the environment in which the decisionmaker operates ("politics"). Even so, some of the selections in this volume could equally well have been included in a volume on British government. Almost all of the selections deal with Britain's two major political parties. The neglect of the Liberals results from considerations of space, not from political prejudice. A few items—notably Sir Martin Redmayne's interviews with Norman Hunt—were chosen partly because they have appeared so far only in inaccessible periodicals and it seemed desirable to make them more permanently available. The Appendix is intended mainly for reference; the documents it contains have not been printed together anywhere else. Footnotes have been brutally deleted throughout.

Another aspect of this book should be commented on. It is the relative dearth of contributions from the so-called "behavioral" school of political science. Of the thirty selections, only four or five are behavioral in orientation. This is partly, of course, because not all subjects lend themselves to this sort of treatment. In addition, a few examples of British work of this type were omitted because they were too technical or too allusive. But the main reason is simply that in this field British work lags some distance behind American. There exists, for example, a substantial literature on voting behavior in Britain, but other aspects of political recruitment and participation have been almost wholly ignored. The parties, in particular, have not been analysed with the rigor of a Leiserson or an Eldersveld. Very few attempts have been made to apply the decision-making approach to either the parties or the government machine. The literature on communications and the formation of opinion is still meagre. Interest in the new approaches to political science has begun to develop in Britain, but the pace is still painfully slow.

What is the explanation? Lack of money undoubtedly has a great deal to do with it; political science research has not been irrigated by foundation funds in Britain to nearly the same extent as in the United States. Lack of manpower is equally important; in 1965 the total membership of the Political Studies Association of the United Kingdom numbered just over two hundred. Graduate training in political science is still in its infancy in Britain. One has also to remember that in Britain—as indeed in Europe generally—political science grew out of the study of law, philosophy, and history. In training and outlook, many teachers of political science in Europe are still primarily lawyers or philosophers or historians. The close relationship which American political science enjoys with sociology, psychology and the other social sciences has yet to be established on the other side of the Atlantic.

Perhaps, however, there is another, more fundamental reason. Andrew Hacker of Cornell University has argued that British academics are close to, and sometimes even part of, their country's "establishment." They are therefore reluctant to probe too deeply into the organization of power in British society. "To do this," Professor Hacker maintains, "would be to lay bare the motives and behavior of their own kind of people." In fact, the explanation is probably less obvious. It is not that British academics are afraid of embarrassing "their own kind of people"; it is that the motives and behavior of their kind of people seem so natural and so normal as not to require investigation. Everything is taken for granted. In this respect, British political scientists manifest the national distaste for corporate introspection which characterizes educated British society generally and distinguishes it sharply from its American counterpart. If British political scientists are ever to probe British politics in depth, they will probably have to adopt a self-consciously "foreign" perspective.

Half a century ago, A. Lawrence Lowell remarked: "A stranger who tries to search out the institutions of a foreign land is often perplexed because the people with whom he talks do not understand the difficulties that arise in his own mind." One of the chief functions of comparative government is to encourage the student to view his native country through foreigners' eyes. It is hoped that this volume will not only stimulate students in the United States but will also cause some Englishmen, at least, to look afresh at their own institutions.

Guide To Terms And Names

Alderman. Non-elected member of local government authority coopted by elected councillors.

Backbencher. M.P. not chosen by his party leader to sit on the front bench in Parliament, i.e., to be one of the party's official spokesmen.

Bevan, Aneurin. Leading left-wing Labour figure; minister 1945–1951; died 1960.

Block Vote. Vote case at Labour annual conference by total affiliated membership of trade union (on pattern of state's vote in American electoral college).

Butler, R. A. (later Lord). Conservative minister 1932–1964 except from 1945–1951; party chairman 1959–1961; defeated for party leadership in 1957, again in 1963.

By-election. Election held to fill parliamentary vacancy between general elections.

Campaign for Nuclear Disarmament (C.N.D.). Organization advocating unilateral nuclear disarmament for Britain, sometimes withdrawal from North Atlantic Treaty Organization; active in Labour Party, esp. 1959–1961.

Castle, Barbara. Left-wing member of Labour National Executive, party chairman 1959–1960; minister in Wilson government.

Central Office. National headquarters of Conservative Party in London.

Chamberlain, Joseph. Radical imperialist statesman; father of Neville; died 1914.

Commonwealth Immigrants Act. Passed by Conservative government against Labour opposition in 1961 to reduce number of Commonwealth immigrants entering Britain.

Conservative and Unionist Party. Formal name of Conservative Party; term Unionist is used mainly in Scotland, Northern Ireland.

Cousins, Frank. General secretary of Transport and General Workers' Union from 1956; supporter of Labour left; minister in Wilson government.

Crossman, R. H. S. Labour publicist of center-left views; party chairman 1961–1962; minister in Wilson government.

Daily Herald. Official Labour newspaper; ceased publication 1964.

Daily Mirror. Popular tabloid with largest daily sale in world apart from *Pravda*; generally pro-Labour.

Daily Telegraph. Conservative "quality" newspaper.

Division. Vote in Parliament; or, part of borough or county designated for parliamentary purposes (roughly equivalent to American congressional district).

Dissolution. Termination of a Parliament's life by the Monarch on the Prime Minister's advice prior to a general election.

Free Vote. Vote in Parliament on which party leaders have refrained from instructing their followers.

Foot, Michael. Left-wing Labour M.P.; author.

Frontbencher. Party leader or M.P. designated one of his party's official spokesmen in Parliament (cf. Backbencher).

Gaitskell, Hugh. Chancellor of the Exchequer 1950–1951; Labour leader 1955–1963; died 1963.

General Management Committee. Chief governing body of constituency Labour party.

Hatfield House. Residence of successive Marquisses of Salisbury.

Heath, Edward. Conservative Chief Whip 1955–1959; chief negotiator during Britain's attempt to join the European Economic Community; Secretary of State for Industry, Trade and Regional Development 1963–1964; Conservative Party leader from July 1965.

Hogg, Quintin (Lord Hailsham 1950–1963). Minister in Conservative governments 1955–1964; party chairman 1957–1959; unsuccessful contender for party leadership 1963.

Home, Sir Alec Douglas- (Earl of Home 1951–1963). Foreign Secretary 1960–1963; Conservative leader 1963–1965; Prime Minister 1963–1964.

Independent Television Authority (I.T.A.). Body appointed by government to supervise commercial television broadcasting.

Jenkins, Roy. Labour M.P., supporter of moderate wing, minister in Wilson government.

Junior Minister. Member of government not included in cabinet or of cabinet rank.

Lloyd, Selwyn. Conservative Foreign Secretary 1955–1960, Chancellor of the Exchequer from 1960 till dismissed by Macmillan (q.v.) in 1962, minister again 1963–1964.

Macleod, Iain. Conservative minister 1952–1963; party chairman 1961–1963; refused to serve under Sir Alec Douglas-Home (q.v.); editor of the *Spectator* (q.v.) 1963–1965.

Macmillan, Harold. Conservative minister 1951–1957; Foreign Secretary 1955; Chancellor of the Exchequer 1955–1957; Prime Minister 1957–1963.

Maudling, Reginald. Conservative minister 1952–1964; Chancellor of the Exchequer 1962–1964; defeated by Edward Heath (q.v.) for party leadership July 1965.

National Union of Conservative and Unionist Associations (the "National Union"). Representative extra-parliamentary organization of Conservative Party.

National Executive Committee. Governing body (subject to annual conference) of extra-parliamentary Labour party.

News of the World. Popular non-political Sunday newspaper.

Ostrogorski, Moisei. Russian author of *Democracy and the Organisation of Political Parties* (1902).

Pannell, Norman. Conservative M.P. 1955–1964; generally associated with party's right wing.

Parliamentary Committee. Executive committee of Parliamentary Labour Party in opposition; often referred to as "shadow cabinet."

Parliamentary Private Secretary (P.P.S.). M.P. acting as unpaid parliamentary assistant to minister or party leader.

Phillips, Morgan. Labour Party general secretary 1944–1961.

Powell, Enoch. Conservative minister 1957–1958; resigned 1958; again minister 1960–1963; refused to serve under Sir Alec Douglas-Home (q.v.) 1963.

Profumo, John. Conservative junior minister 1959–1963; resigned as result of Christine Keeler scandal.

Question Time. Period in House of Commons during which ministers are questioned on matters affecting their departments.

Smithers, Sir Waldron. Conservative M.P. associated with extreme right wing; died 1954.

Socialist. Term used favorably by Labour supporters to describe themselves, unfavorably by Conservatives.

Spectator. Pro-Conservative weekly review.

Standing Committees. Non-specialist House of Commons committees to which legislation is normally referred for detailed consideration.

Sunday Express. Popular pro-Conservative newspaper.

Sunday Pictorial. Popular tabloid, ceased publication 1962.

Sunday Times. Pro-Conservative "quality" newspaper (having no connection with *The Times,* q.v.).

Thomson, Lord. Newspaper proprietor; owner of television companies.

Times, The. Leading national newspaper; generally pro-Conservative; noted for its high moral tone under the editorship of Sir William Haley from 1952.

Transport House. National headquarters of Labour Party in London (also headquarters of the Transport and General Workers' Union).

Trades Union Congress. National trade union body.

Westminster. Borough of London containing Parliament, many government offices; term often used as shorthand for British political world generally.

Whip. Member of Parliament or peer charged with organizing votes of party's parliamentary supporters.

Wilson, Harold. Labour minister 1945–1951; party leader from 1963; Prime Minister from 1964.

I. Citizens and Electors

Jean Blondel

1. AN URBAN SOCIETY

Britain has had representative institutions for many hundreds of years but became a democracy only in this century. All adult males had the vote by 1918. Women over the age of 30 were enfranchised at the end of the First World War, and those between the ages of 21 and 29 in 1928. In this selection, Jean Blondel discusses one of the major factors which has conditioned the functioning of British democracy. Professor Blondel is French and naturally compares Britain with Continental countries rather than with the United States.

Britain is probably the most homogeneous of all industrial countries. It is homogeneous because it is small, but this is not the only reason, for some smaller countries, like Belgium or Switzerland, have more social diversity than Britain. Moreover, sources of diversity are also present in Britain, as is shown by the division of the United Kingdom into four countries, England, Wales, Scotland, and Northern Ireland. What makes Britain appear homogeneous is the fact that the population is not uniformly spread in these four countries but highly concentrated in a small area. In the early part of the nineteenth century, the population of England became much greater than that of the three other countries combined and a century later Southern Ireland seceded from the United Kingdom. As a result, over 80 per cent of the fifty-two million British people now live in England.

Nor is this all. Even in England, one would find more diversity if the population were uniformly spread over the 50,000 square miles from Land's End to Margate and from the Isle of Wight to Cumberland. In fact, the population is concentrated in a strip of territory of about half the total area of England. This strip, roughly 300 miles long and less than 100 miles wide, contains the main centres of population. Outside this strip, in the extreme North, in the South-West, in East Anglia, densities are lower. In the twenty-five geographical counties which form the thickly populated area, there live thirty-five million people, over 80 per cent of all Englishmen and two-thirds of the population of the British Isles.

The population is not only heavily concentrated in the centre and South-East. It also came to be agglomerated in large conurbations on a scale which has not been

From Jean Blondel, *Voters, Parties, and Leaders: the Social Fabric of British Politics* (Baltimore, Md., 1963), pp. 21–26. Reprinted by permission of the author and Penguin Books, Ltd.

1

achieved in other industrial countries. The inhabitants of the central strip do not live in small villages and medium-sized towns as does the population of Belgium or Holland. They are not scattered over the area: they crowd into huge urban areas which spread tentacles over miles of road and often come very near to joining each other. Moreover, many other large towns lack the distinctive character which cathedral towns, for instance, have. No industrial country has such a large proportion of its population concentrated in so few urban areas. While almost two-fifths of the British people live in the seven major conurbations and almost one-fifth in the largest of all, the Metropolis [London], the rural districts house a mere 20 per cent of the population. Indeed, many of those who live in "rural" districts are commuters who belong to the large centres and have simply "overspilled," by taste or necessity, into the neighbouring countryside.

This is not, of course, the only side of the picture. At the extremities of the country, in the South-West of England, in Wales, in Northern Scotland or in Northern Ireland, large towns are rare or even absent. Only 26 per cent of Welshmen live in towns of 50,000 inhabitants or more; 30 percent of the Scots live in landward areas and 45 per cent of Ulstermen in rural districts. The largest town in Cornwall has only 35,000 inhabitants and one-tenth of the total population of the county. Overall, however, large urban areas weigh much more in the social structure of Britain than they do in that of France, Italy, or even Germany. So much population and so many economic activities have been concentrated in the central part of England that the other parts have had, willy nilly, to follow the lead.

Within the central part of England the predominance of London increases the homogeneous character of the country. Germany never really had a capital; Italy has two; the supremacy of Paris has had to be imposed. London did not become the political, social, economic, cultural capital of the country as a result of a decision taken by some seventeenth- or eighteenth-century monarch. It has long been unchallenged, even though its predominance may still be resented in many parts of the provinces. Its location is such that it is within easy reach of the large majority and can easily service large masses of people. At least half the British people can go to London on business and return home on the same day. Things might have been different if, as Paris is to most Frenchmen, London had been as distant to most British people as it is to the Scots.

Hence the centralization of business, of the administration, and of the media of mass culture in the Metropolis. Hence the unique development of a national press covering all Britain daily and offering the same national news at the expense of regional and local information. Radio and television may have helped to centralize even the most diverse countries; nowhere except in Britain is it possible for the citizens of a country of fifty-two million inhabitants to go from one part of the country to another and find, as a matter of course, their favourite newspaper on their breakfast table. If a Frenchman or a German moves 200 miles, he will realize anew, every day, that he now belongs to a new community, because he will have to read a regional newspaper. An Englishman may find, while talking to his new colleagues, to his neighbours, that the accent has changed, that some customs are different; he might be treated as a "foreigner." At least one thing remains solid, and that is the mass culture which he absorbs every day.

Britain is homogeneous not only because of its conurbations and because of London. It is also homogeneous because it does not possess, like other European countries and even North America, a "peasant class," living independently from the rest of the community and having developed its own traditions.

In the first place, Britain has a small agricultural population. Agriculture diminished so rapidly in the course of the nineteenth century that, around 1930, it seemed on the point of disappearing altogether. The fall has been halted, largely because of the panic caused by the Second World War: agriculture is now well protected and it is in no danger of losing its present position in the economic life of the country. But there has been no movement of workers back to agriculture and increased production has been almost entirely due to mechanization. No large country in the world has a smaller proportion of its population working on the land. While agriculture employs one man in ten or even one man in five in other industrial countries, it only employs one man in twenty in Britain.

The agricultural community is not only smaller than elsewhere; it is different. It is much more integrated to the social structure of the nation than it is in other countries. This is because, while English agriculture was transformed by an economic revolution in the eighteenth and nineteenth centuries, the type of social revolution which took place on the land in other parts of Europe never took place in Britain. After 1789, in France and in many parts of Western Europe, agrarian reform was one of the main political battles. Tension between landlords and farmers mounted. Landlords were forced to abandon their rights in some areas; in others they voluntarily renounced them. Almost everywhere in North-Western Europe the traditional hierarchy between landlord and farmer was broken.

In Britain, at any rate in much of England, this pressure on the landlords did not materialize. In fact, the landlords were often the originators of the economic revolution of the eighteenth century. They introduced new methods. Stock raising and sheep farming were often substituted for agriculture proper. Manpower was saved and many rural workers were forced out of the land. The farmers who remained were not only probably more prosperous than their counterparts on the Continent; they also continued to accept the traditional social hierarchy of landowners, farmers, and labourers. The landed gentry succeeded in keeping, if not its privileges, at least its social status.

As a result, a *peasantry* did not develop in Britain, while it developed in many continental countries. Independent smallholders — independent, but usually not well-off — formed, and still form, a class of their own in France, as they also do, although to a more limited extent, in many parts of North-Western Europe. They also form an independent class in the United States. These peasants are at the margin of industrial societies. They are self-employed; in a sense, they might even be said to be "capitalists." But they are "capitalists" living in precarious conditions. They often distrust the "organization" of modern industrial societies and attack the State on semi-anarchistic grounds. They are sometimes ideologically radical. But their radicalism does not lead them necessarily to ally themselves with the industrial workers. . . . They often form parties. They reject the centralization which modern societies impose. They loathe the bureaucracy which is the instrument of that centralization. They have an individualistic approach to politics. In Britain, where the rural population is small, where the economic conditions under which it lives are different, where the social structure on the land has remained more traditional, these disruptive tendencies have been avoided. Society did not have to reckon with the members of the farming community as an element apart. Political parties have dealt with them as if they were engaged in an "occupation" or an "industry" like any other.

British society is therefore much more integrated than most societies on the Continent. Despite regional differences and apart from the extremities of the country which are out of reach of this uniform culture, Britain is essentially a homogeneous nation in which the major distinctions are not based on geography, but on social and economic conditions. One cannot begin to describe the structure of France, Germany, the United States or even Belgium or Switzerland, without first considering in detail profound regional differences which are sometimes as important as national characteristics. These differences cut across nation-wide social and economic problems. But, in Britain, national class differences are the main divisions of society. The British class system may be complex, although it is perhaps no more complex than the class system of other industrial countries. It may be different, as it clearly is in some of its aspects. It is, at any rate, the main line of division between the British people. One of the differences between Britain and other countries is perhaps that class divisions play a much greater part in the structure of British society simply because, elsewhere, local characteristics often unite people of all classes to an extent which is rarely attained in Britain.

Mark Abrams

2. CLASS DISTINCTIONS IN BRITAIN

Class distinctions pervade British life to a degree almost inconceivable in the United States. "England," said George Orwell, "is the most class-ridden country under the sun." Differences in class can be detected in speech, dress, manners, and even in the sports the English play (the upper classes play rugby, everybody else soccer). The country supports two educational systems: a State system for the poor and the lower-middle classes, and a private (called "public") system for the well-to-do. As might be expected, these class divisions constitute one of the major influences on voting behavior. Dr. Mark Abrams is managing director of a leading market research firm. His article was first published in 1958.

Almost three years ago I took part in a survey that tried to measure the amount of class consciousness that exists in this country. Our equipment consisted of two unlabelled black and white photographs: one was of a manual labourer in his working clothes, and the other was of a business executive, also in his working clothes. We showed these photographs to a small but representative sample of all the adult men in Britain and then asked them to try and describe each of the two men in the photographs. What social class did he belong to? How did he earn his living? How did he spend his leisure? What newspapers did he read? Was he a smoker? How much time did he spend in pubs? Was he the sort of man they would like if they met him? Were they, in fact, likely to meet such people in their everyday affairs?

Practically no-one had any hesitation in answering these questions. They took one look at the photo of the manual labourer, immediately affirmed that he was working-class and then went on to describe his way of life fluently and in detail. It was the same when we showed them the photo of the business executive; he was invariably labelled middle-class and a full account of his behaviour and interests was poured out apparently without the slightest difficulty.

The imagined life of the working-class man went something like this: He earned his living at such jobs as bricklayer, 'bus driver, farm labourer or railway porter. On weekdays he read either the *Daily Mirror* or

From Mark Abrams, "Class Distinctions in Britain," in *The Future of the Welfare State* (London, 1958), pp. 61–75. Reprinted by permission of the author and the Conservative Political Centre.

the *Daily Herald;* on Sundays he read both the *News of the World* and the *Sunday Pictorial.* There was almost complete agreement about the way he spent his leisure. His favourite recreations were said to be visiting the pub with his friends, betting, and watching football matches; fairly high up the list came "going to the pictures" and "watching television"; practically no-one thought he would spend any time visiting a theatre or reading books. Over 80 per cent. of the working-class men interviewed said that if they met the man in the photo they would probably like him very much and, in fact, that he *was* a type they often met. But only half the middle-class respondents said this was someone they might like very much and even fewer that he was a type they might meet frequently.

The imaginary portrait given us about the photograph of the middle-class man was very different; most people saw him as a doctor, a barrister, a company director or a works manager; they thought his daily paper was either the *Daily Telegraph* or *The Times* and that at the weekend he read the *Sunday Express* or the *Sunday Times.* The leisure interests attributed to him were clear-cut; well at the head came driving a car, reading books, attending the theatre, watching cricket and playing golf. Very few people saw this man spending much time going to the cinema, watching football matches or sitting in a pub with his friends. Little more than 40 per cent. of the working-class men interviewed said that if they met the man in the photograph they would probably like him very much, and only 30 per cent. felt that he was a type they met frequently. Of the middle-class men in the sample appreciably higher proportions both thought they would like him and recognised him as the sort of man they met frequently. (It should not be assumed that the above accounts of working-class life and middle-class life accord with reality; rather, they are stereotyped images.)

A second and more recent inquiry into British class awareness was part of [a] national readership survey carried out in 1956. This involved questioning 6,000 people who constituted a highly representative sample of all persons aged 16 and over in Great Britain. Each person was shown a list containing twenty-two occupational types (e.g. coal miner, doctor, railway porter, etc.) and asked: "Which of these would you describe as middle-class and which as working-class?" and "Which of those you've described as working-class comes nearest to being middle-class?"

Less than 1 per cent. of the 6,000 men and women interviewed said they were unwilling to answer these questions on the grounds that they did not perceive people as being members of a class. The other 99 per cent. participated in the labelling without any hesitation, although when dealing with *each* of the twenty-two listed types some 3 or 4 per cent. said they were unable to classify that particular type. . . .

The size of the sample used in this survey was large enough to permit separate analyses for particular sections of the sample. From these two conclusions emerged: First, not only is the total population able to recognise clearly the class labels of most of the people on our list, but the labellings given by men and women, young and old, rich and poor are practically identical. Secondly, people in particular occupations normally give themselves exactly the same social rating as that given them by the rest of the community. . . .

The readiness of society to recognise some people as solid middle-class, others as lower middle-class, and still others as working-class does not necessarily mean that they have an hierarchical ranking of these groups in their minds. To justify this claim we can turn to the survey carried out by Professor Glass and his colleagues. Here public opinion was specifically tested as to the relative social prestige of a number of occupations. Each member of the sample was shown a list of thirty occupations and asked to rank them in relation to each other according to their social standing in the community. Of Professor Glass's thirty occupations, sixteen (with minor differences in nomenclature) occurred in the [readership survey] list. Comparing the two sets of lists we find that middle-class medical officers, company directors, executive civil servants and works managers come at the top of the social prestige scale; lower middle-class farmers, school teachers, news reporters, newsagents and routine clerks come in the middle of the social prestige scale; and working-class bricklayers, coal hewers and railway porters come near the bottom of the scale of prestige.

I think, then, that we have enough evidence for concluding that we are a class society — the British people willingly grade their fellow men into class-designated groups and they regard these groups as forming a hierarchy of prestige. If this is accepted then we can turn to considering how many groups there are, the size of each of them and what are the distinctive characteristics of each class.

On the basis of [our] findings, I would suggest that we can think most profitably in terms of four social classes — the upper or solid middle class, the lower middle class, the upper working class and the lower working class — and that a first guide to the dimensions of these classes is to be found in the survey already mentioned.

In this survey interviews were carried out through the whole of 1956 with a sample of 16,000 people drawn at random from the Electoral Registers. In the course of the interview there was recorded for each respondent the precise occupation of the head of his or her household, and in the light of these occupations each respondent was given an alphabetical coding. Thus, household heads who were doctors, company directors, research scientists, senior university teachers, factory managers, headmasters, technicians with professional qualifications, etc. were designated by the letters AB. At the next level (designated C1) there were grouped teachers, junior civil servants, owners and managers of small shops, skilled clerical workers, medical auxiliaries, librarians, etc. At the third level (designated C2) came firemen, charge hands, skilled

workmen — e.g. electricians, toolmakers, cabinet makers, linotype operators — and shop assistants. Finally in the fourth group (designated DE) there were placed unskilled labourers, agricultural workers, railway porters, cleaners, etc. The findings of the survey showed that:

> 15% of all heads of households were AB — or in "solid" middle-class occupations.
> 20% of all heads of households were C1 — or lower middle-class occupations.
> 30% of all heads of households were C2 — or upper working-class occupations.
> 35% of all heads of households were DE — or lower working-class occupations.

Apart from the occupational differences between these four classes, what others are there? Perhaps the most immediately perceived one is the difference in earnings. Broadly speaking the middle-class householder has today over £1,000 a year and most of them over £1,500. In the lower middle-class the range that comprises most incomes is from £750 to £1,000. In the upper working-class it is normally from £500 to £750 and in the lower working-class usually below £10 a week.

Much greater disparities prevail when we consider, not income, but wealth. The latest Savings Survey to be published suggests that the net assets (excluding insurance policies and the value of any business owned) of the average householder in each class varies from about £10,000 in the middle class to roughly £2,000 in the lower middle class, to about £700 in the upper working class. In other words, among the 15 per cent. of middle-class householders the average wealth is at least thirty times larger than the corresponding figure among lower working-class families.

The differences in wealth and income already discussed are, of course, themselves the generators of many of the other differences in ways of living pursued by the four classes. They will, for example, generate differences in the ownership of durable consumer goods. The figures in Table 1 . . ., also taken from the readership survey, show how sharp these differences are today. In the "solid" middle-class household a telephone, a lawnmower, a car, and a television set are almost taken for granted; and in nearly 40 per cent. of these homes there is a refrigerator. In the average lower working-class home all these aids to comfortable living are very largely absent — with

one exception: the television set; this is the one item of equipment they share in common with their "betters." The hysterical tantrums indulged in by some middle-class critics of the "high-living" working classes are hardly justified by these figures.

TABLE 1   OWNERSHIP OF DURABLE CONSUMER GOODS, BY SOCIAL CLASS

Commodity	Middle class (AB) %	Lower middle class (C1) %	Upper working class (C2) %	Lower working class (DE) %
Refrigerator	39	14	6	3
Washing machine	46	29	25	14
Telephone	73	32	10	4
Lawn mower	77	55	35	21
Car	63	28	18	7
TV set	58	52	54	36

Perhaps one of the most widely discussed differences between the classes is that of educational background. Whatever may be the future achievements of the 1944 Education Act, the position in 1957 is that 60 per cent. of the people in the solid middle class enjoyed some form of full-time education

beyond the age of fifteen, while only 5 per cent. of the lower working class left school after reaching that age. The readership survey, in which all respondents were asked: "How old were you when you finished your full-time education?", provides figures in Table 2.

TABLE 2.   TERMINAL EDUCATION AGE BY SOCIAL CLASS

Terminal Education Age	Middle class (AB) %	Lower middle class (C1) %	Upper working class (C2) %	Lower working class (DE) %
19 or over	17	5	2	—
16 – 18	43	27	8	5
15 or under	40	68	90	95
Total ..	100	100	100	100

An alternative way of expressing some of these facts is as follows: Of all adults in Britain today who have enjoyed full-time education after reaching their nineteenth birthday, 60 per cent. are in the solid middle class, 25 per cent. are in the lower middle class and only 15 per cent. are in either section of the working class. Conversely, of all those who left school at fifteen or younger, only 7 per cent. are now in either of the two middle classes, and 93 per cent. are in the working class. . . .

There is one further area of class differences that I would like to discuss — voting behaviour. Here one has to proceed by in-

ference and by the use of sample surveys; both these suggest that there is a close relationship between class and Party loyalties. In the average parliamentary constituency approximately 14 per cent. of the electors belong to the solid middle class. But in constituencies where, at the 1955 General Election, the Conservative candidate obtained a majority of the combined Labour and Conservative vote, it was found (again in the survey) that the proportion of solid middle-class electors exceeded 16 per cent. Conversely, in those constituencies where the Conservative vote was less than 50 per cent. of the combined Conservative and

Labour vote, it was found that solid middle-class voters were 10 per cent. or less of the total electorate. The inference that can reasonably be drawn from the figures in Table 3 is that a high proportion of middle-class

TABLE 3.   CONSERVATIVE VOTES AND
MIDDLE-CLASS ELECTORS

Conservative vote as percentage of combined vote	Middle-class (AB) as percentage of all electors
Under 30	4.5
30–39	5.8
40–49	10.1
50–59	16.3
60–69	21.2
70 and over	26.1
All constituencies	14.4

electors is causally associated with Conservative victories and that the former produces the latter.

The other source of material that throws some light on the relationship between class and Party is the public opinion polls. Those taken round the time of the 1955 General Election suggest that in the middle classes at least 75 per cent. of those going to the polls voted Conservative; and that in the working classes over 60 per cent. of the voters chose the Labour candidate. What might be called a "normal" post-war voting situation is given in round figures in Table 4. They suggest that middle-class voters strongly appreciate the Conservatives as their Party. Working-class voters feel the same about Labour, but not so uniformly.

TABLE 4.   PARLIAMENTARY VOTING BY SOCIAL CLASS

Party	Middle class (AB) %	Lower middle class (C1) %	Upper working class (C2) %	Lower working class (DE) %
Conservative	85	70	35	30
Labour	10	25	60	65
Liberal, etc.	5	5	5	5
Total . .	100	100	100	100

R. T. McKenzie and Allan Silver

3. WORKING CLASS CONSERVATISM

It has often been pointed out that, if every worker and his wife voted Labour, the Conservatives would never win in Britain. The working classes substantially outnumber the middle classes. Yet, as Professors McKenzie and Silver show, the Conservatives have dominated British politics since the 1880s; Labour has won an absolute majority in the House of Commons on only four occasions — in 1945, in 1950, in 1964, and in 1966. How is this paradox to be explained? The following selection suggests one possible line of inquiry.

Since 1886 there have been thirteen British elections which have produced a House of Commons in which a single party held a

"working majority" of seats; and on eleven of these thirteen occasions it was the Conservative Party which found itself in this

From Robert T. McKenzie and Allan Silver, "Conservatism, Industrialism and the Working Class Tory in England" in *Transactions of the Fifth World Congress of Sociology* (1962), pp. 191–202. Reprinted by permission of the International Sociology Association, Geneva and the authors.

position. The most heavily urbanised and industrialised electorate of any democracy has only twice returned a parliament in which a party of the Left has had a working majority.

The Conservative achievement is particularly striking if it is recalled that the modern party was born (after 1832) specifically of resistance to the idea of political equality and that it was, in its beginnings, largely out of sympathy with industrialism. In addition its leadership, always drawn overwhelmingly from the upper and upper-middle classes, had faced a preponderantly working class electorate without the advantage of explicit religious support of the sort that has bolstered the Right in the preponderantly Catholic countries of continental Europe.

What accounts for the Conservatives' success in holding power alone (or in Conservative-dominated coalitions) for three-quarters of the period since Britain became a political democracy? In part the answer lies in the fragmentation of the non-Conservative vote. At the beginning of the period the Liberals split (in 1886) over Gladstone's proposals for Irish Home Rule and an important wing of the party entered what was to be a permanent alliance with the Conservatives. Meanwhile after 1900 the emergent Labour Party drained off working class support for the Liberals; and when the latter were again wracked by bitter quarrels during and after the first world war Labour was able to supplant the Liberals as the second party in the state. The Socialists, in turn, virtually fell apart in 1931; and again, twenty years later, after their only period of majority rule Labour became absorbed in internecine conflict which was to last for almost a decade. Meanwhile the Liberals, who had continued to poll a small but significant share of the electoral vote, began to regain marked public support (in by-elections at least) during the early 1960's. The Conservatives, although often deeply divided during the years since 1886, were a far more cohesive political force than their op-

ponents on the left. Undoubtedly this was a major factor in enabling them to retain their parliamentary ascendancy, even though their share of the total votes cast in elections during the period 1886–1959 was no more than 47%.

But Conservative electoral success in Britain is not solely or even primarily the consequence of the fissiparous tendencies of the British Left (or of its political ineptitude, striking though that has been). A much more important consideration is the fact that the Conservatives have been one of the most successful of all Right-wing parties in coming to terms with the political implications of industrialism and the "age of democratic revolution." . . .

Certain of the more pessimistic (and frightened) continental conservatives concluded that the answer to the problem of social disorganisation raised by the industrial and democratic revolutions lay with "the Pope and the executioner." But British Conservatives (who in any case could not rely on the Pope) were wise enough for the most part to eschew the assistance of the executioner; they perceived that the answer lay with the reinforcement of those institutions in British society which would help to maintain cohesion and strengthen consensus in that society.

The greatest of nineteenth century British Conservative leaders, Benjamin Disraeli, recognised as vividly as did his contemporary Karl Marx the existence of "the two nations" in nineteenth century industrial Britain. Disraeli and his followers rejected of course the Marxist view that this division was the inevitable precursor of a revolution out of which a new consensus would be established in a classless society. But they also rejected the view of those Liberal advocates of laissez-faire who were prepared to depend on the self-regulating mechanisms of the market automatically to produce a harmony of interests. Nor were they in the least attracted by the doctrines of Social Darwinism.

The Conservatives accepted the inevitability of the class system since they believe that it reflects the innate inequality of men. They realised however that conflict was immanent in the worker-owner relationship, and they therefore tried to redress the balance of interests when it shifted too far in the direction of the owners of industry. Hence their willingness to sponsor legislation recognising trade unions and governing the condition of work in factories. In addition they, rather than the Liberals, took the initiative in bringing the urban masses within the pale of the constitution by the first major extension of the franchise to the urban working classes in 1867. But above all else the Conservatives under Disraeli's inspiration, attempted to ally themselves with the forces of social cohesion within British society; they championed the monarchy and the system of "orders" reflected in the peerage, religion, nationalism, (and toward the end of the century, imperialism), indeed all the institutions and forces likely to eliminate domestic strife, to ensure stability and to override sectional interests.

In what was perhaps the most important address ever made by a British Conservative Leader, Disraeli, in his Crystal Palace speech in 1872 declared that the fundamental purposes of Conservatism were to maintain the institutions of the country; to uphold the empire of England; and to elevate the condition of the people.

With characteristic audacity Disraeli hereby claimed for his party a unique role as custodian of the national interests (as a contemporary Conservative publication puts it "there is no textbook of Conservatism, except the history of Britain"); but Disraeli also demonstrated the wisdom of British Conservatism by coupling with the national appeal a concern for the welfare of the masses. This programme was to prove attractive not merely to the upper strata of British society, but also to a large section of the working class which has remained unmoved by appeals to class solidarity even though, by sheer weight of electoral numbers, the working class has been in a position to control the levers of political power for the past eighty years.

From their earliest beginnings the Conservatives had been able to rely on the support of the "squirearchy" and of a large part of "the landed interests"; in addition, by the turn of the century they had become the acknowledged champions of the business community; and, with the decline of the Liberals, they were to inherit the preponderant part of the middle class vote. But these sources of electoral support would not have enabled the Conservatives to maintain their parliamentary ascendancy had they not also been able to win and retain the support of a very considerable proportion of the working class, which from 1884 onwards represented two-thirds of the electorate. It would appear that at most elections the Conservatives have won about one-third of the working class vote and that this working class element has constituted about one-half the party's total electoral support.

The phenomenon of working class Conservatism has long been a source of exasperation to the Left in Britain. After the general election of 1868, (following the passage of the Second Reform Act of 1867 which enfranchised a large proportion of the urban working class) Engels wrote to Marx:

What do you say to the elections in the factory districts? Once again the proletariat has discredited itself terribly. . . it cannot be denied that the increase of working class voters has brought the Tories more than their simple percentage increase; it has improved their relative position.

Ninety years and thirty-three elections later a considerable section of the proletariat was, in the view of the Left, still "discrediting itself terribly." After the Labour Party's ejection from office in 1951, an official party publication brooded over the failure of universal suffrage to produce the expected result:

Once the mass of the people have the vote, Socialists were convinced that Conservatism and all that it stood for would be swept away. Their victory seemed certain, for conservatism which was based on privilege and wealth was inevitably a minority creed, whereas socialism, with its appeal to social justice and economic self-interest, would recruit the big battalions of the poor and under-privileged, whom the vote would make the masters of political democracy. . . Yet it is clear that events have falsified these predictions. . . The question which must now be asked is why the fruits of universal suffrage have taken so long to ripen. How is it that so large a proportion of the electorate, many of whom are neither wealthy or privileged, have been recruited for a cause which is not their own?

One need not accept the assumptions underlying either of these quotations to recognise that working class Conservatism has been a major factor in determining the distinctive pattern of modern British politics.

The Tory Worker Today

This section of the paper provides a very brief preliminary account of some findings from research undertaken by the present writers into the nature of contemporary working class Conservative allegiance in England. A sample survey undertaken in 6 urban constituencies — in London, Manchester, Halifax and Coventry — yielded 604 working class voters, including 178 Conservatives. The research was not concerned with the social psychological mechanisms of particular voting choices, nor with the effects of an electoral campaign, but rather with the relatively enduring conditions out of which party affiliations emerge under the pressures of events, issues and propaganda.

Two kinds of approaches to the material are possible: straight-forward comparisons of working class Labour and Conservative voters, and internal analyses of the population of working class Conservatives. In the former — the comparative — procedure, we ask what characteristics are associated with the frequency with which working class electors vote Conservative. In the latter procedure, we are less interested in the frequency of working class Conservative voting, and more in the ·conditions and consequences of differences in the social

and ideological bases out of which this behavior emerges.

The most general impression one gets from a comparison of Labour and Conservative working class voters in this sample, is of a prevailing homogeneity between the two groups. There is little difference between them in terms of sex, income, or occupational skill level and only a moderate difference in terms of age. No comparable studies exist to provide a base line, but previous research does suggest that an earlier tendency for working class Conservatives to be older and have lower incomes than Labour voters is disappearing, though the Conservatives are still somewhat older.

These aggregate results conceal some diverging trends: among the lower income group, older voters more frequently vote Conservative than younger; and, while age and sex separately are either moderately related or unrelated to voting Conservative, older working class women vote Conservative with considerably more frequency than do other groups. We shall return to these findings later, in another context.

The political and social perspectives of Labour and Conservative working class voters differ where one would expect them to — with respect to objects of partisan concern like the issue of nationalization, key power sources such as the trade unions, big business and the upper classes, and the parties themselves. Yet the differences are not such as to over-ride an impression that conservative values pervade much of the urban working class, including many Labour voters. There is, for example, a widespread dislike or distrust of trade unions: more than half of the entire sample agree that unions have too much power. The unions are often perceived — even by working class Labour voters — as unduly disruptive or officious — and there is a good deal of feeling that strikes are called too frequently, despite the far lower strike rate of Britain compared to that of the United States. The organic view of society, promulgated by the great Conservative spokesmen, Burke

11

and Disraeli, finds a responsive echo in the contemporary urban working class. For such reasons, it is hard to think of working class Conservatives in Britain as normatively deviant from working class political culture; on the contrary, they seem to express aspects of a wide national consensus.

It is also difficult to think of working class Conservatives as apathetic, ignorant or alienated people—a kind of psychological *lumpen-proletariat*. Working class Conservatism cannot, apparently, be ascribed to political pathology in ways analogous to the alleged link between the "authoritarian personality" and clinical pathology. In fact, the working class Conservatives in our sample tend to be better informed than the Labour voters in terms of political knowledge; somewhat more of them (to take but one example,) knew the name of the Leader of the Labour Party. Furthermore, Conservative voters show no signs of a greater sense of political futility. In short, the Conservatives appear to be as integrated as Labour voters into the political process in contemporary Britain.

Conservative working class voters proved to be much more committed to their party in terms of a range of criteria than Labour voters. While Labour is widely perceived as more concerned with the interest of the common man, it is often perceived as more solicitous than efficacious, while the Conservatives are widely seen as more efficacious than solicitous. In short, it is widely believed that the Conservatives have a capacity to get things done—a superior executive ability—which appears to offset their lesser concern with the class interests of manual workers.

"Concern for the interests of the common man" is almost the only criterion on which Labour is consistently ranked higher than the Conservatives. With respect to foreign policy, Commonwealth relations, national prosperity, and the sense of patriotism, the Conservatives are evaluated as far superior by Tory voters, and as almost the equal of (or superior to) Labour by Labour voters. In fact, Conservative voters in the working class appear to enjoy greater congruence between voting behavior and broad perceptions of the parties than do Labour voters, who seem to be linked to Labour almost entirely in terms of class interest. In a political culture which values so highly the Burkean themes of consensus and national identity, this suggests that working class Conservatives may be under less ideological cross-pressure than Labour voters.

Let us turn, for the moment, from the comparative analysis of working class Conservative and Labour voters, to consider the population of working class Conservatives alone. Here, we can no longer rely upon the dichotomous choice situation imposed by a two-party system to provide the categories of analysis. Rather, it is necessary to develop and impose analytic categories derived from the historical origins of working class Conservatism in Britain.

Both Marx and Disraeli conceived working class Conservatism to be based on what Walter Bagehot, in *The English Constitution*, called "deference": the voluntary abnegation of power by the working class in favor of an hereditary, or quasi-hereditary elite. A reading both of Bagehot and of Conservative propaganda directed at the working class suggests the following set of definitions of "deferential" Conservatism:

1. Deferentials prefer ascribed, socially superior political leadership.
2. Deferentials prefer power to originate from the elite, rather than from the mass franchise.
3. Deferentials form and express political judgements in terms of the intrinsic characteristics of leaders, not pragmatically in terms of issues or the outcome of policy.
4. Deferentials view political outcomes benefiting the working class as indulgent or paternalistic acts by the elite, not as flowing from the machinery of government or the economy.
5. Deferentials prefer continuity to change.
6. Deferentials view the Conservative Party as more patriotic than the opposition.

We have also used a typological opposite to deference—working class Conservatives whose perspectives tend to run counter to these traditional values; these people we have called "seculars." The question then becomes: are all, or almost all, working class Conservatives deferentials—as envisioned by commentators so diversely committed as Marx, Disraeli and Bagehot; if not, what are the conditions and consequences of these two bases of working class Conservatism?

It is necessary to illustrate at least the single most important criterion used to define deference and secularism. We asked respondents to explain their choice for prime minister between two men—one of them the son of a banker and MP, a graduate of Eton and Oxford, and an officer in the Guards; the other, the son of a lorry (truck) driver who went to a grammar school, won a scholarship to a provincial university, entered the Army as a private and was promoted to officer rank. We have, then, caricatures of ascribed, elitist leadership and achieved leadership of working class origin. A few illustrative quotations will give the flavor of the distinction between deference and secularism in this criterion:

Deferential responses: [Respondent prefers son of MP.] Because he should have the brains or instincts of parents. The qualities to make a prime minister are in the breeding. When it comes to critical questions like whether the country should go to war you want someone with a good headpiece who knows what he's doing. It's born in you.

The MP's son. Breeding counts every time. I like to be set an example and have someone I can look up to. I know the other man has got a long way on his own merits, and I do admire that, but breeding shows and is most important in that position.

Secular responses: [Respondent prefers lorry (truck) driver's son.] He has struggled in life. He knows more about the working troubles of the ordinary person. Those who inherit money rarely know anything about real life. This man has proved he is clever and can achieve something without any help from others.
Either of them because it depends upon their individual ruling ability.

Using this criterion alone, it was possible to compare working class voters for the two parties. Deference is considerably more common among Conservative than Labour voters. Half the Conservatives, but only one-fifth of Labour voters, preferred the prime minister of elite social origin. It seems that deferential perspectives continue to sustain the Conservatism of very many working class voters in contemporary urban England.

Among working class Conservatives, it was possible to classify individuals on the basis of more of the six criteria defining deference and secularism. When we look for social differences between these two ideological kinds of working class Conservatives, the factors of age, sex and income that failed to discriminate—or did so decreasingly—between Labour and Conservative voters, come to life: deferentials tend strongly to be older than seculars and to have lower incomes; and there is a marked, but lesser tendency for fewer women than men to be seculars.

Insofar as youth and higher incomes are linked to postwar social change—to which women can be thought of as less exposed than men—secularism may be displacing deference as an ideological basis of working class Conservatism in Britain, although it is not possible of course to establish this conclusion by means of observations at one point in time. Moreover, the themes and motifs of traditional, hierarchical Conservatism—so richly available in British culture—may well be available for resuscitation under the impact of future events.

Some political attitudes of deferentials and seculars diverge. Seculars for example are less often unconditionally committed to the Conservative Party: almost all the deferentials, but only half the seculars, told us that they would definitely vote Conservative in an imminent, hypothetical election—a result obtained long before the pressures of the campaign, and of the necessity for choice, precipitated long-standing loyalties. There is a moderate, but consistent tendency for seculars to be more frequently "leftist" on a variety of issues and judgements. There is considerable evidence to suggest that seculars are more concerned with social mobility: many more of them than deferentials endorse a complaint that it is "too hard to get ahead in Britain." Finally, seculars seem to be more sensitized to economic deprivation: among low income working class Conservatives [but not those with high incomes], seculars are much more likely to identify with the working class than are deferentials.

Keeping in mind that deferentials are considerably older than seculars, we can now suggest why, as we have reported, low income has a conservatizing effect among older working class voters, but seems to move younger ones in the direction of Labour. Low income may be tolerated by deferential Conservatives and, indeed, be experienced as calling for increased reliance upon the traditional elite. But for seculars, low income may represent a severe strain upon their commitment to the Conservative Party—a commitment based upon pragmatic rather than traditional grounds. The political impact of low income, then, depends on the values and perspectives upon which party loyalty is based. Analogous reasoning may account for the uniquely high level of Conservative voting among older, working class women: both their age and sex combine to leave them relatively unexposed to secularization among Conservative voters; hence, they have a lessened capacity to withdraw support from the traditional elite.

We can also suggest why the classic demographic correlates of working class rightist voting—age, sex and income—do not obtain, or are decreasing, in contemporary Britain. We are, perhaps, witnessing a shift from the politicized ethos of earlier working class protest in what has been called the "post-political" age. In the earlier context, traditionalist ideologies like deference were linked, in the working class, to low income (among unskilled rural migrants from traditional backgrounds), to women [relatively insulated from change], and to the older (who had been socialized into traditional values); hence, these characteristics in turn were often linked to rightist voting. But as working class Conservatism is stabilized in Britain on the basis of ideologies appropriate to industrial culture, like secular Conservatism, the earlier empirical correlations between working class rightist voting and these demographic attributes begin to diminish.

Does this mean that something like Jacksonian, or more generally egalitarian perspectives, are emerging in the working class electorate? Not necessarily. Even in the United States, Robert Lane has suggested that inegalitarian values have important functions for the industrial working class. And, as Gabriel Almond has argued, the traditional elements in modern political culture can be seen not as deviant anachronistic or atavistic, but as serving critically important expressive and symbolic purposes. Where would this be true more strongly than in the peculiarly and triumphantly mixed political culture of Britain, in which traditional themes bear so close a relationship to the very sense of nationality?

The data contain other suggestions as to the future of deferential values in the working class electorate. For example as younger working class Conservatives appear to abandon deference—at least for the present—younger Labour voters may be moving towards deference. Thus, while proportionately more younger than older Conservatives tend to prefer the lorry (truck) driver's son as prime minister, more younger than older Labour voters prefer the candidate of elite origin. It is possible that, while secularism is "modern" for working class Conservatives, it is less so for Labour voters. It is as if deferential predispositions among working class voters for both major parties are converging towards a common level.

It may be, then, that as recent social change in working class Britain—the expanded horizons, improved education, higher income, slow erosion of class boundaries—is diluting deference among Conservatives, the greater integration of the working class into British society is confronting Labour voters with traditional themes to which they had been hostile or unexposed. These traditional themes, deference among them, may in the Britain to come begin to lose their intimate connection with the Conservative Party and become more than ever norms for the good citizen regardless of party loyalty. Indeed, the data show that the connection between deference and Conservative voting is far stronger among older than among younger workers. Thus, deference may be declining among Conservative working class voters, increasing or maintaining itself among Labour voters, and thus becoming less factional and more consensual among the working class electorate.

At the moment, however, it appears that post-war social change in urban Britain has acted less dramatically to change the frequency with which working class electors vote Conservative than to shift the social and ideological basis of working class Conservative allegiance from the older and poorer to the younger and better paid, from deferentials to seculars. The Conservative Party is well prepared by its history to cope with this change. But one hundred years after the Reform of 1867, the decline of deference among working class Conservatives sharpens the party's need to attract the increasingly prosperous descendants of the Victorian working men whom Disraeli and his followers enfranchised.

Five years after that Reform, Bagehot, fearing the domination of the "poor ignorant people," saw deference as crucial to "the happy working of a delicate experiment." As working class Conservatives come to include fewer of the poor and the deferential, the shape of the party's relationship to its working class voters remains to be clarified by time, research and the course of events.

II. *Grassroots*

A. H. Birch and H. J. Hanham

1. THE PARTIES IN GLOSSOP

Most Englishmen scarcely participate in politics, of course, beyond voting in local or national elections. Those who do take a more active part generally belong to their local Labour party, or Conservative association, or Liberal association. Like most European political parties, the parties in Britain are organized into branches with individual memberships (although Labour also allows trade unions and other organizations to affiliate on a corporate basis). The branches in particular localities are grouped together into constituency parties or associations for parliamentary purposes. The following selection describes the activities of the Conservative and Labour parties in the small town of Glossop in north Derbyshire. Glossop forms part of the High Peak parliamentary division.

During recent years it has become common to speak of British political parties as highly disciplined and centralized bodies. At the parliamentary level the discipline is apparent, and it may be natural for the observer at Westminster to regard the local branches as no more individual than platoons in a regiment. Seen from the periphery, however, the parties take on quite a different aspect. Wherever one looks in England one finds local party organizations which are self-perpetuating and self-contained, busy with their own affairs, not greatly troubled from day to day by party leaders, party bureaucracy, or even by party policy. Local parties are highly individual, conditioned more by their environment than by directives from central office, and largely independent in managing their own business. It would be unwise to be dogmatic about what their business is: sometimes it is local government, sometimes social life, sometimes personal rivalries and ambitions, often a mixture of all three. The . . . party branches in Glossop provide interesting and perhaps characteristic examples of these general truths. . . .

THE CONSERVATIVE PARTY

Formal Organization

The Glossop Conservative Association is in all but name the Conservative Club: the two titles are used indiscriminately in the

From A. H. Birch, *Small-Town Politics; a Study of Political Life in Glossop* (New York, 1959), pp. 44–53, 60–74. Reprinted by permission of the Clarendon Press, Oxford, and the authors. The section on the Conservative Party is by H. J. Hanham.

rule book, and the Association is affiliated as a club to the Association of Conservative Clubs. Most members pay their subscriptions to the club, which is expected to transfer 90 per cent. of the money so raised to the Divisional Association; others pay the Divisional Association directly, in which case 10 per cent. of their subscription is credited to the Glossop Association. There is nothing unusual about the club itself. Membership is open to anybody over the age of eighteen who "shall pledge himself to support the Leader of the Conservative Party and to abide by the Rules of the Association." There is a president, chairman, treasurer, secretary, and a committee of fifteen members — five to form a quorum — and provision is made in the constitution for the election of up to four patrons and as many vice-presidents as are willing to subscribe a guinea. Most of the routine work of the club is delegated to one or other of the sub-committees. . . .

Differentiation between the social and political activities of the club is more obvious in the appointments of a separate club Secretary and a political agent who is also sub-agent for the High Peak Association. The latter organizes the half-dozen political meetings which are held every winter and is in charge of the local electoral organization. But his real importance is derived from the fact that he represents the High Peak Association, and as such is the centre of party activities in Glossop.

The financial position of the Association is complicated by the need to maintain a large building, very little of which is in everyday use, and by the financial liabilities which its construction imposed. A considerable mortgage was raised at the time, presumably in expectation of a considerable income from letting the hall, and this has still to be paid off. This end is now in sight, but the burden is not yet cast off, and the club subscription of 10s. 6d., although sufficient to cover working costs and the redemption of the debt, leaves very little margin. Local elections are in general financed by the candidates. . . .

Membership

Party membership has different meanings for different parties and it is very difficult to say anything useful about the membership of a party which places so little emphasis on the collective role of members as does the Conservative Party. The Labour Party still clings to the idea that the party should be something like a band of comrades, a crusading movement, but the Conservatives have never adopted this attitude. They tend to look upon party associations simply as a means of bringing like-, and right-, minded people together, and prominent Conservatives not infrequently have the slenderest connexions with local organizations. For these reasons it is difficult to know what interpretation to put on the Conservative claim to some 1,000 members, including club members, in Glossop. Certainly very few of them are active, and many are behindhand with their subscriptions. Many of the leading citizens, particularly business and professional men, have little or no contact with the Conservative Club. They content themselves with voting Conservative at elections and showing which way their sympathies lie in private conversation. But it is from this group that the Conservatives, here as elsewhere, try to draw their councillors: "We try to get business men every time," was the comment of a leading party worker. . . .

A survey of the rank and file party members suggested that they are drawn from all types of occupation so as to form a pretty fair cross-section of the town's workers. The most striking characteristics of the members, as a group, are the paucity of women, not more than one-sixth of the total, and the large number of Anglicans. Only about a third of the members are not either active or nominal churchmen. The small number of women may be attributed partly to internal feuds, but it is much more obviously accounted for by the predominantly masculine character of the Conservative Club. The Anglican majority is not surprising in view of the history of the party in the town.

Leadership and Influence

The present position of the party cannot be fully understood without taking into account the peculiar difficulties which arise from the social position of its leaders. As shopkeepers and owners of small business concerns in an industrial town, they are apt to feel ill at ease in the company of the professional men, retired army officers, and country gentry who tend to dominate the party in the rest of the constituency. They feel both that the divisional leaders look down on them socially, and that these leaders are out of touch with the realities and problems of life in an industrial town. Certainly the kind of speech which a party organizer has to make in Buxton is necessarily different from the kind which would appeal to Glossopians; and as the divisional leaders live in Buxton and the surrounding countryside they tend to talk in a language to which the Glossop Conservatives cannot respond. This leads to a certain uneasiness in social relations which, combined with resentment at the location of the headquarters and some transport difficulties, discourages the Glossop delegates from attending the divisional meetings as often as they might. . . .

On the other hand, the Glossop leaders are not as respected by their own supporters as an outsider would expect. Many of the rank and file party members, as well as the working-class Conservative voters, still seem to expect the kind of leadership they had from the wealthy families who once patronized the party. They are not willing to give the party the help, financial and otherwise, that it now needs from its supporters, and their attitude seems to be that if the present leaders are not wealthy and powerful enough to run the party in the way that the Woods did, so much the worse for the present leaders.

The result of all this is not that disagreement is rife among the party leaders, but simply that the state of morale is rather low. No one is producing new ideas for activities that would attract young people to the party. The organization of election campaigns is left almost entirely to the sub-agent, who is efficient, but cannot do everything single-handed. . . .

The consequence of this state of affairs is that few young people are coming into the party and there seems no obvious reason why there should be any increase in the number of active Conservatives in the town. It is the national prestige of the party and the voter's deep-laid reluctance to change his allegiance which keep the Conservative cause alive.

Party Activities

The political activities of the Glossop Association are restricted to evening meetings in winter and the contesting of elections. Since there is no party caucus and the Conservative councillors and aldermen form a small minority, there is little party, as distinct from individual, activity on the Council.

The winter meetings are the great attraction of the year, and one of them usually outshines all the others. On this occasion the speakers are usually a junior minister [when the Conservatives are in office] and the Member. At other meetings the Member makes a short address and the local leaders are given an opportunity for a formal or informal speech on local issues or about their grievances. About fifty people usually attend these meetings, which are informal and are held near the bar in the Conservative Club. However, apart from providing a home for party functions, it cannot be said that the club itself is noticeably political. . . .

THE LABOUR PARTY

Formal Organization

The Labour Party, like the other two parties, is handicapped in its organization by the scattered nature of the High Peak Division and the poor communications

18

within it. Because the Division is a difficult and expensive one to organize, the Glossop Party gets little, except during a general election, in return for the sizeable contributions it makes to the revenue of the Divisional Party. However, there is none of the tension between the Borough Party and the Divisional Party that affects the Conservatives: the Glossop Labour Party is the second strongest borough party in the division, and the meetings of the Divisional Management Committee rotate between five centres of which Glossop is one. The part-time agent for the division visits Glossop fairly frequently and is on good terms with the leaders of the Glossop Party.

Within the Borough of Glossop there were formerly two party branches, one at Glossop and one at Hadfield, but in 1934 the national rules of the Labour Party were changed so that it became no longer possible for a single borough within a division to have more than one branch. Under the new rules a Ward Group should be organized in each ward, and the General Committee of the Borough Branch should consist largely of delegates from the Ward Groups. The Hadfield Branch was wound up in consequence of this change, but the Glossop Labour Party has never organized Ward Groups. As the members in the other two wards all live within ten or fifteen minutes' walk of the Labour Club, this is understandable, but Hadfield is too far away for members to get to the club except by bus, and membership in the Hadfield Ward languishes accordingly.

The Labour Club, which is the headquarters of the party, is a small terraced house near the centre of the town. The back parlour has been converted into a bar, with a dart-board and tables at which members sometimes play dominoes, and the front and upstairs rooms are used for meetings. No distinction is drawn between club membership and party membership, and subscriptions are paid by members when they visit the club so that the party has no need to send workers from house to house to collect dues. Enough money is made by

the sale of drinks to pay all the expenses of the club, including the wages of the steward. As party meetings are held free of charge on club premises, and as the club provides a convenient focus for the organization of money-raising activities like jumble sales, the party gains a certain amount of financial benefit from the existence of the club.

Whether the club is helpful to the party politically is, however, a matter of some dispute. Its main disadvantage is simply that it obviates the need for the party to organize the collection of dues. The establishment of a team of dues collectors, who call regularly on members, gain experience in canvassing, and get to know the residents of their street or area, is an important step in the organization of any party branch. . . . It is significant that in Buxton, where there is a population of similar size but no Labour Club, the Labour Party has established teams of dues collectors, has organized a Ward Committee in each ward, and now has nearly three times as many members as the Glossop Party. A further disadvantage of the club, it is said, is that it emphasizes the social rather than the political aspects of party membership. Too much should not be made of this, however, as other studies of Labour Party organization have shown that in any case only a small proportion of members are seriously interested in political activity. . . .

The finances of the Glossop Labour Party can be simply described. Each member pays an annual subscription of 6s., of which 2s. 9d. goes to the Divisional Party, 6d. to Transport House, and the remaining 2s. 9d. is kept by Glossop. The only other sources of revenue are the donations which municipal candidates and trade-union branches make to the municipal election fund and the grants which the Entertainments Committee of the Labour Club makes to the party. The money for these grants is raised partly by social activities like whist drives and raffles which are organized by the Entertainments Committee. . . .

This account of the organization of the party would not be complete without some discussion of the position of the Divisional Party. As has been said, the geography of the High Peak Division makes it a very difficult one to organize, and this difficulty is increased in the case of the Labour Party by a perennial shortage of money and the knowledge that electoral success is an eventual hope rather than an immediate prospect. However, the divisional agent is a lively and energetic man who does a good deal to overcome these difficulties, even though he has to combine the task with a full-time job on the railway, the duties of branch secretary of the N.U.R., and membership of an urban district council.

The agent's main functions are to extract subscriptions from the branches for the divisional campaign fund, to organize meetings in co-operation with the branches, and to take charge of the campaign during a parliamentary election. The budget on which he has to work is fairly small, and in the year 1952–3 he overspent by about £50 which came out of his own pocket but was subsequently repaid. . . . [A] total revenue of a little over £400 puts the party at a considerable disadvantage compared with the Conservatives, and they are slightly worse off than the much smaller Liberal Party. However, the adoption in 1952 of a candidate sponsored by the Amalgamated Engineering Union has somewhat improved the party's financial position, as the A.E.U. now makes an annual grant towards the agent's expenses which, although not large, is sufficient to relieve the immediate pressure. More important, the A.E.U. has guaranteed to pay the greater part of the cost of the election campaign, and this made a considerable difference in 1955. . . .

Membership

During the past three years the number of members has remained fairly constant at between 160 and 180, and the turnover appears to be small. The members are drawn from all age groups in a way that reflects the age distribution of the electorate, and about one-third of them are women. The Labour Party has thus been considerably more successful in attracting women members than the Conservative Party, less than a fifth of whose members are women, but not as successful as the Liberal Party, in which the sexes are about equally represented.

Most of the members are industrial workers and members of their families, and when we interviewed a sample of the rank-and-file members we found that they were drawn from the various types of occupation in roughly the same proportions as the whole body of Labour voters: about three-quarters of them are industrial workers or their dependants and the remainder work in shops or offices. The people from the professional and managerial groups who vote Labour tend not to join the party unless they are seriously interested in political work. There are only a handful of them among the rank-and-file members, but they play a prominent part in the leadership of the party. Of the nine Labour councillors in 1953–4, four were engaged in professional and managerial occupations.

Analysis of the religious affiliations of members shows that about half of them are Nonconformists, about a quarter of them are Roman Catholics, and the rest are either inactive Anglicans or not religious: there are very few active Anglicans in the Party.

Leadership and Influence

The leading members of the party are by no means united on questions of policy and organization, and, as is usually the case, the formal organization of the party is a very poor guide to the distribution of influence. The most influential member is not on the Executive Committee, while the chairman, although a popular and energetic man, has very little influence on decisions. Our observations of party activities over a period of twelve months made it clear that there are three distinct groups which compete for influence, to which we shall give the convenient, if not precisely accurate, labels of the "older" group, the younger "moderate" group, and the "left-wing" group. . . .

The main issues of controversy between these groups relate to the organization and tactics of the party rather than to questions of policy. . . . The older group believe that they have more influence on the Council by collaborating with other councillors, particularly Liberals, than they could have by adopting a strict party line; they believe that councillors should be free to speak and vote as they please rather than be tied to the decisions of a party caucus; they think that it is usually better to nominate one candidate in each ward, and concentrate all efforts on his campaign, than to nominate two and run the risk of the Labour votes being split so that neither of them is successful. The left-wing group hold the opposite view on each of these matters, and while some of them admit that the personal influence of the older Labour members may owe a good deal to their freedom from strict party rules, they add that this is procured at the cost of failing to build up an active and efficient party organization which might one day secure a majority over both the other parties on the Council.

This disagreement came to a head over the proposal made in 1952 to adopt the Standing Orders which the Labour Party prescribes for its branches, and which would bind Council members to decisions taken at a caucus meeting prior to each Council meeting, with representatives of the local party present. In 1952 a motion that this procedure be adopted was put to the Executive Committee by two members of the "left-wing" group and accepted by a majority vote. The chairman and one other member of the committee (and of the left-wing group) were accordingly appointed to attend meetings of the Labour Group on the Council as observers, with the right to speak and the duty of reporting back to the committee on the activities of the group.

However, when the two observers turned up at the next meeting of the Group they were refused admission. The Labour councillors, it seems, were agreed both on the desirability of their being free to disagree in Council and on the undesirability of their meetings being "observed" by representatives of the party Executive.

The party chairman was naturally somewhat annoyed by being locked out in this way, and at the next meeting of the Executive he moved that the issue should be referred either to the Divisional Executive or to the North-West Regional organizer of the party. However, one of the "moderate" group immediately threatened that if this were done he and at least one other councillor would resign, and after a rather heated discussion it was eventually decided to discuss the matter at a full party meeting, at which the divisional agent would be invited to take the chair. At this meeting four members of the "left-wing" group spoke in favour of keeping to the Standing Orders which had just been adopted and four councillors opposed this course, including the two most influential members of the "older" group, neither of whom was on the Executive. The meeting decided to reverse the decision of the Executive and continue as before.

This incident demonstrates very clearly that the distribution of power within the party is determined by the relations between groups of members rather than by the formal organization. The left-wing group included nearly all the officers of the party but they had very little influence over policy; the leading members of the older group were not even on the Executive but, when it came to a showdown, they carried the day. The members of the moderate group often differ from the older group on matters of Council policy, but generally support them on matters of party organization and strategy, as they did on this occasion. . . .

Party Activities

The activities of the Labour Party may be considered under a number of heads: the discussion of party policy; the propagation of policy; the nomination of candidates for elective office; the conduct of election campaigns; and the activities of Labour members of the Council.

In practice there are hardly any organized discussions of general policy within the party. There are no ward groups, there are no general meetings of members except the Annual General Meeting and the very infrequent special meetings which are called to discuss some particular problem of party organization, and there is no General Management Committee. The Executive Committee meet once a month and discuss local issues which have arisen: for instance at one meeting they considered a complaint made by the Trades Council that unpleasant fumes were being emitted by a chemical works, and asked a Labour councillor who was chairman of the Health Committee to report on this. The Executive Committee also deal with the choice of candidates and with the organization of election campaigns, but they do not discuss questions of national policy and they only rarely discuss questions of local policy such as the Council's housing programme or the problem of attracting overspill population. Matters like this are normally left for members of the Labour Group on the Council to deal with. . . .

The Glossop Party does not propagate Labour policies much more than it discusses them. Public meetings are occasionally held at which well-known Members of Parliament expound the party's programme, but there is rarely more than one of these each year. In addition, the candidate for the High Peak has recently adopted the practice of visiting Glossop every month or two and holding a series of short street-corner meetings with the aid of a loud-speaker van. With these exceptions, public meetings are held only during election campaigns. . . .

The party helps its candidates in municipal elections mainly by putting out publicity, but this is done on a much smaller scale than is usual in cities. Instead of an election address for each candidate there is normally a simple pamphlet mentioning all the Labour candidates in Glossop. . . . The campaign does not make much of a stir; the party's efforts probably make little difference to the result; it is the activities and personal qualities of the candidates that decide the issue.

In national elections the circumstances are very different. Most people have a fixed allegiance to one party and most of those who do not have a fixed allegiance make up their minds how to vote in any particular election some time before the campaign begins. Practically everyone sees the election as a contest between the national parties rather than as one between individual candidates, and the personalities of the candidates have very little effect on the way people vote. In these circumstances the local campaign that is waged by the parties has — in the High Peak as in most other constituencies — something of the character of a ritual, which has to be gone through but seldom makes any real difference to the result. It is, however, a ritual to which a great deal of importance is attached. The Labour Party spends between two and three times as much money on a parliamentary election in Glossop as on a municipal election, notwithstanding the fact that the campaign clearly has less influence on the voters in the former case than it has, or might have, in the latter. The techniques adopted are substantially the same as those used in constituencies up and down the country, and need not be described in detail. . . .*

*See the selection beginning on page 101. [Editor's note]

R. L. Leonard

2. SELECTING CANDIDATES

A journalist once described the process of candidate selection as "the secret garden of British politics." There are no primary elections in Britain, and all of the political parties regard the selection of parliamentary candidates as their own private affair. Yet the process of selection is important. It determines the caliber of the men and women who will govern Britain, particularly since most seats are safe seats. It also constitutes one of the few areas of real autonomy remaining to local associations. Contrary to widespread belief, the Conservative and Labour national headquarters can make suggestions to the constituency parties, but they cannot dictate to them. R. L. Leonard was himself a parliamentary candidate in 1955.

The procedures of the three main political parties for selecting candidates differ in a number of important details, but are basically similar. In each case the selection is the responsibility of the local constituency party and the influence of the party headquarters is relatively minor.

A pamphlet published by the Conservative Central Office for the guidance of local associations states: "Subject to certain simple Party rules each association has complete freedom to select the man or woman of its choice." There are well-established procedures within the Conservative Party which limit, however, the degree of local variation in methods of selection.

The Executive Council of a Conservative association wishing to select a new candidate appoints a selection committee, usually of about six members, who would be amongst the most influential and senior members of the association. The Chairman of the association is invariably included unless, which is not infrequently the case, he has ambitions to be selected himself. The purpose of the selection committee is to consider all the possible aspirants for the candidature and reduce them to a small number from which the Executive Council may make its choice.

The constituency chairman is expected to obtain from the Central Office a list of names of suitable people, together with biographical details. One of the vice-chairmen of the National Union, assisted by the Standing Advisory Committee on Candidates, is responsible for maintaining an official list of approved potential candidates from among whom a number of names would be sent. Any member of the Conservative Party may apply to be included on the official list, and he is then interviewed by the Vice-Chairman or by members of the Standing Advisory Committee, and, if approved, his name is added to the list.

Together with the names obtained from Central Office, the selection committee considers any members of the constituency association who have expressed an interest in the candidature and also the names of Conservatives who may have written asking to be considered. If it is a safe Conservative seat there may be a large number

From R. L. Leonard, *Guide to the General Election* (London, 1964), pp. 85–94. Reprinted by permission of Pan Books, Ltd.

of these and it is not uncommon for a selection committee to have over a hundred names from which to choose.

The selection committee quickly whittle this number down to about seven or eight, and in the case of a safe seat few of the applicants would have much chance of surviving to this stage unless they were nationally known figures, were obviously extremely well qualified or were personally known to a member of the selection committee.

The seven or eight people chosen are invited to attend to be interviewed by the selection committee which then chooses normally two or three names from whom the Executive Council may make its final choice. Occasionally, however, when the selection committee decide, in the words of the Central Office pamphlet, that "a candidate is available whose record is so distinguished and whose qualifications are so outstanding that his adoption is practically a foregone conclusion" only one name is put forward to the Executive Council.

Before this stage is reached the names of any of the surviving nominees who are not included on the approved Central Office list are submitted to the Standing Advisory Committee for endorsement. If endorsement is refused and the constituency proceeds to select a nominee in spite of this, he is not regarded as an official party candidate at the ensuing election. Cases of an association selecting a candidate who has not been previously approved, are, however, extremely rare.

The nominees put forward by the selection committee attend a selection conference of the Executive Council. Each makes a short speech (normally limited to a period varying between 10 and 30 minutes) and answers questions put to him from the floor. A secret ballot is then held to choose who will be the candidate. There is no provision in the party rules as to the conduct of this ballot. It is possible for the nominee leading on the first ballot to be chosen forthwith, even though only a minority may have voted for him. It is far more usual, however, for an exhaustive ballot to be held, with the bottom candidate falling out if no overall majority is obtained on the first ballot.

The Executive Council's choice is submitted for approval to a general meeting of the whole association. This is normally a formality, but there have been occasions in which the Executive Council's choice has been challenged at this stage and another name substituted.

Money nowadays plays no significant part in the selection of Conservative candidates. This has not always been so. Up till 1948 it was very common for Conservative candidates to defray the whole of their election expenses and in addition to pay a large annual subscription to the constituency association. Consequently wealth was a prerequisite for potential Conservative Members, with very few exceptions.

The shock of defeat in 1945, however, led to a comprehensive reappraisal of the organisation of the Conservative Party following the report of a Committee presided over by Sir David Maxwell Fyfe (now Lord Kilmuir). Its recommendations, which were accepted by the party, have fundamentally altered the financial relationship between Conservative MPs and candidates and their constituency associations. Under the new rules a Conservative candidate is precluded from making any contribution whatever towards the election expenses, other than his personal expenses. The maximum contribution which he may make to his association is £25 a year as a candidate, and £50 a year as an MP. In no circumstances, state the Party rules, may the payment of a subscription be made a condition of adoption.

There can be no doubt that the new rules are substantially adhered to, and the result has been that a large number of Conservative candidates without private means have been selected in the period since 1948. Whilst wealth is no handicap in the Conservative Party and rich men are often selected as candidates, money no longer plays a direct part in their selection.

The Labour Party's selection procedure is laid down in more detail in the party rules, and it is complicated by the existence of two classes of membership, individual and affiliated (principally trade unions) When a constituency party decides to select a candidate, its Executive Committee first consults with the regional organiser of the party to agree on a timetable for the selection. The regional organiser is the representative of Transport House and it is his responsibility to ensure that the selection takes place according to the party rules. When the timetable has been approved by the General Management Committee of the constituency party, the secretary writes to each local or ward party or affiliated organisation inviting them to make a nomination before a certain date, normally a minimum period of one month being allowed for this.

No person may be considered for selection unless he or she has been nominated by a local party or affiliated organisation. There is no provision in the Labour Party for members to nominate themselves, though if a member has good personal contact with organisations with the right to nominate it is often not difficult for him to obtain a nomination.

Like the Conservative Central Office, Transport House maintains a list of possible Parliamentary candidates. It is in two parts: List A contains the names of individuals nominated by trade unions and in respect of whom the appropriate trade union is prepared to assume financial responsibility for the candidature. List B consists of persons nominated by constituency Labour parties and for whom no financial responsibility has been assumed.

The Executive Committee of a constituency party may ask for copies of either list for its own reference or to circulate to affiliated organisations, but there is no compulsion on them to do so, and frequently, particularly in the case of safe Labour seats, they make no effort to obtain the lists. There is little point in local parties in safe Conservative areas consulting list A, as trade unions are rarely willing to sponsor candidates who have no prospect of being elected. The more hopeless the seat, however, the more likely is a party to make use of list B and to write to perhaps a large number of the people included, asking them to accept nomination.

The number of nominations made varies enormously. In a "hopeless" rural constituency many miles from a large centre of population there may be as few as two or three. In a safe Labour-held seat in a borough, with many affiliated organisations, there is likely to be anything from ten to twenty-five nominations, and even the latter figure is often exceeded. . . .

When the period for nomination has passed it is the responsibility of the Executive Committee (which itself has the right to make one nomination) to consider all the nominations received and to draw up a short list. If there are fewer than half a dozen nominations this is normally unnecessary, but this is a rare event, except in strong Tory areas. The Executive Committee may decide to interview all the nominees before drawing up a short list, or it may send them questionnaires to fill in. Often, however, it does neither.

The Executive Committee usually recommends a short list with from four to six names and this is reported to the General Management Committee for its approval. It is open to any member of the GMC to move the addition, substitution, or deletion of names and this occurs with considerable frequency, though more often than not amendments are voted down.

People on the approved short list are then invited to a selection conference of the GMC whose procedure is not unlike that of the Executive Council of a Conservative association, though an exhaustive ballot is prescribed in the party rules. The choice of the GMC does not have to be confirmed by a general meeting of members, as in the case of the Conservative Party, but his candidature must be endorsed by the National Executive Committee of the party.

It is paradoxical that financial considerations now play a greater part in the selection of Labour candidates than of Conservatives. The restrictions on individuals are similar—no Labour candidate may subscribe more than £50 a year to his constituency party, and this rule is seldom transgressed. In fact the average Labour candidate or MP undoubtedly subscribes less to his constituency party than his Conservative counterpart.

The monetary element in the Labour Party is represented by the system of trade union sponsorship of candidates, which goes back to the early days of the party when there was no individual membership and every candidature had to be sponsored by an official organisation. Under the so-called Hastings Agreement, dating from the Labour Party conference at Hastings in 1933, a trade union is permitted to contribute up to 80 per cent of the election expenses incurred on behalf of its nominee and a maximum of £420 a year, or 60 per cent of the agent's salary, to the constituency party.

There is thus a strong temptation for hard-up constituency parties to choose a sponsored candidate, and this applies especially in safe Labour seats in industrial areas. Many constituency parties take a pride in choosing the best nominee available irrespective of financial considerations and many sponsored nominees are able and public-spirited men. There have, however, certainly been cases where more competent nominees have been passed over in favour of a mediocrity whose principal recommendation has been the income which his selection would ensure.

Under the party rules no mention of financial matters may be made at a selection conference and the regional organiser, who attends on behalf of Transport House, strictly enforces this rule. The significance of the distinction between trade union and local party nominees is likely, however, to be appreciated by at least the most alert of GMC members. But it is at the short-listing stage that sponsorship carries the greatest weight. For the Executive Committee of a constituency party is acutely aware of the difference that a sponsored candidate can make and, composed as it is of the dozen or so people with the greatest responsibility for the party's affairs, financial worries are likely to be very much on its mind. If an Executive Committee is determined to have a sponsored candidate it will recommend a short list made up entirely of those with financial backing, and there are fairly frequent examples of this occurring in safe Labour seats.

It is a difficult problem, as it is probably only the sponsorship system which enables a fair number of people from manual occupations to go straight from the workbench to the House of Commons and thus enable Parliament to contain a reasonable cross-section of the nation. If the system were abandoned it might result in the long run in the House being composed merely of people of the professional and middle classes, with a solid block of miners remaining as the only representative of manual workers. It is to be hoped, however, that one day the Labour Party will devise some method of supplanting the sponsorship system, without losing what has always been one of its most attractive features—the very wide range of background and occupation from which its candidates are drawn. . . .

A few general points may be made about selection procedures of all parties. One is the small number of people involved in making the choice. The drawing up of the short list—a vital stage—is the responsibility in the Conservative Party of less than a dozen people and in the Labour Party of less than 20. The final selection is seldom made by more than 200 people and most often by between 50 and 150. In the Liberal Party the numbers involved are [even] smaller.

The Selection Conference

The actual selection conference is the most dramatic stage in the selection process, and it is one that imposes considerable strain on the would-be candidates, as the author knows only too well from personal experience.

The nominees are asked to attend a conference lasting anything up to three or four hours, though most of the time they are cooped up in an ante-room with the other contenders while procedural matters are being discussed or one of their number is making his speech. There is a certain tactical advantage in being the last to speak (the order is normally decided by lot), but this is often offset by the tension of waiting until all your rivals have spoken. All one can hear of the proceedings are occasional muffled sounds of applause from which one imagines that one's rivals are making an extremely good impression. In fact the audience normally goes out of its way to encourage the nominees whose ordeal they can imagine, and are very free with their applause.

At last it is your turn. You are ushered into the conference, which as often as not is housed in a bleak Nonconformist church hall or school, but may occasionally be in the more regal surroundings of the council chamber of the Town Hall. Before you are perhaps 80 people, predominantly middle-aged, and you search eagerly for the encouragement of a familiar face, probably in vain.

You reach your seat on the platform, shake hands with the chairman, who announces that you are Mr X, whose biographical details have been circulated to all the delegates. You have 15 minutes to speak and another 15 minutes for questions. After 14 minutes the chairman will sound a warning bell and after 15 you will be stopped — if necessary in mid-sentence.

You stand up, try to show a confidence which you do not feel and launch into a well-prepared speech, which has been carefully timed in front of your bedroom mirror to last 14 1/2 minutes. In the event, you have either sat down after 9 1/2 minutes or are rudely cut short after 15 minutes — less than a third of the way through your oration. You then deal rather better than you had expected with three or four questions and are surprised to hear that another 15 minutes have gone by.

Back to the ante-room and the interminable wait while a succession of ballots is taken. At last after two or three false alarms the regional organiser of the party will come into the room, look at you straight in the eye and announce that Mr Y has been selected. You shake hands with Mr Y and utter a few modest words of congratulation. Meanwhile that blithering idiot Mr Z, is slapping Mr Y on the back and saying he had always known that Y would be chosen.

Back to the conference chamber with the other nominees. Deafening applause. The chairman says that all the nominees were absolutely first class (even if this was patently not the case). They would have liked to have chosen all of them, nevertheless they had to make a choice, however difficult, and the mantle had fallen on Mr Y. He was quite sure that such excellent people as Messrs W, X and Z would have no difficulty in being chosen soon by another constituency, and the members of his constituency would follow their future careers with interest. Then votes of thanks all round, a few words from the selected candidate and a final rousing call from the chairman to rally round the ensure that Mr Y becomes the next member for the constituency.

Austin Ranney

3. THE CHOSEN FEW

What sorts of men and women are the selection conferences looking for? In Conservative-held seats, the sitting Conservative M.P. will usually be readopted. The same is true in Labour- and Liberal-held seats. A few members retire voluntarily at each election, but only very rarely is a sitting M.P. denied readoption on political grounds. (For one of the rare exceptions, see the selection beginning on page 130.) To discover the criteria used by selection conferences when adopting new candidates. Austin Ranney accordingly analysed the characteristics only of nonincumbents.

1. Assets and Liabilities

We have assumed that the constituency organizations in the most winnable constituencies consider larger numbers and wider ranges of aspirants than those in the least winnable, and that by comparing the characteristics of the non-incumbents adopted in each category we could learn something of what the local selectors regard as assets and liabilities for candidature. The most significant differences found were as follows:

Previous Candidatures. In all three parties persons who have fought previous parliamentary contests are markedly overrepresented in the most winnable constituencies, and newcomers are equally overrepresented in the least winnable. So having already been a candidate seems to be a substantial asset for moving to a winnable seat.

Age. In all three parties each older age group from the twenties through the forties wins a higher proportion of the most desirable constituencies than the next younger group; among the Conservatives, but not Labour, the proportion declines for those in their fifties, still more for those in their sixties, and even more for those in their seventies. Labour candidates are gen- erally older than Conservative or Liberal, although most of the difference reflects the much higher average age of Labour candidates sponsored by trade unions.

Sex. Central Office expresses much more concern than Transport House with the local selectors' prejudice against women candidates; but both parties give about the same small fraction (5 and 7 per cent) of their candidatures to women. The Liberals have a slightly higher proportion of women, but they can rarely afford to be as selective as the major parties.

Local Connections. Despite the absence of a local residence rule and the presumed centralization of British politics, almost a third of the Conservatives' candidatures by non-incumbents and over a quarter of Labour's have gone to persons with personal connections in the constituencies for which they were adopted. However, local connections seem to be an advantage in some constituencies but not in others: the preference for local candidates in both parties is most marked, not in the rural areas as one might expect, but in the ten largest English, Welsh, and Scottish cities outside London—and, for Labour only, in the mining areas where the National Union of Mineworkers dominates most selections.

Reprinted with permission of the author and the copyright owners, The Regents of the University of Wisconsin, from Austin Ranney, *Pathways to Parliament* (The University of Wisconsin Press, 1965), pp. 276–279.

Education. Neither Labour nor Liberal candidatures show any significant relationship between education and constituency winnability. Education as measured by years of schooling is little more significant in the allocation of Conservative candidatures. But education measured by the social prestige of schools attended is highly related to the distribution of Conservative candidates among the more and less desirable constituencies: persons who have attended public schools are heavily overrepresented in the best constituencies, while persons who have not fight a disproportionate number of hopeless constituencies. University attendance, on the other hand, makes little difference: the public-school-and-Oxbridge candidates have done no better than the public-school-only group; and the secondary-and-Oxbridge group have done no better than the secondary-and-no-university group.

Occupation. One of the most striking differences between the two major parties is in the occupational groups which win the highest proportions of the best candidatures: civil servants and farmers are favored by the Conservatives, while trade union officials and political organizers do best with Labour—members of the ruling "establishment" and of old county families for the Tories, and full-time servants of the movement for the Socialists.

Ideology. By all accounts the aspirants' general political ideologies and specific views on the issues of the moment play almost no role in the selection of Conservative and Liberal candidates. Both factors have been somewhat more prominent in Labour selections because of the sharp and persistent factional fight between Left and Right. But even so, ideological considerations have been decisive in only a minority of Labour selections, and left-wing CLPs have often chosen right-wing candidates and vice versa.

Personality. Activists in all three parties testify that the greatest asset an aspirant can have is the right kind of personality or character. Some of the specific qualities mentioned are common to all the parties: skill at public speaking, ability to get on well with people (especially with local party workers), a willingness to serve the local organization as well as the national party, and so on. But the parties' images of the ideal candidate also differ in several significant respects. Most Conservatives speak of wanting a man of character—solid, loyal, dependable in a tight spot, not flashy or brilliant. Most Socialists, on the other hand, speak of wanting a dedicated servant of the movement. But to most trade unionists this means a man who has worked with his hands, served his union faithfully, and accumulated the seniority that entitles him to parliamentary candidature. To most individual CLP members it means an intellectual who has proved his devotion to certain causes—nationalization, racial equality, nuclear disarmament, equal educational opportunities, or whatever. And to most Co-operative party members it means a man who has worked faithfully in the co-operative movement. . . .

2. Candidates, Party Members, and Party Voters

Labour voters and party workers are drawn mainly from the lower-middle and working classes, while Conservative and Liberal voters and workers include much higher proportions from the middle and upper ranks of British society. These differences are paralleled by differences between the parties' candidates, although the differences *within* the Labour party are even wider than those between Labour and its opponents.

However, no party's roster of candidates is a representative cross-section of its voters or workers. The candidates are generally of higher social status; they have substantially more formal schooling; more by far have attended high-prestige schools; and they hold mainly business, professional, or white-collar jobs, while many more of their voters and party workers are manual laborers. Socially, then, each party's candidates do not represent its rank-and-file;

rather they occupy a considerably higher level in the party hierarchy. As Guttsman well sums it up:

If we ascend the political hierarchy, from the voters upwards, we find that at each level—the membership of political parties, party activists, local political leaders, M.P.s, National Leaders—the social character of the group is slightly less "representative" and slightly more tilted in favour of those who belong to the middle and upper levels of our society. Ability and availability, deference and assumed superiority contribute to this pattern at each level. For major politicians are initially made by minor politicians and the "political leaders in miniature" who man the local party Executives and Management Committees tend to choose as candidates men who are like themselves or who are socially above them.

This social gap between party leaders and party workers and voters is not unique to Britain; it appears to some degree in all western democracies no matter how class-identified may be their political parties ideologically. There are good reasons why

it does. Most candidate selectors do not intend to choose the aspirant most like themselves for the honor of candidature; rather they try to choose the aspirant most likely to make the best candidate—one who will work the most effectively with the local organization and appeal most strongly to the local voters. The selectors know that a good candidate needs, among other things, time away from his job to campaign, an ability to express himself well in public, and a reputable position in society. And in Britain as elsewhere, persons in the upper reaches of the educational-occupational scale are more likely to have these advantages than those in the lower.

Thus in social status, personality, and outlook the parliamentary candidates of all three British parties, like their counterparts in other democracies, resemble each other more closely than they resemble their respective supporters. They may not constitute a ruling class in the traditional sense, but they are certainly a political élite.

Richard Rose

4. HOW MILITANT ARE THE MILITANTS?

Walter Bagehot, writing a hundred years ago, assumed that party activists in the constituencies would invariably hold more extreme views than the responsible politicians at Westminster. Local party opinion, he maintained, "could not be moderate." Essentially the same view is often expressed today. Both major parties in Britain certainly contain extremists—extreme Tories as well as extreme socialists. But are they in the majority? Richard Rose in 1961 produced some evidence to suggest that they are not.

The constituency party militant is one of the stock figures in British politics. He is a crank, a blueblood, or a Blimp, always pressing the sane men in the House of Commons to follow the wild men outside. Militants do the donkey work of politics,

and in turn are said to bray like asses when given the chance to speak their minds. The Annual Conference of the Conservative Party sometimes seems to be managed by people who have this pessimistic picture of human nature.

From Richard Rose, "Who are the Tory Militants?" in *Crossbow* (London, autumn 1961, vol. 5, no. 17), pp. 35–39. Reprinted by permission of the author and Bow Publications, Ltd. Cf. Dr. Rose's article "The Political Ideas of English Party Activists" in *American Political Science Review* (June 1962, vol. LVI, no. 2), pp. 360–371.

Nigel Nicolson's experiences at Bournemouth provided final confirmation for doubters that the Conservative rank-and-file are extremists to a man.* Press treatment of Tory women's conferences has fostered the belief that they are also extremists to a woman.

In private, one may make fun of Conservatives who are zealous in a faith that the leadership quietly abandoned some years back. But the Nicolson affair suggests that the extremist views of militants may be no laughing matter. They hold the power to nominate or eject MPs. Since most Conservatives sit for safe seats, their power is greater and more immediate than that of the electors, who must accept what the local party wills. The only thing lacking in this picture is evidence that it is drawn from life, and not from the fertile brain of journalists. One job of academics . . .is to do research to find out whether the "obvious" is also true.

The resolutions which constituency parties submit to party conferences provide a rich source of material for investigating the views of militants. Resolutions are one of the two ways that militants have of making their voices heard in the national councils of the party. It is reasonable to assume that over a period of years these resolutions will fairly reflect the views of the small handful of people who dominate constituency parties. In order to find out how militant are the militants, I analysed the 1,959 resolutions put down for Conservative conferences between 1955 and 1960 inclusive, omitting 1959 because resolutions were not published then. Each resolution was assigned to one of four categories—Right, Left, Partisan or Non-partisan.

Right-wing resolutions are those calling for action which would widen the existing gap between the two parties, usually by adopting a reactionary policy, for instance, a major reduction in death duties. This, incidentally, was the concern of constituencies as different as Reigate and South-East Leeds at the 1960 Conference.

*See the selection beginning on page 130. [Editor's note]

Left-wing Conservative resolutions, few in number, are those more in harmony with Labour than Conservative policy. For instance, the safe Conservative seat of Nottingham South requested [the 1960] conference to endorse legislation securing rights for tenants.

Resolutions scored partisan are those which endorsed a policy on which all sections of the party agree. These include pious denunciations of nationalisation, and pious hopes for a bright and sound economic future. These resolutions are eminently suitable for conference publicity. Non-partisan resolutions are those which urge views which are not the subject of differences between the parties, either because they are impeccably non-controversial, such as South-West Hertfordshire's plea for greater emphasis upon responsibility and moral values, or because they are the product of interest groups working within both parties. For instance, a resolution urging more research into the nation's educational resources could come from any Conservative constituency party; the resolution actually presented in these terms last year came from Dick Crossman's party at Coventry East, and was moved at the Labour Conference.

Systematic analysis of conference resolutions along these lines immediately shows that the stock picture is incorrect. Exactly half the resolutions pressed by Conservative parties are non-partisan — though, of course, not necessarily non-political.

TABLE 1
CONSERVATIVE CONSTITUENCY RESOLUTIONS

Type	No.	Per cent
Right-wing	505	26
Partisan	403	21
Left-wing	62	3
Non-partisan	989	50

The figures were not much different for the Labour Party, notwithstanding the strong emphasis upon ideological hair-splitting among Socialists. Non-partisan resolutions constituted 42 per cent of those submitted to Labour conferences in the same period.

The quantity and bias of resolutions appear to be much influenced by passing moods. The lowest number were filed at the 1955 conference, when the post-election euphoria still existed. The highest number came in 1958, when the Government was losing ground in by-elections. Items in the news appear more likely to stimulate resolutions than beliefs treasured from the glorious days of the pre-Socialist 1930s. The one exception is Suez. There were only four resolutions on foreign policy in 1956, and only four in 1957.

One-third of all Conservative constituencies do not even bother to submit resolutions to conference. Another sixth only submit resolutions on an average of once every five years. The party which annually sends in at least one resolution is an exception rather than the rule. Balfour is reported once to have said that he would as soon take orders from his valet as from a Conservative Party conference. Apparently, many constituency workers are as loath to give advice as a modern-day Balfour would be to accept it. Such deference among middle-class party workers is perhaps even more important than deference among the working-class.

Appropriately, the prize for conspicuous concern with policy-making goes to Harrow East, which for most of this time was represented by Ian Harvey, himself an advertising man. The Harrow party submitted a total of forty-six resolutions to five conferences. Enfield East and West and Southall are the other associations submitting more than thirty resolutions in the period. None of these Middlesex associations showed an above average degree of extremism. Many of their resolutions were of that delightful degree of froth and stately emptiness which might qualify them for spotlighting—and their sponsors as speakers from the rostrum.

The number of constituency parties which are above average in extremism is little more than one-tenth of all Conserva-

tive parties, even though the definition of high extremism does not require even half the resolutions being reactionary. Only 11 per cent fall in this bracket, whereas 66 per cent of parties filed no extremist resolutions in the period. The seats which show high extremism form no particular classification: they include South Kensington and Southwark, but not Chelsea or Bermondsey. None of the county constituencies surrounding Hatfield House in Hertfordshire falls in this group, nor does Bournemouth East, which sent in four extremist resolutions out of twelve.

A look at the topics chosen for discussion and the views put forward helps to explain why extremism is not as rampant as it might be.

TABLE 2
CHIEF TOPICS FOR PARTY RESOLUTIONS

Topic	Right	Partisan	Left	Non-Partisan
Economic affairs	121	142	28	64
Housing	22	35	4	107
Industrial relations	73	37	7	16
Party organisation	5	8	3	112
Education	33	18	2	72
Pensions	6	2	–	104
Taxes	56	17	–	29
Compulsory purchase	16	79	–	4
Crime	63	13	4	11
Transportation	5	1	–	82

A similar analysis of Labour resolutions shows that there are a number of issues—education, transportation, pensions and welfare services—where militants in both parties do not apply partisan standards most of the time, even though three of these topics are the subject of clearcut ideological differences. Even militants appear on some issues to be concerned with getting "more," be it roads, schools or pensions, rather than with implementing fine points of party principle. This is the outlook of consumers, not ideologues. It indicates the extent to which active party members may put their pressure group ties even ahead of their party links. Or, in the case of farmers, militants may simply regard the

Conservative Party as a tool to use in furthering their demands as farmers. Differences between the parties appear sharpest on issues such as economic and industrial affairs, where interest group and ideological principles are virtually identical, and on foreign affairs, where there can only be ideological differences, since all belong to the same interest group.

Perhaps these interest group ties explain why even where the Conservative Party is strongest, in quiet seaside resorts and deep in the heart of rural England, the passion for Gladstonian finance without Gladstone has cooled off. Safe Conservative seats (that is, held by margins of more than 10 per cent in 1955 and 1959) appear little more likely to voice extremist views than hopeless ones.

TABLE 3

ELECTORAL STRENGTH AND POLICY VIEWS

Category (1955, 1959) (England only)	No.	Partisan Resolutions (per cent)	Extremist Resolutions (per cent)
Twice safe	213	48.4	29.3
Twice marginal	123	49.8	25.0
Twice hopeless	110	49.7	20.2

The relationship between electoral strength and right-wing views is statistically significant—but not politically significant. It means that a safe seat is likely to submit one more extremist resolution than a hopeless seat in a fourteen year period. Safe seats may appear reactionary for two reasons. One is that the Almighty, in His infinite wisdom, chose to make so many of them. The other is that among the twenty-eight associations which are consistently extremist and prone to submit many resolutions, safe seats form a disproportionately large number—67 per cent, as compared to 42 per cent in England as a whole.

A few comparisons between MPs' views with the views of their constituency parties indicate that there is, in the majority of cases, no sign that one influences the other. For instance, of sixteen Conservative MPs who were right-wing rebels on Suez, eight came from constituencies that had not once voiced a view on any subject in the period. Only three, John Biggs-Davison, Norman Pannell, and Lord Lambton came from constituencies which were high in extremism. Perhaps the most noteworthy party in the group is that at Kidderminster, which sent in only one resolution in five years. . . .

Just as the parties nominating Suez extremists appear to be a cross-section of winnable seats, so do the parties nominating Privy Councillors.

TABLE 4

POLICY VIEWS OF PRIVY COUNCILLORS' CONSTITUENCY PARTIES

Category	Privy Councillors	Per cent of total Privy Councillors	Parties in this group (per cent)
No extremism	32	63	66
Low extremism	1	2	4
Average extremism	7	14	19
High extremism	6	12	11

MPs who found their cónstituencies showing a deeper blue than the front bench have been a mixed lot; they include Lord Amory (when Chancellor), Ernest Marples, Sir Harry Hylton-Foster, Pat Hornsby-Smith and Sir Winston himself. Iain Macleod's party at Enfield West has been exceptionally busy in cheering the team on, filing thirty-three resolutions, of which only four have been pointing in a back- wards direction. Saffron Walden, like Bromley,* has kept discreetly silent throughout the period. Perhaps their members fear that a resolution put down in praise of a specific policy in the summer may be obsolete by the time of conference in October. . . . One thing that emerges quite clearly from analysing resolutions is evi-

*The former constituencies, respectively, of Mr. R. A. Butler and Mr. Harold Macmillan. [Editor's note]

dence of the *multiplicity* of reasons why people may become active party workers. The desire to uphold the standards of Conservatism (in its nineteenth or twentieth century forms) is only one of them. . . .

The real opposition to change does not come from rank-and-file workers. Opposition comes from factions which draw support from all ranks of the party, from noble marquesses down to humble voters. Simi-larly, the Party Leader is also able to count on some support from all levels of the party. The leaders need not worry about pressure from what Americans call the grass-roots; their lawn-mower can cut the grass-roots down to size. Major changes within the party can only be precipitated when there is first of all a quarrel among the gardeners as to whose hand one wants to guide the machine.

III. *Attitudes and Ideologies*

David Butler

1. THE PARADOX OF PARTY DIFFERENCE

Edmund Burke in the eighteenth century defined a political party as "a body of men united for promoting by their joint endeavors the national interests upon some particular principle upon which they are all agreed." This definition is obviously not wholly satisfactory; it fails to distinguish between parties and pressure groups, and it lays overmuch stress on the purely ideological aspects of party. Nevertheless, most political parties — even the Republicans and Democrats — are associated with some principles, however ill-defined. In the following selection, David Butler examines a popular myth about parties in Britain and America.

Most teachers of politics in the United States and in Britain would agree that Lord Bryce's picture of the Republican and Democratic parties as "two bottles, each having a label denoting the kind of liquor it contains, but each of them empty," has been too long with us. A rather smaller majority would agree that the picture offered by Professor Schattschneider and others of the clear contrast between the British parties has been much overstated. I do not wish to add to the controversies on the theme — many and profitable though they have been — but merely to offer a graphic device which has been used with some success before audiences on both sides of the Atlantic to illustrate the nature of the differences within and between the party systems of different countries.

For the purposes of this device, one assumption that admittedly begs the question must be made: that political positions can be explained in terms of a spectrum running from extreme left to extreme right and that everyone can be classified in terms of his particular place on that spectrum. This assumption is grossly arbitrary, of course. A man may be to the left on some issues and to the right on others, while in relation to many issues the terms "left" and "right" are meaningless.

However arbitrary this notion may be, it is not altogether unrealistic. Some such view underlies a large amount of everyday political conversation and reporting. And a host at an academic or political cocktail party will be amazed at how rarely he has to tremble in indecision if he distinguishes

From David Butler, "The Paradox of Party Difference" in *American Behavioral Scientist,* Vol. IV, no. 3 (November 1960), pp. 3–5. Reprinted by permission of the author and the *American Behavioral Scientist,* a division of Sage Publications, 150 Fifth Avenue, New York, New York 10011.

between his guests' drinks by taking the glass of his more right-wing guest in his right hand. It is quite possible to make a rough estimate about where a politician or an elector stands along a spectrum from radical red to reactionary violet. Furthermore, with the use of the questionnaire and other techniques, more precise scaling can be achieved, as Angus Campbell, Herbert McClosky, and others have recently shown.

The popular picture of the spread of opinion between right and left in British and American parties is probably much like that shown in Figure I. The overlap between the positions of Conservative and Labour M. P.'s is very slight; the overlap between Republican and Democratic Congressmen is fairly complete. The grounds for believing in the total confusion of the American party system and the relative clarity of that in Britain are made blatantly plain.

But the picture is transformed if averages and not extremes are considered, if attention is focussed upon the way in which opinion is *concentrated* in each party and not upon its potential range. Frequency distributions, showing how people holding right and left opinions are distributed within each party, would probably have the shape of Figure II. In this figure the distance between what may be loosely termed the centers of gravity, the positions of the median supporter of each party, are about the same in Britain and the United States. Indeed, if the right wing of the Democrats, so largely drawn from the South, was eliminated, the American contrast would be appreciably more striking.

Even without this consideration, however, it can be argued that there is in fact a greater difference between the two American parties than between the two British parties. In some recent periods the issues in the area between the party centers of gravity — for example, acceptance of the welfare state or of international involvements — have been bigger and more genuinely controversial on the western side of the Atlantic.

A simplified expository device must not be mistaken for an exactly observed picture of reality. These curves are not based on precise measurements. Different observers might have very different views on how individuals and issues should be classified. It would be possible to draw and defend curves that would illustrate the substantial identity or the total contrast between the parties in either or both the countries. Each theorist must decide for himself the extent of the paradox which the device is designed to explain — the paradox that parties whose views seem very largely to overlap can be so very different, while parties whose views seem quite distinct can be so close to each other. Moreover, each theorist must decide for himself how much of the political struggle can be explained within the terms "right" and "left," and how much must be regarded as mere feuding between sections or interests of a kind that cannot be fitted into any such ideological classification.

But if the concepts of "right" and "left" can throw light on any area of party conflict, then this graphic device can be used to clarify other problems. For example, the gap between the parties obviously varies with time. Figure III suggests a possible interpretation of recent British politics: the spread of opinion between the Conservative and Labour parties — and to some extent within the Conservative party — diminished greatly between 1935 and 1955.

Similar diagrams drawn for the United States would show the Republicans and Democrats overlapping greatly in the early 1920's, drawing widely apart with the coming of the New Deal, and overlapping greatly once more in the 1950's. . . .

But perhaps the most valuable application of this sort of diagram is a demonstration of the conflicting elements *within* parties. Thus far we have tacitly assumed that we are illustrating the distribution of views among M.P.'s [and] Congressmen . . .

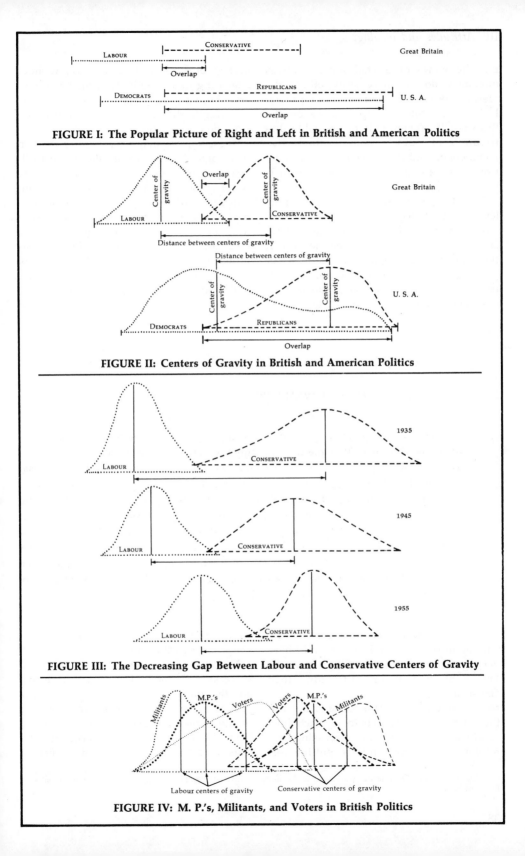

FIGURE I: The Popular Picture of Right and Left in British and American Politics

FIGURE II: Centers of Gravity in British and American Politics

FIGURE III: The Decreasing Gap Between Labour and Conservative Centers of Gravity

FIGURE IV: M. P.'s, Militants, and Voters in British Politics

But the views of elected representatives obviously do not necessarily mirror the views of those who vote or work for them. It is worthwhile to superimpose on the British half of Figure II the possible distribution of opinion among the active members of, and the passive voters for, the Conservative and Labour parties, which is done in Figure IV.

This diagram illustrates the essential dilemma of party leaders in Britain, and elsewhere: their most loyal and devoted followers tend to have more extreme views than they have themselves, and to be still farther removed from the mass of those who actually provide the vote. Party leaders have to conciliate those who support them with

money or with voluntary work, without alienating that large body of moderate voters whose attitudes make them most likely to swing to the other party and thus to decide the next election.

These various diagrams are no more than pedagogic devices, arbitrarily drawn to illustrate propositions that must occur to any serious observer of party politics. In conjunction with voting records or survey-based indices of "rightness" or "leftness," they do offer a useful technique. They can help separate out, more clearly than has hitherto been practicable, the extent of present and past ideological cleavages within and between democratic parties.

Labour Party

2. THE DEBATE ON PUBLIC OWNERSHIP

The British Labour Party has been wracked by internal dissension ever since its foundation in 1900. Sometimes foreign and defense policy have aroused controversy. At other times domestic policy—especially the question of nationalisation—has been disputed. Ultimately, however, the argument has revolved around the issue of whether Labour should pursue policies of gradualism and moderation, or whether it should cling to the cause of root-and-branch socialism. Hugh Gaitskell, the party leader, tried to settle the issue finally following Labour's defeat in the 1959 general election. This selection consists of extracts from Gaitskell's speech to the 1959 party conference, and from the debate which followed. Many delegates spoke in Gaitskell's favor, but a sampling only of the critical speeches has been quoted.

THE CHAIRMAN: We now come to the debate upon the General Election, and I have very great pleasure in calling upon the Leader of the Labour Party, Mr. Hugh Gaitskell, to open.

THE RT. HON. HUGH GAITSKELL, M.P.: It is not the purpose of this debate to reach final conclusions. We are not discussing any resolution. The Executive is putting forward no proposals. So this afternoon I speak for myself alone. . . .

The stark fact is that this is the third successive General Election we have lost and the fourth in which we have lost seats. This is a grave development which we are bound to take very seriously indeed. For an Opposition to suffer three successive defeats is almost unprecedented in British

From *Report of the Fifty-Eighth Annual Conference of the Labour Party*, Blackpool, 1959 (London: The Labour Party, 1960), pp. 105–137. Reprinted by permission.

political history. In the past the pendulum has always swung against the Party in power after one or at most two periods of office. It has not been swinging in these last few years. And this trend is all the more serious for a Party like ours which assumed, and quite naturally, that while there would be ups and downs in the long struggle for power, nevertheless over the years our advance would be inexorable. This is no longer happening today. That is why there is no room at all for complacency.

What has caused this adverse trend? It is, I believe, a significant change in the economic and social background of politics. First, there is the changing character of the labour force. . . . Everywhere the balance is shifting away from heavy physical work and towards machine maintenance, distribution and staff jobs. . . . It is an inevitable result of technological advance. But it means that the typical worker of the future is more likely to be a skilled man in a white overall, watching dials in a bright new modern factory than a badly paid cotton operative working in a dark and obsolete 19th-century mill. The second great change is the absence of serious unemployment or even the fear of it. True, we had a minor recession and there are still parts of the country which have considerable unemployment. But, taking the country as a whole, the contrast with 1939 and still more with 1932 is staggering. Today we talk of unemployment as being serious if it rises above 2 per cent. In the inter-war years it was never less than 10 per cent. It permeated the lives of the British people. . . .

Of course, we not only profoundly welcome the change to full employment but we take great pride in the part we played in bringing it about. For the change would never have occurred but for the insistence by the British Labour Movement that a government with the will and the power could maintain full employment and that, therefore, the power of the State over the economy must be increased. This is exactly what has happened. . . .

To full employment we can add the Welfare State — another of our achievements of which we are proud and which has also had profound consequences. We point out rightly how much remains to be done. Indeed, we fought the election to a very large extent on the improvements which are so urgently needed. But this is not to deny that, for the majority at least, the protection of the Welfare State has already made a profound difference. Unfortunately, gratitude is not a very reliable political asset.

Moreover, the recent improvements in living standards have been of a special kind. There has been a particularly notable increase in comforts, pleasures and conveniences in the home. Television, whether we like it or not, has transformed the leisure hours of the vast majority of our fellow-citizens. Washing machines, refrigerators, modern cookers, have made women's lives a good deal easier. . . . Most obviously, perhaps, there is the increase in the cars. Not only have many more got them but many more are expecting to get them. . . .

Again and again, especially talking to candidates in the Midlands and the South, I have heard the same story of the relatively prosperous younger married couples who, having moved from older houses in solid Labour areas to new attractive housing estates, usually built by Labour councils, then lost their Labour loyalty and voted Conservative. . .

In short, the changing character of labour, full employment, new housing, the new way of living based on the telly, the frig., the car and the glossy magazines — all these have had their effect on our political strength. Of course, one can exaggerate the importance of the effect, but when we are talking, as we must, of swings of one, two, three and five per cent, even a small change can be of decisive importance.

It is easier to describe these changes and their political effects than to prescribe the remedy. It may be this which has led to what I can only describe as defeatism in some quarters. But defeatism is as bad as complacency. We should firmly reject the idea, even the whisper of it, that perhaps we should be content to remain in permanent Opposition until somehow in 20 or 30 years' time the country comes to its senses and condescends to elect us to power. It is our job to get back into power as quickly as possible so that we may do the things in which we believe for our country and the world. If we lose sight of this we condemn our movement to decay and decrepitude. The British people will not be interested in a party which is no longer concerned with power. They do not take kindly, in politics or war, to those who have given up the will to battle.

What then is the answer? Some rather desperate remedies have been proposed.

It has been suggested that we should make a pact with the Liberals. We can toss that one out of the window straight away. It is not just a matter of being prejudiced against it—though most of us probably are. There is no evidence that it would do us any good. . . .

It has also been proposed that we should change our name. I have had several letters to this effect from people who are alarmed by the snobbery of some of the new suburban voters. We should toss this out of the window too. Our name is one which evokes the loyalty of many millions of British people. And I doubt if the snobs would be much influenced if we did change it.

There is a third desperate suggestion which also goes out of the window right away—the proposal that the Labour Party should break with the Unions. We have heard it before. And from the same quarter we've heard the suggestion that the Unions in their own interests should break with the Labour Party. It's not a friendly quarter. And the advice is not disinterested. I have always looked upon the Trade Union Congress and the Labour Party as part of the same great Labour Movement and our close integration as one of our greatest strengths. I see no reason to change my mind. I hope our trade union friends feel likewise. . . .

Now let me be more positive. I do not believe that the social and economic changes of which I have spoken were bound to react against us. They did so simply because we did not take them sufficiently into account. We assumed too readily an instinctive loyalty to Labour which was all the time slowly gradually being eroded. We failed to appreciate that we should have to make a special conscious effort to win over these younger, newer, social groups.

Sometimes I think we seem to do the opposite and give the idea that clerical, administrative and other white collar classes of workers, whose numbers are growing, are not welcome in our ranks. This is a pity and it creates a false impression. If you look at the parties in the House of Commons today you will see that ours is a far better cross section of the community than the Tories who are still overwhelmingly drawn from a single social class. Yet, somehow, we let the Tories get away with the monstrous falsehood that *we* are a Class Party and they are *not*. We must surely now attend to this.

We should put more stress on the issues which specially appeal to younger people. I believe these include the cause of Colonial freedom; the protection of the individual against ham-handed and arrogant bureaucracy; resistance to the squalid commercialism which threatens to despoil our countryside and disfigure our cities; a dislike of bumbledom in all forms; a greater concern for sport and the arts.

It is sometimes said that we appeal too much on behalf of the underdog. True, the underdogs are fewer than they used to be, and consequently they bring us fewer votes. But I cannot accept that we should cease to appeal on their behalf. To me that would be a betrayal of Socialist principles. And I believe too that young people still respond more to idealism than to purely materialistic and selfish causes. . . .

Above all our object must be to broaden our base, to be in touch always with ordinary people, to avoid becoming small cliques of isolated doctrine-ridden fanatics, out of touch with the main stream of social life in our time. We should be missionaries, not monks, a mass party not a conspiratorial group.

There are also some handicaps which we must try and eliminate. For example, we still sometimes give an appearance of disunity. This may seem strange, since in fact we were more united than for many years past. But between elections at least we do argue with each other a great deal in public and this tends to give the impression that we're always at sixes and sevens, incapable of ever speaking with a single voice, or of managing our own affairs properly, let alone those of the nation. Is it a forlorn hope to suggest that we might all spend more of our time putting over our policy, and less in pointing out why we think it should be a different policy? How wonderful it would be if we could always be as united as we generally were in the last General Election. . . .

Now I turn to public ownership and nationalisation. There seems no doubt that, if we are to accept the majority view of those who fought this election, nationalisation —on balance—lost us votes. No one suggests it was the main cause but anything which appears to have swung votes against us deserves careful and, as far as possible, dispassionate study.

Why was nationalisation apparently a vote loser? For two reasons I believe. First, some of the existing nationalised industries are unpopular. This unpopularity is very largely due to circumstances which have nothing to do with nationalisation. London buses are overcrowded and slow—not because the Transport Commission is inefficient but because of the state of London traffic and the way the Tory Government have neglected it all these years. The backward conditions of the railways are not really the result of bad management but of inadequate investment in the past which has left behind a gigantic problem of modernisation. . . .

The second reason, I believe, why nationalisation was a vote loser was the confusion in the public mind about our future policy. This confusion was again in large part the result of gross misrepresentation. What the voters disliked was not so much our policy but what they came to think our policy was. Our moderate, practical proposals were distorted out of all recognition by our opponents. Thousands and perhaps millions of voters were induced to think that we intended to nationalise any and every private firm, however efficiently it might be operating—a chemical factory in this constituency, an engineering works in that, a motor car firm in the other. . . .

But although much of the misunderstanding was due to the campaign of the Institute of Directors and the Tory Central Office, perhaps we gave them some help. Perhaps we were not sufficiently precise about what we were going to do or why we wanted to do it. This brings me to the central problem of future policy on public ownership.

I agree with neither of the two extreme points of view. Some suggest that we should accept for all time the present frontiers between the public and private sectors. We cannot do that. It would imply that everything works so perfectly in the private sector that we shall never want to intervene. . . .

At the same time I disagree equally with the other extreme view that nationalisation or even public ownership is the be all and end all, the ultimate first principle and aim of socialism. I believe that this view arises from a complete confusion about the fundamental meaning of socialism and, in particular, a misunderstanding about ends and means.

So I want now to set out what I at any rate regard as the basic first principles of British democratic socialism. Of course, we have tried to do this on many occasions. I had a go at it in a very few sentences when I last spoke in this hall at the T.U.C. just at the beginning of the General Election campaign. But that was off the cuff. I thought that this afternoon I had better be a little more formal.

So I say, first, we express what G. D. H. Cole once called "a broad, human movement on behalf of the bottom dog"—on behalf of all those who are oppressed or in need or hardship. Thus, at home, our first concern is naturally for the less fortunate—the old, the sick, the widowed, the unemployed, the disabled ,and the badly housed; abroad, it is reflected in a deep concern for the well-being of peoples much, much poorer than ourselves, badly in need of help.

Secondly, we believe in social justice, in an equitable distribution of wealth and income. We do not demand exact equality. But we do demand that the differences should be related not to the accident of birth and inheritance but on how much of effort, skill and creative energy we each contribute to the common good.

Thirdly, we believe in a "classless society"—a society without the snobbery, the privilege, the restrictive social barriers which are still far too prevalent in Britain today.

Fourthly, we believe in the fundamental equality of all races and of all peoples, and in the building of an international order which will enable them to live together in peace. We detest equally the arrogant postures of white supremacy and the exercise of unbridled power by large nations over small ones. Suez, Hungary, Hola are words of infamy to us. For we believe quite simply in the brotherhood of man.

Fifthly, British socialism has always contained an essential element of personal idealism—the belief that the pursuit of material satisfaction by itself without spiritual values is empty and barren and that our relations with one another should be based not on ruthless self-regarding rivalry but on fellowship and co-operation. It is hard to convey this idea in plain language. But we can, surely, agree that without it our socialism would be the poorer.

Sixthly, we believe that the public interest must come before private interest. We are not opposed to individuals seeking to do the best they can for themselves and their families. But we insist that the pursuit of private gain should not take precedence over the public good. The idea of public planning in the interests of the whole community both for economic and social reasons is certainly a basic principle of socialism.

Finally, we believe that these things must be achieved with and through freedom and democratic self government. We intend to maintain this for ourselves and, so far as lies within our power, to help others to enjoy it too.

These I believe constitute the essential first principles of our democratic socialism. Everything else—nationalisation, controls, our particular policies on housing or education or old age pensions—constitute only the means to realising these principles in practice. For example, the extension of public ownership may help towards a more equitable distribution of wealth: by securing for the community profits and capital gains which would otherwise accrue to wealthy private shareholders. It was for this reason that we decided that the State and other public agencies should be free to hold shares in private industry. But public ownership is not itself the ultimate objective; it is only a means of achieving the objective. . . .

As I have already said I am against starting on a new election programme now. But I do think that we should clear our minds on these fundamental issues and then try to express in the most simple and comprehensive fashion what we stand for in the world today.

The only official document which embodies such an attempt is the Party Constitution, written over 40 years ago. It seems to me that this needs to be brought up to date. For instance, can we really be satisfied today with a statement of fundamentals which makes no mention at all of colonial freedom, race relations, disarmament, full employment or planning? The only specific reference to our objectives at home is the well-known phrase:

To secure for the workers by hand or by brain the full fruits of their industry and the most equitable distribution thereof that may be possible, upon the basis of the common ownership of the means of production, distribution, and exchange. . . .

Standing as it does on its own, this cannot possibly be regarded as adequate. It lays us open to continual misrepresentation. It implies that common ownership is an end, whereas in fact it is a means. It implies that the only precise object we have is nationalisation, whereas in fact we have many other Socialist objectives. It implies that we propose to nationalise everything, but do we? Everything?—the whole of light industry, the whole of agriculture, all the shops—every little pub and garage? Of course not. We have long ago come to accept, we know very well, for the foreseeable future, at least in some form, a mixed economy; in which case, if this is our view—as I believe it to be of 90 per cent of the Labour Party—had we better not say so instead of going out of our way to court misrepresentation?

I knew I should say some things that would not be palatable to everybody this afternoon. It would have been very nice in some ways to have made a speech which contained so many bromides and so little controversial matter that it was certain of a very large number of cheers. But I do not conceive that to be my duty today. I would rather forego the cheers now in the hope that we shall get more votes later on. I do not want deliberately to advise a course of action which could only involve me in leading this Party to another electoral defeat, and I will not do so.

I am sure that the Webbs and Arthur Henderson who largely drafted this Constitution, would have been amazed and horrified had they thought that their words were to be treated as sacrosanct 40 years later in utterly changed conditions. Let us remember that we are a Party of the future, not of the past; that we must appeal to the young as well as the old—young people who have very little reverence for the past. It is no use waving the banners of a bygone age. . . .

I hope, then, that the Executive will during the next few months try to work out and state the fundamental principles of British democratic socialism as we see and as we feel it today, in 1959, not 1918, and I hope that in due course another Conference will endorse what they propose. I hope that the Executive in doing this work will tilt the balance to the future rather than the past, so that what is decided will be and will seem relevant in 1970—even, if you like, in 1980. After that we can have another look at it again. . . .

It is right that we should have had this discussion; not to have had it would have been appallingly complacent. But we must be careful not to overdo it, not to overdo the self-analysis. We must not expend all our time on it, and we must not get it out of perspective. Before I sit down, I would like to remind the Conference of some of the other things in the election. I think of the grand, tumultuous, gay, good-humoured meetings, the passionate excited longing of the crowds that we should win. . . .

I ask myself what most of these people want of us now. They see the need for our re-thinking; they have been doing some themselves, some of it very sensible stuff, too. But what they wanted above all was that we should win, and why they wanted us to win was so that we could carry out the programme in which both we and they believe. What they want us to do now first of all is to go on fighting for the things we fought for in the election, and they are dead right. . . .Our defeat, comrades, must not be a depressive or a sedative, but a supreme challenge, a challenge to keep up the spirit of attack, the spirit of attack again and again and again, until we win. For in this way, and in this way only, we shall keep faith with the millions of people who had faith in us at the last General Election, and the millions of people abroad who still look to us for leadership, because they, like us, believe in the imperishable ideas of democratic socialism. (*Prolonged Applause*).

THE CHAIRMAN: Now we move on to the general debate. . . .

MR. M. FOOT (*ex-officio* Candidate, Devonport): . . .

We had at the beginning of this Conference from Barbara Castle what I thought was one of the finest statements for socialism I have ever heard at a conference. She showed quite clearly how public ownership is bang up to date; she showed quite clearly how it is a modern doctrine; she showed quite clearly how it refers to many of these other aspects of our society about which we say young people are especially interested and are certain to be interested in the years ahead. . . .

I do not believe Hugh Gaitskell made the same kind of speech. I do not think it was a speech which stated those principles anything like so clearly. . . .

What is this philosophical argument Hugh Gaitskell makes about ends and means? Many of the ends Hugh Gaitskell described at the end of his speech are in such general terms that the Tories could agree with them, too. They do not carry them out — that is the difference — but so far as the words are concerned they say they believe in social justice; they believe in freedom; they use the same kind of words and therefore it is a fallacy to try to separate the ends and the means because socialism, in my view, is a doctrine which reveals how only by mobilising the resources of the community can you achieve the ends. That is what socialism is.

Therefore, when Hugh Gaitskell says in his speech that he wants to have less argument in the Party about policy, when he says we should be united as we were in the election — when he makes a speech like that he does not contribute to the unity. If Hugh Gaitskell had stated the case for public ownership in the terms Barbara Castle did this morning this Party would be much more united than it is after Hugh Gaitskell's speech.

Therefore, I say that in the months ahead we are bound to have arguments about policy. We have to make in those months ahead one of the most critical decisions that has ever been made in the history of this Party: whether we are going to go the same way as the German Social Democratic Party or whether we are going to realise that in order to win an election we have to change the mood of the people in this country, to

open their eyes to what an evil and disgraceful and rotten society it is. This is what we have to do and if we really applied our mind to that I am sure we could do it. . . .

Mr. G. Roberts (*ex-officio* Candidate, Ormskirk): . . .

Let us turn to the attack, and let us come to this Conference not to find if we are satisfying the public opinion of the moment, but let us come to this Conference to find ourselves, to find truth, to find socialism, to find what we believe in. Do we really believe that society should be run for human greed? If we do not, that is the best possible and the only possible reason for public ownership. Let us go from this Conference to form a progressive policy, a Socialist policy, a forward policy. If we have to go into the wilderness, if we have to go into opposition, let us do so at least with honour! Barbara Castle said that the Tory Party was an amoral Party. Let us show at this Conference that we are basically a moral Party, who believe in truth and believe in socialism! If we do that, it does not matter whether we become the Government in 1964 or 1974 or 1984. When we do form a government, I know that we have something to offer the people of this country. We have a new world to offer them, and a new society, not a botched-up old system. Let us go forward from this Conference! Let us go forward and not turn back! . . .

Mr. F. Singleton (*ex-officio* Candidate, Harrogate): I do not know why most of you joined the Labour Party, but I know why I did. I joined the Labour Party because I believed it was an instrument of social change that was going radically to alter the fundamental basis of our society. I thought there was a lot wrong with our existing society and that the Labour Party was the political instrument of change. There are other instruments of change — social, even religious, and in other forms educational — which may bring about change; but I believed the Labour Party was the main political instrument for change. It seems to me that the poeple who wish to water down our socialism and to make small the differences between our kind of society, the way of life that we represent, and that of the other political Parties are so blurring the image that this Party presents to the public that we are going to find that the average independent voter is going to say, "What is the difference between these Parties except that one wants to put one set of faces in Downing Street and the other another set?" . . .

MR. FRANK COUSINS (Transport & General Workers Union): . . .

There are a lot of different views about what happened and what was the cause of the defeat. My views are different from Hugh's. I do not think we portrayed ourselves sufficiently well as a Party in opposition to the Tories. Let us give over pretending we have to get half a million Tory people to change their allegiance to us at voting time. There are five million or six million people who are Socialists in embryo waiting for us to go out and harness them to the power machine we want to drive, and the sooner we get on with that job the better for all of us. . . .

I was a bit disturbed by Hugh's reference that, whilst we are going along as we are now, there may be need to revise the Constitution in the modern circumstances in which we find ourselves. It seemed a bit peculiar that there had been no consultation with the N.E.C. I think I am a fairly powerful man in my own organisation, but if I were going to give a public airing to a change in the Constitution of my Union I should wait until I had talked to the Executive before doing it. If the idea is that all we need to do is to add something to our Constitution there could be something to be said in favour of that. But if, as I gather, [Clause Four] is likely to be revised to make a different reference to our attitude towards public ownership, I would suggest, with the greatest respect to our Leader, that no way. . . is going to change that one. . . .

MR. BENN LEVY (Chelsea C.L.P.): . . .

I think, myself, that we are now at this Conference at a very crucial stage in the history of the Labour Party. We have to choose. We have heard two voices from the platform, Barbara Castle's and Hugh Gaitskell's. If there is any person in this hall who thought those two voices were speaking the same language, then he is very deaf indeed. One might even be forgiven for thinking that one of them at least was addressing a different Party Conference! What we have to decide, and we had better decide it sooner than later, is which of those voices is the voice of the Labour Movement. Can there really be any doubt?

MR. CHARLES PANNELL (ex-officio M.P., Leeds West): I had hoped to come to a great religious Socialist revival. Instead of that, I find myself in the middle of the biggest belly-ache I have ever come across. . . .

[Hugh Gaitskell's effort to amend the party constitution ended in failure. He could not rally enough support on Labour's National Executive Committee. The N.E.C. would accept no more than an informal "amplification" of the party's aims. See also the selection beginning on page 81.

3. THE DEBATE ON THE INDUSTRIAL CHARTER

The Conservative Party was stunned by its overwhelming electoral defeat in 1945, and many observers wondered how it would react. Would the Tories swing to the right? Or would they accept the need to adopt more "modern" policies? R. A. Butler, with the support of Winston Churchill, the party leader, fought to persuade Conservatives to accept Labour's social reforms and to admit the need for economic planning. In drafting *The Industrial Charter*, he was assisted by young men like Reginald Maudling who later became prominent party figures. The *Charter* contained the main statement of Butler's moderate political philosophy. The debate on it reached a climax at the 1947 Conservative conference.

THE CHAIRMAN: We will now take Resolution No. 6 standing in the name of Mr. Ian Orr-Ewing on behalf of the Hendon North Conservative Association.

That this Conference, in welcoming the Industrial Charter as a basis for discussion, recommends that the Committee which prepared it should be kept in being in order that the Charter can be kept fully up to date, and in order that the Party may be able, at short notice, to publish an industrial programme based on this charter.

I have, as you know, various amendments to this Resolution, and I am going to call the one in the name of Mr. Maudling, the main amendment.

MR. C. IAN ORR-EWING, O.B.E. (Hendon North): In moving this Resolution I think we should first like to congratulate Mr. R. A. Butler and his Committee on the magnificent work they have done in the preparation of this Charter (*Hear, hear*.) Following our requests for a restatement of the Conservative policy at Blackpool last October, much painstaking work has been undertaken, and the result is a first-class document based on practical common sense.

The twenty-eight Resolutions dealing with the Industrial Charter alone ensure that this afternoon much healthy discussion is going to take place. When this is over I hope we can move to the second part of the Resolution, and thus send this Charter forward with the wholehearted support of this great Conference.

I have read with care the various attacks on this Charter by certain sections of the Press and a part of the Conservative Party. I hope this Conference will show that these people represent only a small minority. The two points with which they seem to disagree are, firstly, the Charter's statement that there is a need for central planning and, secondly, the Charter's attitude to nationalisation. It is contended by a few that in those two respects we are in danger of deserting Conservative principles. I refute this contention absolutely. Surely the great strength of Conservatism is that it is not tied to a hidebound doctrine; it is not anchored to any rigid political theory. The Conservative policy I think is like some great building resting on sure foundations, whose main structure remains the same but

From *National Union of Conservative and Unionist Associations, 68th Annual Conference*, Brighton, 1947 (London, National Union of Conservative and Unionist Associations, 1948), pp. 46–54. Reprinted by permission.

whose rooms are modified so that they can serve most effectively the needs of each succeeding generation. As I read the history of the last eighty years there has been a slow but steady growth in the amount of planning which it has been necessary for the Government to undertake. The Conservatives have endorsed the [wartime] Coalition plans for full employment, and this automatically committed us to the retention of strong powers at the centre. . . .

Now let us briefly consider the Charter's recommendations in connection with nationalisation. Here again I believe the Charter has taken a most sensible and objective view. It is true the Conservative Party is opposed in principle to monopolies, whether these be run by the State or by big industrial concerns. We are opposed to monopolies because we believe they concentrate power dangerously, and because they are inefficient and therefore eventually react on the volume of our exports. However, when we take office, almost our first need will be to do everything in our power to unify the country. We will not get it by rushing into denationalisation as a matter of principle. If we want co-operation from all our citizens we must show that we are not going to indulge in purely party politics. On platforms and on paper we have condemned the Socialist Government because they, at a most crucial time, have insisted upon proceeding with their political experiments in reorganisation. We blamed them for concentrating on nationalisation plans when there have been such very serious problems ahead. When we take up the reins let us resolve that we will not fall into the same errors, that we will never put our political beliefs before the needs of this country. This country may be very sick when the present doctors (whom we suspect to be "quacks") have finished with their experimental operations, and when more qualified men are called in we may need to bind up the nation's wounds. We may have to leave some of the scars of nationalisation whilst we build up the patient's strength in all possible ways. . . .

THE CHAIRMAN: I now call on Mr. Maudling on behalf of the Barnet Division Conservative Association to move his amendment.

To delete words after "Charter" in first line to "in order" in fourth line.
To insert after "Charter" in first line "as a clear restatement of the general principles of Conservative economic policy, recommends that the Committee which prepared it should be kept in being and should take full account of constructive suggestions put forward for insertion in the Charter."

MR. R. MAUDLING (Barnet): I believe that this amendment is very important, but I have only five minutes in which to move it. I am not going to try to argue the merits of the job. I want to make one point, that whatever view this Conference takes of the Charter that view must be recorded today clearly, decisively, and without possibility of equivocation. . . .

I do not suggest in the amendment that the Charter is a final document. We do not have final documents in this Party because our policy grows and progresses all the time, but it makes it clear that this is a Charter of Conservative economic policy. On the basis of this Charter we will produce an industrial programme for the next election, however soon it comes—and the sooner the better. Do not, I beg you, be misled by any argument that, unless every single person here accepts every single word in the Charter, then you cannot take a decision. You would never take any decisions on that basis. That is precisely the argument that can be used to prevent a decision being taken on the Charter by people who know that the decision will be voted, and do not want to have that decision recorded.

Finally, I would if I may, commend this amendment to you out of a deep conviction that, on the basis of this Industrial Charter, our great Party can rise again to its full strength, its full stature, to lead our dear country out of the mist and fog in which we are wandering, on to the heights where once again we can walk in prestige and prosperity. There is no other way. (*Applause*). . . .

SIR WALDRON SMITHERS, M.P. (Orpington): I have five minutes in which to convince you that the existence of the Conservative Party, therefore of Britain, depends on the rejection of the Industrial Charter (*Cries of dissent*). There can be no compromise with Socialism or Communism. You must not let the Conservative Party become infected with the Socialist bug. The Conservative Party must stick to its principles or perish. If good principles of Government are applied, good results will inevitably follow. Disraeli's three principles were: to maintain our Constitution, to preserve our Empire, and to improve the conditions of the people. They must be applied in that order. Material prosperity can only be built up on spiritually reinforced foundations.

Remember the principle that you passed at Blackpool: to defend the Christian religion and to resist all attacks upon it. The command is "Seek ye first the Kingdom." The Industrial Charter puts the cart before the horse. The crisis is not an economic, a financial or a dollar crisis; it is a spiritual and moral crisis. Britain is in danger of losing her soul, and the Conservative Party, of all Parties, offers it a lifebuoy—the Industrial Charter. If Britain loses her soul she loses her power to recover economically and financially. If the people want Socialism and so-called Social Reform, they will not come to the Conservative Party for it, as the by-elections prove. The Industrial Charter is "milk and water Socialism" (*Cries of dissent*). Our slogan must be "Freedom." Let people trade freely. Put the responsibility for recovery on the only place where it can be put, on the shoulders of each individual man and woman. Let them do it of their own freewill, and by no other way. Do their duty to God and their neighbour. Duty first; the rights of men third, a bad third.

To remove all controls and regulations inside three months would cause an upheaval, but that upheaval would be as nothing to the complete disaster which will inevitably follow if it is not done. The ap-

pointment of Sir Stafford Cripps as the Economic Leader of Britain was inevitable; administration under the various Ministers had broken down; and now we have one Dictator, which will increase delay, create frustration and spell disaster. The Charter says one Cabinet Minister would be in charge of Government Economic Policy, instead of bunches as now.

I have some justification for saying what I have to say today. On four or five occasions, mine has been the only voice, or one of two, to rise against Socialist Bills, and the awful thing is that I have been proved right. No personal credit is due to me at all, because I simply base my political action on principles. I am certain I am right in attacking the Charter now. How many of you have really read it, and studied it word for word. Today each one of you has an opportunity to influence the future of Britain. Think for yourselves. Do not be afraid of the Central Office or the platform. Vote according to your conscience. By rejecting this Charter you can save the Conservative Party and save England.

MR. ERIC HARRISON (Orpington): As the Member of Parliament for Orpington has just addressed the Conference in condemnation of this great Charter, I would like to say that the Orpington Division of the Conservative Association has not so far passed a resolution on this matter either one way or the other, but it is my duty to inform this Conference that Sir Waldron Smithers, in condemning the Charter, may be speaking for himself, but he is certainly *not* speaking for the overwhelming majority of Conservatives of the Orpington Division (*Hear, hear*). . . .

We of the Orpington Division greatly respect our Member of Parliament. I warmly pay tribute to his many fine qualities, and it was indeed partly out of personal respect for him that we have so far passed no resolution one way or the other. But there is undeniable proof that an overwhelming majority of Conservatives in the Orpington Division have warmly welcomed and endorse this great Charter. . . .

MR. FRANK BURROW (Lancaster): I have listened with some interest, and not a little amusement, to the speeches which have gone before me. The only one which I think was sincere and came from the heart of a true Conservative was that of Sir Waldron Smithers. The attitude of mind of a number of speakers today seems to be despair following defeat. We seem to have forgotten those three basic principles of Conservatism laid down by Disraeli, and we have taken up a "pink Socialism" which can offer no good to anyone. . . . We have seen in this year so many things of a grievous nature. We have had the Industrial Charter. We have had "Design for Freedom"; and we have had several other documents which are not in line with Conservative Party policy. I ask you, though, believe me, I know it is a hopeless task, but still I ask you, this afternoon not to pass this Charter as Conservative policy, because it is not in line with those basic principles of Conservatism laid down by Disraeli and because it does not offer an alternative to Socialism. It merely offers a milk-and-water form of Socialism.

I appreciate that Mr. Butler and his Committee put a great deal of work into this Charter, but from my discussion with the working-class people—I hate that phrase, but I use it—with the ordinary workers in the fields and in the factories, I say that they will rather have Socialism in its cold-blooded form than any watered-down form. Therefore I ask you to defeat this motion this afternoon, and to give back to the Conservative Party, a better, a truer, and a genuine Conservative policy.

SIR JOHN MARLING, BT., O.B.E. (Stafford): Pink Socialism, my foot! Milk-and-water Socialism, rubbish! We all know that. . . .

The Charter was produced four months ago by some of the best brains in the Party. It was four months ago that it was published with all the arts of modern publicity at our disposal, and it has been acclaimed throughout the country practically without any opposing voice at all, except those of our political enemies. Then, four months ago, our new flag was run up to the masthead. Is this the time now to run it down to

examine the spots, to see if we want to change some of them? Surely now is the time to nail the flag to the masthead in the midst of battle. . . .

THE RT. HON. R. A. BUTLER, M.P.: It really does not seem necessary for me to make a very long speech. . . . I cannot honestly say that I have had many quarrels with Sir Waldron Smithers. He asks us to adhere to the Ten Commandments. The second great commandment is this: Thou shalt love thy neighbour as thyself. If Sir Waldron will follow those precepts in his public life, as he does in his private life—no man is a better Christian than he is—I feel sure we shall get along well enough together. Meanwhile, if this Conference supports the Charter, they will, in fact, be supporting that very principle, which is the basis of the Charter—love thy neighbour by giving him a better opportunity.

I unhesitatingly come down on the side of the amendment. I think it is essential for this Conference to decide in favour of the Charter unequivocally. I do not believe that we can redraft the Charter itself. I will just answer the last speaker by saying that I think he was speaking sound common sense. . . .

I do not think it is necessary for me to spend much time on the criticism we have received. I think it only necessary for me to stress that in its essential features the Charter represents the core of the Conservative tradition and the direct opposite of Socialist philosophy. It also represents an attempt to re-state Conservatism in the light of modern economic theory. It is essential for us, as a Party, to embrace the new world and seize its opportunities, and not proceed looking backwards. I believe we have a sublime opportunity to put forward the one economic theory which will really work in the modern world. What is that—the liberation of enterprise, thus bringing out the best in human nature, and a definition of the place of government in a free society. How I describe it in short is, "Private initiative in the public interest." Since the days of Bolingbroke our Party has always believed in using the power and majesty of the State in order to serve the best interests of our citizens and to preserve the maximum amount of freedom.

The real struggle is not . . . between those who are clinging to the old world and those who are embracing the new. The difference is between those who are ready to take action on new lines, as we are, and those who are not ready to take such action. It is the Labour Movement by its creation of monopolies . . . and its capitulation to sectional interests among its own supporters, which is adhering to the slogans of "monopoly and vested interests." I am certain that we should accept the main line of the Charter, which is strong Central Government policy. To those who criticise this I would remind them that the laying down of priorities, which has been one of the cardinal points in Socialism, cannot be done unless you have a strong Central Government policy. It is precisely because we have weak central guidance that the country is in the mess it is. We do not claim that the State should interfere right throughout. I am sure that is contrary to all our own philosophy and contrary to all common sense. We say that the State's long finger should not reach down into those matters in which public interference clogs and delays action, and in which personal endeavour alone can ensure progress and ensure liberty. . . .

I have been thinking that this is our 68th Annual Conference. It was about sixty-four years ago that our Leader's father, Lord Randolph Churchill, stirred up the National Union and brought vigour into their ranks. I remember working for several years now in the old Post-War Problems Committee, helping our leader who must take the final decision on all those matters and must himself promulgate the policy when the time comes. Now the Conference has a chance to give its endorsement of some work which we have tried to do at your request from

Blackpool. Please give us this authority. . . .

We want authority to go ahead with this development policy. I believe that is vital to our Party, and I believe that we can inspire ourselves by the words used by Lord Randolph Churchill in October, 1883, when he was speaking: "If you want to gain the confidence of the working classes, let them have a share, and a large share—a real share and not a sham share—in your Party Councils and in your Party Government"; and I would add "in industry." If you wish that to be the case you may be sure that our Party has a great future, and if you believe that, you can show it most readily by endorsing the Charter this afternoon and taking it quite clearly from me and my fellow-members of the Committee that we will listen to any constructive suggestions. This is only a beginning, and when we have your immediate approval we can then go ahead to better work and better tasks. (*Prolonged applause.*)

THE CHAIRMAN: You have heard that very important statement from Mr. Butler. The mover and seconder of the Resolution have agreed to accept the amendment. . . .May I read it very carefully, to make quite sure what the Conference is voting on?

That this Conference, in welcoming the Industrial Charter as a clear restatement of the general principles of Conservative economic policy, recommends that the Committee which prepared it should be kept in being and should take full account of constructive suggestions in order that the Party may be able, at short notice, to publish an industrial programme based on this Charter."

Is everybody agreed to vote on that? (*Agreed.*)

(The Motion, as amended, was put to the Conference and carried, with three dissentients. At a later stage, the Chairman announced that the Motion had been carried unanimously at the overflow.)

Jo Grimond

4. A THIRD PARTY?

The British Liberal Party has never fully recovered from the 1916 split between its two leaders, H. H. Asquith and David Lloyd George. During the interwar years it was gradually replaced by Labour as the second major party. In recent years, however, there have been persistent signs of a Liberal revival. Jo Grimond was elected party leader in 1956 and set out to establish the Liberals as a radical, nonsocialist alternative to the Tories. At the 1964 election the Liberals won more than three million votes.*

British politics for the last hundred years and more have been carried on by what may be called a two-bloc system. . . . One bloc provided the Government. The other bloc criticized, obstructed and raised grievances. . . .

The convenience of straight disagreement between a conservative and a progressive bloc is obvious. You can then have periods of change interspersed by periods of consolidation. The dialogue goes on in all life and to some extent in each person. It is easily understandable and comforting to our general notions. The awkward situation arises when there is no agreement among progressives about the direction of progress. Luckily when there is such a disagreement it seldom runs through the whole political field and it seldom splits the progressives into equal halves.

In the nineteenth century the progressive side of politics was engaged in freeing people, industry and trade from eighteenth-century paternalism. There were, of course, progressives who saw the dangers of carrying this process too far. But the main stream of progressive thought—through Adam Smith, Bentham, the Mills and Ricardo —was fairly plain. Towards the end of the century it became widely apparent that the

process had in fact gone too far. Humanitarians were horrified at the disintegration of society. They were indignant at the slums. They revolted at the price we were paying for the Industrial Revolution. They saw that in the general rush towards freedom, one of the winners was original sin. . . . So men, having seen the teaching of Adam Smith hopelessly distorted, and faced with what appeared to be the breakdown of a homogeneous society, looked round for some creed which might satisfy morality and a desire for the common good: a creed which would also be strong enough to restrain the imps escaped from Pandora's Box and might once again speak in the name of the whole citizen body. They called in State Socialism. Faith in the power of the state to improve society was not confined to Socialists. The whole progressive movement was infected by the natural and proper belief that a great deal of good could be achieved by state action. . . .

But as a creed for today Socialism has fundamental defects. It has lost its moral force. It is committed to certain views which are dubious in the economic field and if applied logically would entail a severe restriction of liberty. It has never developed a political theory of its own and

---

*In 1966, although their total votes fell, they increased their parliamentary representation from nine to twelve. [Editor's note]

From Joseph Grimond, *The Liberal Challenge* (London, 1963), pp. 297–315. Reprinted by permission of the author and Hollis & Carter, Ltd.

III. *Attitudes and Ideologies*

even now few of its adherents still give any thought to the relation of Socialism and Democracy. The result of the movement towards Socialism has been the all-powerful state, with the evils which it has entailed. I am not suggesting that Socialists deliberately willed Bismarck, Hitler, Stalin or Mussolini to power, any more than Liberalism deliberately willed the hard-faced exploiters of the nineteenth-century. Of course, just as many Liberals fought the evils of *laissez-faire*, so the Socialists were among the first to denounce the vice of the all-embracing state.

But nevertheless, as Liberalism must take its share of the blame for making the break-up of society respectable in the nineteenth-century, so Socialism bears some guilt for spreading the tentacles of the state in the twentieth. Socialism did not realize until too late how damaging to human relations the new tyranny might be. It gave little thought to how an executive might be controlled and it constantly justified interference with liberty. The decline of the nation state obviously puts a Party so closely associated with it into difficulties.

The Labour Party is often accused of being a class Party—and a fusty class Party at that. So long as we run a class system it is not unreasonable to have class Parties. The danger is that the Labour Party has a vested interest in keeping this class system. It has a vested interest in maintaining a class of "outsiders" when what is wanted in this country is to have a better "inside". . . .

Further the Labour Party has a broad streak of nationalist, restrictionist feeling. Socialist planning still emphasizes "physical" controls. By "physical" controls are meant the curbing or stimulation of certain operations in the economy; for instance a limit on the building of petrol stations to free resources for municipal housing. With this goes naturally suspicion of new developments such as the Common Market, which are outside our tradition and may dilute control over our own affairs. Mixed with other emotions CND too has a share of isolationism.

Socialism in the sense of an ethical belief in co-operation as against competition and a revulsion against profit is confined to a small section of the Labour Party. In the 1930s, whether a Socialist could conscientiously be rich, or own shares, was a subject for earnest discussion. Now few Socialists are averse to taking profits, expenses, and high salaries. The modern case for nationalization, in so far as it is argued at all, is put forward not so much for ethical, as for practical reasons.

Some Socialists seize on the Galbraith thesis of public squalor in the midst of private affluence. They claim that it is true of this country as well as America and can only be cured by further nationalization. The link in the reasoning is that without some profitable nationalization a Labour Government will never get the money to improve the public services—taxation being so unpopular. Some Socialists too claim that the state must control the commanding heights of the economy. Which industries fall under this description is not clear. Sometimes coal, steel, the railways, and chemicals, industries historically "basic," seem the kind of industry intended, though the importance of coal and the railways —perhaps soon even steel—is decreasing. . . . These strands in Socialist thought add up to a recognizable body of opinion. It has swayed the Party against the Common Market and rapped down any tampering with Clause 4.

But there are clearly other opinions on the progressive side of politics. Politics cannot be channelled within a predetermined number of Parties tailored to suit politicians. While the Right may usually find one Party because there is only one way of standing still, the progressives, who want to move, find there is more than one direction in which they may go.

Opposing strands of political thought—the Liberal Party

There are many people who want to change in the opposite direction, away from a nationalist, conservative, restrictionist policy. They want planning, but of a type which relies on fiscal measures, skilful management of currency and credit and the sophisticated techniques of guiding the economy as a whole rather than imposing clamps on this operation or that. As for the "commanding heights," there are those who see the need for some over-all plan for the economy but do not see the relevance of nationalizing a few industries. . . .

These were the people who wanted to join the Common Market. These are the people who see that Britain, because she was not invaded, has kept her old class-ridden society. They realize that it is not only new machinery and buildings that we need but new methods and above all opportunities for new men. They are not in awe of the conservative and established — they want quicker promotion and promotion by merit. They hear nationalization as an echo from an old controversy.

These people also represent an identifiable point of view. They rest on a different base. Their politics flow from wider interests than the established attitudes. They are concerned about individual relationships. Where are they to find political leverage? It is to them the Liberal Party looks. . . .

The Conservative Party

The Conservative Party thrives on the fear of many people for what change may bring. It is not difficult to persuade those who are well-off that change would be a mistake. Nor at the other end of the scale are the very poor usually keen on change unless they are driven to desperation. For them the margins are so small that they must cling to what they have. There is then a large middle range of people who, if things are going well, at least have hopes of the future. This makes them conservative in the present.

The appeal of the Conservative Party also unlocks a mixed bag of emotions and prejudices. Nationalism, suspicion of foreigners and the unfamiliar in general, association with tradition, glory, success, especially financial and social success, can all be played upon by Conservatives.

Of course, the Conservative Party embraces many people who are not wholly conservative. It is not usually a reactionary Party in the sense of being a Party which wants to undo much of what more progressive Parties have achieved. The very lack of *reactionary* spirit highlights its *conservatism*. It sees insuperable difficulties in any change. However badly some existing method works it is assumed that it is better than any alteration. It accepts whatever is. A good example of the conservatism of the Conservative Party is its treatment of the nationalized industries. They were monuments of Socialism. They were anathema to the Party. Play upon the fears of nationalization has been the stock-in-trade of Conservative propaganda since 1951. Yet no effort has been made to denationalize them for many years.

At every Election Tory meetings ring with denunciation of Government expenditure. Yet under Conservative Ministers it rises steadily. The taxation system does not work — evasion is widespread — yet Tories have done nothing radically to change it. In the face of the Tories' inability to change even those features of our government which they are supposed to dislike, what chance is there of them summoning the will or energy to promote any new reforms?

Along with inertia the Tories have the habit of putting off decisions as long as possible and hiding away the realities of modern choice in cupboards where perhaps they hope they will not be noticed. They tried to back out of Suez shouting that it was a great success, spoiled by someone else (the favourite Tory technique of blaming the other fellow). They tried to ignore the Common Market for as long as possible and then edge towards it hoping no one would notice. . . .

The mingling of what is more strictly a conservative mentality with what might be described as the Tory mentality results in some peculiarly distinctive features of the Conservative Party — for, of course, the Conservative Party is not the only home of conservatives; there are conservatives outside it. The word Tory means robber, I am

53

told. That may be a little blunt. But there is a strain of authoritarianism in the Conservative Party which at its best may be called paternal and at its worst is upper-class, overbearing and acquisitive. The best of Toryism is feudal. Once the obligations of feudalism withered the Party never found another justification anything like so compelling, nor a philosophy so attractive. Now too often feudalism has degenerated into the assumption that there is some deference due to the rich and the upper classes. This strain too not only suffers from xenophobia but rejoices in so suffering. It admires a certain toughness for the sake of toughness, as can be seen in its attachment to the gallows and the birch and in the general tone of much of its propaganda. It is inhumane. This Tory strain has not taken over the Conservative Party but it has achieved its negative successes within the Party. It has landed us with a hideous and cruel compromise over the death penalty, and it has the Commonwealth Immigration Bill to keep it happy. . . .

New Party Divisions?

Three Parties, or indeed even more, allowing for Scottish and Welsh Nationalists, correspond to the present pressures in politics if they were properly aligned. . . .

At present three Parties are perfectly consistent with the British system. It has never been a two-Party system. If we are to continue the two-bloc system the natural division at present would be a Conservative Party faced by two Parties of change, the larger of which would be a liberal, radical Party embracing as well as the Liberal Party some people now voting Conservative and a large part of the Labour Party; the smaller being a Socialist Party. . . .

There would be dangers in a break-up of the [present] Party structure. Might it not lead to a situation in which everyone was so comfortable, so to speak, so well disposed to everyone else that there was even less appetite for change and less will to face unpleasant decisions than there is now?

But this danger is with us now. Already there is a disposition in politics not to block other people's log-rolling so long as they allow your log a free roll. Demands are frequently made that this or that subject should be taken out of Party politics. Anyone who listens to debates in the House of Commons must be aware of how often Ministers plead the public interest as a reason for giving no answer to questions, or of those appeals to the Opposition not to vote because of the bad effect it will have on world opinion. These evasions are often unnecessary and harmful. There is a danger in too much "statesmanlike" behaviour. But at present it arises because of the distortion of the Party system, and it will not be cured by strengthening the grip of the present Parties.

The immediate rate of change within the Party system may be determined by the development of two factors. These factors have a bearing on the progress towards a dominant position of a Liberal Party. The first of these factors is the connection between the Party and an interest.

Must a Party be based on interest? On this I indicated right at the outset of this book that it need not—indeed cannot—be based on an interest in the old simple sense. Instead of digging themselves into the class and interest structure people are in various ways trying to break out of it. Culture is more general. Television is a great leveller. Status symbols are more universal. The economic divisions are altering. It is the middle rank of university teachers, workmen in certain towns of high unemployment, some small farmers, who feel the economic pinch, and these are not a homogeneous interest. The young less than ever want to take on their parents' clothes, real or figurative.

But the importance for a Party of attachment to some interest is that this gives it money and organization, and enlists on its side some of the inertia with which politics is heavily burdened. At times of stress it gives it a hard core of unthinking support. All this may not be enough to give a majority by itself; but can a Party rise without such an interest? And has a progressive radical Liberal Party any roots in any such interest?

Hope for Radical Development

He would be a naïve politician who, after visiting Tyneside or Clydeside, declared that the old working-class interest had disappeared. Every Liberal struggling up without benefit of patronage on a budget of not more than one-fifth to one-tenth of other Parties, and with the bias of the means of communication in the main against all he or she fights for, must often sigh for the bloc vote, the bloc reaction. But there is likely to be a change, a change of emphasis only if you like, or a change which will for some time only affect a part of the nation, but a change nevertheless. People are more interested in consumption; they are in every sense more mobile and they are more interested in political questions such as Defence. Add to this that Liberalism has an interest—a strong interest—among the new educated class, the technicians, scientists, teachers (it has lately been relatively strong in the universities) and in the growing middle class. The success of the Liberal Party in local government I regard as its most striking advance. It brings it back into the practical political field and it leads to a great number of people identifying themselves not in the vague sense of being liberals (with a small 'l' very often) casting a forlorn vote in a general election, but in the sense of having seen some concrete results from their Liberal activity.

The other factor is the "presidential" aspect of general elections.

It is said that general elections will always be a gladiatorial contest between champions of two Parties. There is no room for a third Party. The electorate will not vote for a situation in which the smaller Party may hold the balance. So, as any change in the Party structure presupposes a period of uncertainty on this point, no

change can take place. The electors, it is said, will be unwilling to risk the election of the Party they like least. This is the old argument of the "wasted vote" or the argument against "letting the Socialist in." In so far as this argument has any validity it is an argument against our present electoral system. Certainly at present the electoral system is little better than a lottery. Such systems should be made for the electors, not the electors for the system. If the electors cannot vote the way they want, then the system should be changed. . . .

Certainly if we are not to have other types of political reform, the case for electoral reform in some seats for election to the Commons is very strong.

But even without proportional representation, though I do not doubt that the trend towards presidential politics, with the Prime Minister and official Leader of the Opposition contending on behalf of monolithic national Parties, makes change more difficult, yet I cannot believe that it can prevent it. It is of course accentuated by those political gossip writers who are not interested in political policies but solely in personalities and who is going to win. It may be that we are going to see another period of non-Tory Government, after a half century during which, with the exception of some five years, the Conservatives have been the effective political power. Even so, it will not be a fair ration for the progressive side of politics. Nor does it look as though it will be founded on a determination to move forward, so much as on echoes of high unemployment from the thirties. In these circumstances, though the evolution of a new social and political structure may be retarded, it will not be stopped—unless people lose interest in parliamentary democracy itself.

I have no doubt that the old propaganda against a Third Party—don't split the vote, i.e. the vote for or against the major Parties which have the most chance of forming a Government—will be telling. It may not, however, be quite so telling as it was. More people are questioning the very framework of politics. Fewer people are terrified of their opponents. More people are anxious for a new departure and do not see it in terms of Tory or Labour, and a lot of people—and very able people—at all levels and in many professions are now actively convinced that Liberal attitudes and reforms are what is needed. Though it is extremely difficult for active politicians to raise questions without being pounced upon for failing to provide exact answers, though the floating of unusual political ideas on the main media of communication is also extremely difficult, yet there is, I believe, a small but growing desire for a fresh departure such as Liberals offer.

At present many of these people find their best hope of achieving the sort of society they want in a radical Liberal Party: a Party different in kind in many ways from the present Tory and Labour Parties, allowing loose discipline and accepting considerable co-operation with members of other Parties for some types of business, a Party advocating structural change not only in politics, but in the civil and legal administration, industry and the hierarchy of social life. . . .

IV. *Followers and Leaders*

R. T. McKenzie

1. A MYTH DESTROYED

Few books have had a greater impact on the study of politics in Britain than Robert McKenzie's *British Political Parties*. First published in 1955, it immediately sparked off an academic controversy which has continued to the present day. The book consists mainly of a history of the distribution of power within the two major political parties. The following selection comes from Professor McKenzie's final chapter and summarizes his conclusions.

Both major parties [in Britain] have consistently exaggerated the differences between their party organizations with a view to proving that their own is "democratic" and that of their opponents is not. The Labour Party customarily argues that the Conservative Leader rules his party with the iron hand of an autocrat; that he is not subject to the effective control either of his followers in Parliament or of the mass organization of the party outside Parliament. Labour spokesmen claim that, in contrast, their own party is fully democratic because their party leaders are subject to annual re-election (at least when the party is in opposition) and both the Leader and the parliamentary party, they claim, are ultimately responsible to the annual conference of the party. The Conservatives habitually reply that the Labour Party in Parliament is in fact subject to the control of a tight-knit clique of party managers at the party head office and of a group of trade union oligarchs; these party "bosses," the Conservatives charge, manipulate the affairs of the party in their own interest and are in no way responsible to the electorate. The Conservative spokesmen draw a sharp contrast between this state of affairs and the position in their own party, where the parliamentary Leader (who is subject to the control of the electorate) is assigned full responsibility for the affairs of the party, although (the Conservatives add) he gives due weight to the views of his party followers both inside and outside Parliament.

All of these descriptions of the power structures of the rival parties, proffered by the parties themselves, are fundamentally misleading. The Conservative statement of the position within their own party is perhaps the least misleading of the four views summarized above (although. . .the Conservative Leader plays nothing like the almost dictatorial rôle Conservative literature would seem to suggest). But the Conserva-

From R. T. McKenzie, *British Political Parties: the Distribution of Power within the Conservative and Labour Parties,* second revised ed. (New York, 1964), pp. 635–642. Reprinted by permission of the author, Frederick A. Praeger, Inc., and Heinemann Educational Books.

tive view of the Labour Party and the Labour Party's own picture both of itself and of its opponents are highly misleading.

Some part of the confusion about the power structure of the parties arises . . . from a careless use of terms and a failure to distinguish between several autonomous organizations which are loosely associated together for common political purposes. Two parliamentary parties face each other in the House of Commons: they are correctly called "the Conservative Party" and "the Parliamentary Labour Party." Each is an autonomous organization which is aided for electoral purposes by a mass organization of its supporters: the Conservatives by "The National Union of Conservative and Unionist Associations," the Parliamentary Labour Party by a body properly known as "The Labour Party." At the regional and national level each of the mass organizations is sustained by a professional staff, the Conservative Central Office and the Labour Party head office. The mass organizations are best understood as voluntary associations of the politically-active members of the population who are prepared to work for the return to office of one or other of the parliamentary parties. Each mass organization represents a reservoir of largely voluntary and unpaid labour of the sort which is indispensable in the era of the mass electorate. All other functions of the mass organization are, and must remain, subsidiary to their primary task as vote-getting agencies. They can and do exact a certain price for their labour; they expect to be, and are, listened to by their leaders. Like Bagehot's constitutional monarch, the annual party conference has the right to be consulted, the right to encourage, and the right to warn. But this is not to say that the members of the mass organization have the right, under the British parliamentary system, to control or direct the actions of their parliamentary leaders.

The evolution of the British political parties in the era of the mass electorate has witnessed two striking developments, both of which reflect the ascendancy and the primacy of Parliament. Until well into the nineteenth century the Conservative Party was no more than a grouping of a few hundred Members of Parliament and Peers who were associated together for sustaining (whenever it proved feasible) a Conservative cabinet. They had neither a professional staff of any size nor a mass organization of voluntary supporters in the country; nor did they need them. They were able to rely for the most part on the allegiance and authority of the squirearchy and the generous financial contributions of a section of the business community to provide the very considerable financial resources which were required to win elections in the days of widespread political corruption. Two developments forced the Conservative Party to transform itself. The first was the rapid expansion of the electorate, especially in 1867 and afterwards; and the second, the drastic tightening of the electoral laws against corruption. Even if the Conservatives had not themselves become aware that these developments would force a transformation of the party, the initiative of the Liberals under Joseph Chamberlain would certainly have forced them to do so. In any event, a combination of pressures forced the Conservative Party to devise a mass organization of voluntary supporters to sustain the Conservative cause and to secure votes at elections. Disraeli and Lord Randolph Churchill provided a new statement of Toryism which succeeded in attracting a wide range of popular support, and a number of hardworking party managers did the job of building the National Union as the co-ordinating agency of Conservative activity in the country.

It was by no means certain (when Ostrogorski wrote at the end of the century) that the National Union or the Central Office (or both) might not manage ultimately to become the controlling influence in the affairs of the Conservative Party. Parliament might, as Ostrogorski feared, ultimately be supplanted by the caucus. But. . .this has not happened. Effective control of the affairs of the Conservative Party remains in the hands of the Leader thrown up by the parliamentary party and those he chooses as his associates; they retain their authority as long as they retain the support of their followers in Parliament. The National Union remains what it was declared to be in its earliest beginnings, a "handmaid" to the party in Parliament although, as befits a more democratic age, it has fairly frequently talked to its masters in a way that no Victorian domestic servant would ever have dared to do. The Conservative Party has been transformed since the mid-nineteenth century; it now has a large popular organization which labours on its behalf between and during elections; but the working of the parliamentary party has been remarkably little affected.

A combination of factors has helped to ensure the autonomy of the Conservative parliamentary party. The first has been the sharp awareness of the dangers of extra-parliamentary control on the part of the leaders of the party. The party had existed in Parliament long before it found it necessary to call its mass organization into being. Its leaders, familiar with the rules and conventions of cabinet government, were instinctively aware of the dangers of allowing the extra-parliamentary party to claim a decisive voice in the affairs of the party. Moreover their authority has been reinforced by the fact that the party has been so frequently and continuously in office during the modern period. (In the 77 years since 1886 the Conservatives have been in opposition for only 21 years.) While the Leader of any party is Prime Minister, and his principal colleagues constitute a cabinet, there can be no debate as to where, in principle, final authority in the party lies. In practice, the party's activists outside Parliament may on occasion become so bitterly hostile to policies of the parliamentary leadership that they can play a considerable part either in changing those policies or in overthrowing the existing Leadership. (This was certainly the case in 1922 when Austen Chamberlain, then Conservative Leader in the Commons and a member of the Lloyd George coalition, failed in his attempt to carry the Conservatives into a permanent alliance with the Lloyd George Liberals.) But, in general, party Leaders in office (whether Conservative, Liberal or Labour) have little to fear from their activists outside Parliament.

In addition, the traditional Conservative concepts of leadership and discipline have tended to discourage (although not to eliminate) the possibilities of rebellion. In all normal circumstances revolt against their leaders is furthest from the minds of even the most militant Conservative party workers. Subtle considerations of social deference towards their leading parliamentarians (especially when they are the Queen's ministers, as they tend to be for so much of the time) reinforce the party's own view that it is the prime duty of "followers" to sustain rather than to attempt to dominate their leaders. Except in comparatively rare circumstances, therefore, the Conservative extra-parliamentary organization does no more, so far as policy-making is concerned, than to fulfil its appointed rôle within the party organization: that is to offer advice (which may or may not be acted upon) to the party's parliamentary leaders.

This should not be taken to mean that the National Union has played a wholly insignificant part in the affairs of the Party. It loomed very large indeed in the great controversies over Tariff Reform before the First World War; it had to be taken seriously into account during the struggle over the Irish Treaty in 1921 and during the downfall of the Coalition in 1922. Baldwin was frequently in trouble with his followers outside Parliament and had to pay close attention to their views during the period of the General Strike and during the great debates on the future of India in the early 1930s.

Since 1945 the National Union appears to have had an explicit influence on party policy only on rare occasions. . . .This may have been one consequence of the post-war "democratization" of the party undertaken by Lord Woolton. The annual conference is manifestly more representative of rank-and-file Conservative support in the country than ever before; right-wing ideological dogmatism has been much less in evidence than it was, for example, in Baldwin's day. But, in addition, for the twelve years after 1951 the party leaders constituted the government of the country and this in itself assured their absolute ascendancy within the party assemblies.

The transformation of the Labour Party in the half-century of its existence has been in one sense diametrically different from that of the Conservatives, although the end product is in certain important respects strikingly similar. While the Conservative Party in Parliament created a mass organization to serve its purposes, Labour began as a movement in the country which created a parliamentary party to give the working class a voice in the House of Commons. A gathering representing some hundreds of thousands of organized trade unionists and a few thousand members of socialist societies decided in 1900 to co-operate together for this purpose. They soon found it necessary to instruct their representatives in Parliament to form themselves into what amounted to a parliamentary party. This body began increasingly to resemble the other great parliamentary parties as it came to rival them in size and strength. By the time the Parliamentary Labour Party had taken office in 1924 its transformation was almost complete. By accepting all the conventions with respect to the office of Prime Minister and of Cabinet government it ensured that effective power within the party would be concentrated in the hands of the leadership of the PLP. When the party has been in power this proposition has been self-evident and largely unchallenged. Each of the two governments formed by MacDonald and by Attlee wielded not one whit less authority than other governments in comparable circumstances; nor were they in any sense subject to external direction

by the party outside Parliament. Indeed, if the Labour Party had been as continuously in office as the Conservatives have been, it is highly likely that the issue of external control of the Parliamentary Party would be as nearly dead in the Labour Party as it is with the Conservatives.

But even with Labour so continuously in opposition the autonomy of the PLP and the authority of its leaders has been demonstrated beyond question. From Keir Hardie to Gaitskell the Leaders have repeatedly refused to accept external direction. They have taken the view expounded by Morgan Phillips, the former Secretary of the Party:". . . the Parliamentary Party could not maintain its position in the country if it could be demonstrated that it was at any time or in any way subject to dictation from an outside body which, however representative of the Party, could not be regarded as representative of the country." And it was particularly significant that, on the day of his election as Leader in 1963, Harold Wilson stated that he did not consider himself bound by the Labour Party conference resolution demanding withdrawal of the American Polaris base from Britain because that resolution had not been accepted by the Parliamentary Labour Party.

The Labour Party's devices for ensuring the ascendancy of the Parliamentary Party and its leaders. . . are infinitely more complex than those which obtain in the Conservative Party. But basically they have depended on the existence of a bond of confidence between the parliamentary leaders and a sufficient number of leading trade unionists to command preponderant support for the policies of the party leadership at the party conference. During most of Labour's history it has been overwhelmingly clear that the initiative in the main areas of policy-making (with the possible exception of industrial relations) has lain with the parliamentary leaders rather than with their trade union allies; the latter appear tacitly at least to have recognized that the leaders of the PLP, as a potential cabinet or "Shadow Government," cannot appear, even in opposition, to be reduced to the rôle of political spokesmen for the trade union movement or for the Labour Party conference, with its dominant trade union block vote.

It was also shown [earlier in the book] that, in all normal circumstances, Labour's parliamentary leaders (who, like their Conservative opposite numbers, will take into account the currents of opinion within all sections of the party in the course of determining their policies) are likely to be sustained by majority support with the PLP and the NEC, and in *both* the trade union and the constituency sections of the mass organization. Except on the rarest occasions in the history of the party it has been a Centre-Right majority in the PLP which has carried the day against a Left minority within each of the constituent elements of the party.

The left-wing activists in the constituencies have been repeatedly disillusioned on discovering that the party's rhetoric about "inner-party democracy" bears so little relation to its practice. R. H. S. Crossman, one of the recent heroes of the activists, has summarized the situation, as the militants tend to see it, with cruel precision:

> . . . since it could not afford, like its opponents, to maintain a large army of paid party workers, the Labour Party required militants — politically conscious socialists to do the work of organizing the constituencies. But since these militants tended to be "extremists," a constitution was needed which maintained their enthusiasm by apparently creating a full party democracy while excluding them from effective power. Hence the concession in principle of sovereign powers to the delegates at the Annual Conference, and the removal in practice of most of this sovereignty through the trade union block vote on the one hand, and the complete independence of the Parliamentary Labour Party on the other.

The only occasion when the party's policy-decision mechanisms broke down completely was in 1960–61 when, on a major issue of policy, the party leadership was unable to win preponderant trade union support in the conference (although at Scarborough in 1960 two-thirds of the constituency delegates supported the parliamentary leadership). And in this profoundly important test case a sufficient number of the dissident unions subsequently reversed themselves in the following year to ensure that the next party conference would fall in line again with the Parliamentary Party.

Thereafter the autonomy of the PLP could hardly any longer be in dispute. But what was in dispute was whether the party could continue to cling to a policy-decision process which conveyed the *public* impression that Labour's parliamentary leaders (and therefore the alternative government) were repeatedly on the point of destruction at the hands of their more militant "supporters." In fact, of course, Gaitskell emerged from the struggle of 1960–61 a more powerful figure in his party than all but a very few Leaders of any of the main parties in this century. And this helped enormously to enhance his personal standing as a prospective Prime Minister. But the opinion polls and other evidence strongly suggests that the Labour Party has suffered grave electoral damage as a consequence of its bitter public quarrels. Yet, incredibly enough, the party has made no move even to re-examine its decision-making processes in almost half a century.

Friction between parliamentary parties and their supporters outside Parliament is no doubt inevitable; the parliamentarians, in determining their policies, must take many factors into account and, whatever weight they may give to the views of their active supporters on particular issues, they cannot allow themselves to be reduced to the rôle of spokesmen of the active minority who control their extra-parliamentary organizations. The Labour Party endowed itself with a party constitution which raised this danger in sharpest form. Yet the leadership group of the PLP, while paying lip-service to the theory of inner-party democracy, has repeatedly and consistently refused to accept direction from its extra-parliamentary supporters.

61

Setting aside the party myths and the inter-party propaganda it is clear that the primary function of the mass organizations of the Conservative and Labour parties is to sustain two competing teams of parliamentary leaders between whom the electorate as a whole may periodically choose. When the electorate has made its choice, the leaders of the successful team don the garments of authority which are provided under the Cabinet system and they retain this authority so long as they retain the confidence of their followers in Parliament (and, of course, of the electorate). Their followers outside Parliament become little more than a highly organized pressure group with a special channel of communication directly to the Leader, the Cabinet and the parliamentary party. Any disposition to take advantage of this special relationship is normally more than neutralized by feelings of pride and loyalty to their leaders and by an anxiety not to embarrass them in the execution of their duties or to provide aid and comfort to the rival team, who are eagerly preparing to overthrow them at the forthcoming election. Most governments at one time or another find it advisable to make concessions on some issue of policy to the clearly expressed views of their followers outside Parliament. But they make such concessions much more frequently to their followers *in* Parliament, on whose day-to-day support in the division lobbies the government depends, than they do to their followers in the country whose allegiance is tested normally only at five-yearly intervals. While the parliamentary party is in opposition it tends to listen more readily to the voices of its supporters in the country; but even while in opposition no major parliamentary party in the modern period has allowed itself to be relegated to the rôle of spokesman or servant of its mass organization.

Saul Rose

2. POLICY DECISION IN OPPOSITION

Most political scientists accept Robert McKenzie's conclusions as they apply to the Conservative Party. But many dissent from his account of Labour's power structure. Some critics maintain that his analysis has been falsified by events since 1955. Others insist that he grossly underestimates the importance of the trade unions in the formation of Labour policy. One of the first to take issue with Professor McKenzie was Saul Rose, a former Labour Party official.

Three years' experience at Transport House from 1952 to 1955 as Secretary of the International Department of the Labour Party have instilled in the writer an appreciation of the danger of generalizing about the Labour Party. Any general statements made in this article are therefore to be understood with the qualification that they relate to those three years when the Labour Party was in opposition. During the period after the war when Labour was in office, the way in which policy decisions were made was certainly different. Even in opposition, it would be rash to assume that an analysis based on earlier years remains valid. In the interests of brevity and clarity no attempt is made to deal systematically with the process of policy formulation, as

From Saul Rose, "Policy Decision in Opposition" in *Political Studies*, vol. IV, no. 2 (June 1956), pp. 128–138. Reprinted by permission of The Clarendon Press.

distinct from policy decision, although the two processes are interrelated.

To see how Labour Party policy is decided it will be useful to look first at the way in which policy is ascertained. Students of politics have a special interest in the process by which decisions on policy are reached; but a far more frequent question in practical politics is "What is the policy?" It is a question which may be asked by supporters or opponents or by the elusive floating voter, by affiliated organizations or by foreign visitors. It arises also in the preparation of official publications.

In principle, there should be an answer. To reply that the Labour Party has no policy on a particular issue may sometimes make an impression of careful deliberation or open-mindedness; but if it happened too often, the Opposition would be in danger of forfeiting its claim to be an alternative government. Also, a noncommittal answer is not likely to be much help to a local party agent who is being harried by opponents. Consequently, whenever the question is asked, the headquarters staff set out to find an answer. If all research fails, that may provide a reason, supposing the matter is sufficiently important, for seeking a policy decision.

Usually the question relates to matters which are currently in the news, and the reply is ready to hand. But there is always a first time for any question, and then the answer has to be sought. It is normally to be found among the following sources:

1. Annual Conference decisions.
2. Resolutions of the National Executive Committee (NEC).
3. Motions of the Parliamentary Labour Party (PLP).
4. Declarations by official spokesmen in the House of Commons.
5. Public statements by the Leader or Deputy-Leader.

These sources are not listed in order of precedence, nor could they be, for reasons which will emerge. Yet the way in which policy is decided hinges on the relations between them.

I. Annual Conference

The Party Constitution assigns wide functions to Conference in respect of policy. One of the Party Objects is "To give effect as far as may be practicable to the principles from time to time approved by the Party Conference." Further, "The Party Conference shall decide from time to time what specific proposals of legislative, financial or administrative reform shall be included in the Party Programme. No proposal shall be included in the Party Programme unless it has been adopted by the Party Conference by a majority of not less than two-thirds of the votes recorded on a card vote." Finally, "The work of the Party shall be under the direction and control of the Party Conference which shall itself be subject to the Constitution and Standing Orders of the Party."

According to the Constitution, therefore, Conference is the supreme authority on policy. It has been questioned whether this is so in practice. Mr. R. T. McKenzie, in his book *British Political Parties* contends: "Like Bagehot's constitutional monarch, the annual party conference has the right to be consulted, the right to encourage, and the right to warn." Whatever may have been the case when Labour was in office, this contention is a considerable underestimate of the role of the Labour Party Conference in opposition.

The Leader of the Labour Party gave a different interpretation in his exchange of letters with Mr. Churchill concerning the Laski episode. Mr. Attlee wrote: "Within the programme adopted by the annual party conference, the Parliamentary Labour Party has complete discretion in its conduct of Parliamentary business and in the attitude it should adopt to legislation tabled by other parties." As will appear, this is not only a more authoritative but also a more accurate statement of the relation between Conference and the PLP. The PLP has complete discretion — within limits laid down by Conference. Although Conference cannot give positive instructions to the PLP, it is nevertheless a higher authority than the PLP inasmuch as it determines the bounds of the PLP's actions. In practice, this applies not merely to the Party Programme but to Conference decisions generally.

To attempt to give the reasons would lead too far afield into the history and structure of the Labour Party. Nor does it really require explanation that the terms of the Constitution have some bearing on the actual position. It is not without significance that the PLP has each year to give an account of itself to Conference, nor that parliamentary candidates must undertake to "accept and conform to the Constitution, Programme, Principles and Policy of the Party." A rift between the PLP and Conference would be a free gift of political capital to the Party's opponents which it is obviously desirable to avoid. Moreover, in considering the relation between the PLP and Conference, it is sometimes overlooked that Conference decisions are mandatory upon the National Executive Committee and the Party headquarters.

The important fact is that Conference decisions are generally regarded as binding, at least to the extent that they are not to be contravened. Arguments may develop about differing interpretations of a Conference decision, or it may be contended that the situation has changed so radically as to make the decision no longer applicable; but no other organ of the Party claims the authority to override Conference. For example, the PLP decision concerning Western European Union in November 1954 was argued largely in relation to the resolution adopted at the previous Scarborough Conference. There was room for differences of interpretation, and the argument persisted; but the question of a West German defence contribution in some form was generally regarded as settled by that Conference.

At Scarborough, as at previous Conferences, there was not the impression that Conference was merely being consulted, warning, or encouraging. Conference was taking a decision which was hard fought and hung in the balance until the last. Some interesting remarks were made by Mr. Morrison about the situation that would arise if the NEC were defeated:

> If the Executive motion were lost today we should be in a chaotic situation in the House of Commons. . . . If the Party is in a state of confusion about this, with a sharp division between the Parliamentary leaders and the Party you will hear about it in the Election and it will not be very convenient. Supposing a Labour Government is returned, which is quite possible, are we going to be faced as a Government, as Mr. Attlee said, with a situation in which we are tied and fettered and cannot think in relation to the facts of a changing situation?

There is an implication here, as there was in Mr. Attlee's speech, that the Conference decision would be binding on a Labour Government. Resisting the temptation to pursue that speculation, it may be said that, *a fortiori,* it would be binding on the Party in opposition. Had the vote gone the other way, it is difficult to see how the PLP could have avoided voting against the Western European Union agreements. At the very least, the opponents of German rearmament would have had the endorsement of Conference for doing so, and would hardly have missed the opportunity. This was the expectation at the time, so much so that speculation centred, not on the consequential action of the PLP, but on the position of the Leader and Deputy-Leader in the event of defeat at Conference. It would be superfluous to multiply illustrations. There would be no need to labour the point had it not been challenged. Participants seem to have fewer doubts than observers that Labour Party Conferences really take decisions which determine policy.

There remains the argument that, nevertheless, the parliamentary leaders can be sure of having their way through their control of the NEC and the support of the block vote of the big trade unions at Conference. Mr. McKenzie puts it as follows:

> To summarize (and to put the matter bluntly), the parliamentary party for the most part re-

ceives the advice it wants to hear from the NEC and the party conference, first, because the PLP normally dominates the NEC by a system of overlapping membership, and second, because the PLP leaders are usually in effective control of the conference since the block votes of the big trade unions are almost invariably cast on the side of the parliamentary leaders of the party.

The presentation of this argument is somewhat confused. The NEC faces Conference collectively, without distinction between the parliamentary leaders and the rest. The argument is presumably that the parliamentary leaders normally control the NEC and the NEC in turn usually controls Conference by means of the block vote of the big trade unions. On this interpretation the NEC acts as a connecting link—one might almost say transmission belt—between Conference and the parliamentary leaders. This makes a tidy pattern—much more tidy than the reality.

II. The National Executive Committee

Much has been said and written about the effect of the block vote and the "steam-roller" of the big trade unions. What is sometimes lost sight of is that it is not very extraordinary that the majority of Conference supports the NEC most of the time. It would be more surprising if it did not —however that majority may be constituted.

The NEC cannot count on automatic support, from any section of Conference, for any policy that it may choose. On the contrary, estimates of the feeling within the Party and probable Conference reactions play a considerable part in shaping proposals made by the NEC. This may be stigmatized as juggling with the Conference votes; it may equally be regarded as an essential part of the democratic process by which the leadership and the rank and file are kept in step. Results are not guaranteed: it is not very exceptional for the NEC to be defeated at Conference or be obliged to make concessions. The support of the big trade unions is by no means invariable. . . .

To attribute NEC majorities at Conference to the consistent backing of the big trade unions is a superficial and partial analysis. It omits the important point that the object of the NEC is precisely to secure majority support at Conference, and that support is normally obtained, both from the trade unions and the constituency parties, in the policy-making process. The association of the trade unions with policy-making is provided by trade union representation on the NEC (although trade union members do not sit as representatives of their respective unions), meetings of the National Council of Labour, and a variety of consultations, formal or informal, with the TUC, all of which help to define the majority view. The participation of constituency parties in policy-making operates through somewhat different channels. The combination of these two continuing processes results each year in Conference decisions which, if the NEC is successful in its policy-making, should normally go in its favour.

The NEC's role is not confined to guidance of Conference. It also makes declarations of policy between Conferences. It regards itself as having the right and the duty to interpret Conference decisions or, if need be, to decide new policy. For example, the Margate (1953) Conference declared that "there should be no German rearmament before further efforts have been made to secure the peaceful reunification of Germany." After the Berlin Conference the NEC came to the conclusion that "further efforts have been made and have been frustrated by the Soviet Union," and accordingly declared in favour of a West German defence contribution. Such decisions are subject to Conference approval and could be repudiated by the subsequent Conference. This is less likely to happen in respect of policy decisions if only because, in the interval, the decision will probably become a *fait accompli* or the situation will change so as to present the question in a different form. The NEC decision in favour of the European Defence Community was not challenged at the 1954 Conference, although it had provoked strong reactions when it was made. By the time of the Conference the breakdown of EDC had caused the decision to lapse, and the debate on German rearmament took place on an emergency NEC resolution, adjusted to the changed situation, and a counter-motion from the floor. . . .

III. The NEC and the PLP

The Constitution prescribes that "The Executive Committee shall, subject to the control and directions of the Party Conference, be the Administrative Authority of the Party." In this, its position differs from the PLP which is not subject to positive instructions by Conference. It might be supposed therefore that the PLP has superior authority to the NEC in deciding policy. In fact, however, their relationship tends to fluctuate. Since both the NEC and the PLP have the right to interpret Conference decisions, the clearest indication of their relative authority would emerge where there is a conflict of interpretation. This very rarely happens, for reasons which will be indicated. But there is one instance which occurred in 1954, relating to National Service.

On 2 March 1954 Mr. Shinwell, on behalf of the PLP, moved an amendment to the Government motion on National Service, regretting that the Government ". . . in particular, has made no proposals for a reduction in the length of National Service." Ordinarily, this would have meant that the Labour Party had decided in favour of a cut in the call-up, and the Labour League of Youth, naturally jumping to that conclusion, embarked on a campaign to the effect that "Two years is too long." At that time, however, a tripartite committee drawn from the NEC, TUC, and Parliamentary Committee was considering the question of National Service, and had not yet reached a conclusion. The PLP had "jumped the gun." Neither the NEC nor the TUC was prepared to be presented with a *fait accom-*

pli in this fashion, so the policy remained in suspense. The PLP amendment did not receive the customary publicity in Party literature, and the League of Youth campaign with some difficulty was called off.

The tripartite committee eventually recommended that there should be a committee of inquiry into the National Service Acts, and this recommendation was endorsed by the NEC. At the 1954 Conference, therefore, the NEC opposed resolutions calling for a cut in the period of National Service, and succeeded in having them all remitted. On 28 April 1955 a motion on National Service was again moved in the House of Commons on behalf of the PLP by Mr. Shinwell. This time it read: ". . . the time has now arrived for a review. . . of the operation of the National Service Acts in the light of existing circumstances and commitments and, in particular, as to whether the period of National Service should still remain at two years." In this instance, therefore — a very exceptional one — of conflict between the PLP and NEC, the PLP fell into line with the NEC and TUC. Subsequently, the General Election Manifesto produced by a joint meeting of the NEC and Parliamentary Committee stated: "A Labour Government will at once submit all problems of defence to a searching enquiry. In particular, it will review the period of National Service."

The role of the NEC in preparing an election manifesto also seems to suggest that in policy decision it carries somewhat more weight than the PLP. According to the Constitution, "The National Executive Committee and the Executive Committee of the Parliamentary Labour Party shall decide which items from the Party Programme shall be included in the Manifesto which shall be issued by the National Executive Committee prior to every General Election." Mr. McKenzie asserts: "It has already been noted that the NEC and PLP must *jointly* decide which items shall be included in the manifesto and there can be little doubt that the influence of the PLP in these discussions is overwhelming, if for no other reason than that the NEC normally includes a majority of PLP members." This assumes a dichotomy between M.P.s and the rest, for which there is no warrant. It is equally true, and more relevant, that in a joint meeting between the NEC and the Parliamentary Committee the NEC has a majority.

What happened at the last election was that a draft manifesto was prepared by the Office. This was considered and revised by the NEC. At that stage the members of the Parliamentary Committee were invited by the NEC to attend a joint meeting to consider the revised draft. The presence of the additional members from the Parliamentary Committee at that meeting did not significantly affect the draft, to which only minor alterations were made. Unquestionably, at the last election, the NEC had the primary role in determining the election manifesto.

This is not to say that the NEC has primacy over the PLP in policy decision — merely that the relations between those two bodies are not so simple as some writers have portrayed them. Ordinarily, while Parliament is sitting, policy is expounded by the Parliamentary Committee and official spokesmen on behalf of the PLP. But the role of the NEC is enhanced when Parliament is not sitting, since it usually meets at least once a month except August whereas the PLP does not meet during recess. The NEC has sole responsibility for policy vis-à-vis Conference at which members of the PLP are present merely ex officio without voting rights. Judging by recent experience, the NEC has the major role in formulating the election manifesto. Finally, there is a tendency for the NEC to take a hand in policy when the PLP appears deadlocked or acutely divided, as over German rearmament.

How are the policy decisions of the NEC and the PLP kept on the same track? That a divergence can occur has been shown in the matter of National Service. Usually the two bodies do not find themselves considering the same questions of policy simultaneously. If a question which is currently being considered in Parliament is raised in the NEC, the Leader or Deputy-Leader or a member of the Parliamentary Committee would indicate the position, and it would usually be left to be dealt with by the PLP. If the NEC felt strongly that it should have a say in the matter, a joint meeting with the Parliamentary Committee or some other form of consultation would be arranged. . . .

It has been alleged [by McKenzie] that the parliamentary leaders are able to control the NEC because of the preponderance of M.P.s on that body. This contention rests on three fallacies. The first is that the policy cleavages in the NEC occur between the parliamentary and non-parliamentary members. During the years 1952–5 there were divergences in plenty, but none that conformed to this pattern. Secondly, there is no automatic tendency for M.P.s on the NEC to support the parliamentary leaders. On the contrary, the regular opposition was the Bevanite group, all of whom were M.P.s. In the year 1952–3 there were 17 M.P.s in a total of 27 NEC members. This is arithmetically a majority; but of those 17, six were constantly in opposition. This wipes out the majority which, for the purposes of the argument, has to be restored by including trade union representatives on the NEC as constant supporters of the parliamentary leadership. The argument therefore starts out from the premiss of a parliamentary majority on the NEC, and ends by depending on trade union support for control by the parliamentary leaders. Moreover, the Bevanite M.P.s sometimes showed a tendency to arrogate more power to the NEC as against the PLP because of their stronger representation on the NEC than on the Parliamentary Committee. Indeed, it might be asserted that the arithmetical majority of M.P.s on the NEC is less significant than the minority of women members, inasmuch as the influence of the women's viewpoint has sometimes been perceptible.

The third fallacy is that the parliamentary leaders direct the NEC. Precisely who are meant by the parliamentary leaders in this context is obscure. Sometimes it appears to refer to the Leader alone; sometimes to the Leader and Deputy-Leader; sometimes to the members of the Parliamentary Committee on the NEC. Whichever is meant, it may be stated that (1) there has been no regular harmony of views between members of the Parliamentary Committee on the NEC; (2) the Leader and Deputy-Leader have not always seen eye to eye; (3) it has not been unknown for the Leader's views to fail to gain acceptance by the NEC.

IV. *The Leader*

As has been indicated, one of the sources for ascertaining policy, and therefore one of the authorities in deciding policy, is a public pronouncement by the Leader whether inside or outside Parliament. This also applies to pronouncements of the Deputy-Leader, though perhaps to a less extent. It holds good for official spokesmen in the House of Commons, but not for members of the Parliamentary Committee as such, who are apt to contradict one another.

The reason for the authoritative character of the Leader's declarations is evident. The object of the Party is to make him Prime Minister. What he says must therefore carry great weight. Does this mean that policy is what he says it is? His pronouncements are one of the sources of policy. What if they conflict with another authoritative source, such as Conference? It need hardly be said that this is a very exceptional occurrence. But there was a problem which arose in 1955 concerning Formosa.

The essentials of the problem were that the 1953 Conference had adopted a resolution, at the instance of the NEC, which stated that "Conference declares that the problem of Formosa should be referred to the people of Formosa. Formosa should be neutralised for a period, and Britain should be prepared to contribute to an international naval force for this purpose. Thereafter, the people of Formosa should be

enabled freely to determine their own destiny." There the matter rested until, early in 1955, a crisis over Formosa appeared in the offing.

The Leader, in an interview given to the *Daily Herald,* took the view that Formosa was an integral part of China. The implication of this was that, as the Labour Government had recognized the Peking Government, the Labour Party also recognized Peking's claim to Formosa. Some members of the NEC were not slow to draw this conclusion. Others, including some "parliamentary leaders," took the view that, although Formosa had been recognized as an integral part of China during and after the war, the 1953 Conference decision related to the new state of affairs resulting from the civil war and asserted the right of the people of Formosa to decide whether the island should be part of China or not. This was the view which prevailed. The statement issued by the NEC in February 1955 reiterated the 1953 Conference decision. This illustration seems to throw a somewhat different light on the alleged nullity of Conference in policy decision and on the control of the NEC by the parliamentary leaders.

In conclusion, another statement of the obvious seems necessary: that the position of the Leader depends very much on who the Leader is. As Professor W. J. M. Mackenzie has pointed out, there is no adequate basis for generalization about the Leader. With a Leader other than Mr. Attlee the position might have been more important or less important: what seems certain is that it would have been different. The assumption of the argument for the supremacy of the parliamentary Leader or leaders in relation to the NEC and Conference is that the Leader(s) has a particular line of policy for which he requires to muster support. As is well known, that was not Mr. Attlee's usual method. He preferred to let the discussion proceed and take the sense of the meeting.

To sum up, policy decision in opposition has not been confined to or controlled by the parliamentary leaders alone. Theirs is an influential role, but so is that of the NEC and of the "rank and file" at Conference. At different times one or other of these bodies emerges into greater prominence. In the nature of things, the bulk of policy decisions is made by the PLP. Yet many of the major decisions flow from Conference or from the NEC. It is illusory to seek one focus of power, and explain the rest as a facade. Perhaps, after all, what the Labour Party believes itself to be is a better guide to what it is.

Anthony Howard and Richard West

3. LORD HOME EMERGES

Until very recently, the Conservative Party chose its leader by a traditional, informal process of consultation. Conservative leaders were not "elected"; they "emerged." This system had worked fairly smoothly. Often an heir-apparent had established himself; even when there was more than one contender, the party's elder statesmen could be trusted to take informal soundings of party opinion. Harold Macmillan's sudden resignation in October 1963, however, subjected the system to severe strain and led to the best-publicized and most brutal struggle for power in the party's history. In this selection, the struggle is described by Anthony Howard and Richard West, two journalists who observed the events at close range. Macmillan, the Conservative Prime Minister, had been under attack from within his own party for more than a year.

For months it had been said—if with increasing despair by Macmillan's Tory enemies—that the party conference would prove decisive. And in the end it was, though not quite in the way that anyone had foreseen. When the special 1.35 p.m. Tory conference train drew out of Euston on Tuesday October 8th the half-dozen Cabinet Ministers on board had, it was noticed, cut things rather fine. Most of them had arrived with as little as five minutes to spare: but what the lesser passengers on the train did not know was that since 10 a.m. that morning the Cabinet had been closeted in its most crucial meeting since the Profumo crisis.

Having waited till the very last moment, Harold Macmillan had decided to confront his colleagues with the issue of the leadership. (The previous night both Lord Home and Lord Poole—against the advice of Macmillan's own family—had plainly told him that it was his duty to retire.) He faced the challenge with his usual dexterity and aplomb: had anyone, he asked, got anything he wanted to say about whether or not he should fight the next election? The hush perhaps betrayed embarrassment rather than enthusiasm, but at least the Prime Minister was provided with his cue for saying, "There has got to be a decision and I must announce it at Blackpool." No one (even after Macmillan withdrew, which he immediately tactfully did) seems to have inquired what exactly this was supposed to mean; but it was generally assumed that the Prime Minister had signified his intention of carrying on. . . .

That wet Tuesday afternoon, [however,] as the diesel locomotive ploughed its way up through Warrington, Wigan and Preston, only one Cabinet Minister—and he had remained in London—was told that the Prime Minister might not, after all, be able to fulfil the plans that he had outlined to the Cabinet that morning. At five o'clock Butler was summoned from his office in the Treasury to 10 Downing Street to be told in strict confidence that the Prime Minister had been suffering some considerable pain for the past twelve hours; he would be seeing his doctors in an hour or two for a medical examination and he would then know if he was fit enough to make the journey to Blackpool later in the week.

The Cabinet Ministers travelling to Blackpool—and they included such senior figures as Iain Macleod (joint chairman of the party and Leader of the House of Commons), Edward Heath (the Lord Privy Seal and formerly Britain's Common Market negotiator) and Henry Brooke (the Home Secretary)—were left in complete ignorance of all this. Even when they arrived at Blackpool's Imperial Hotel they were given no indication that anything might be subject to change in the battle-plan for the conference which had been discussed in the Cabinet room that morning. A crowded press conference at 7 p.m. thus found Iain Macleod . . . replying confidently to a rapacious American questioner: "I am quite certain that the Prime Minister on Saturday will make the position about the leadership absolutely clear." When one or two other reporters gamely tried to press for information on what had really been said at the Cabinet meeting, they found themselves brusquely snubbed. "You are wasting your time on this one," Macleod somewhat impatiently pointed out. "What is discussed in Cabinet is never revealed or commented upon." But conscious that it had none the less been given a wink the press conference soon broke up, and as they pushed their way out the journalists agreed almost without exception that they were in for a dull

week, until on Saturday afternoon Macmillan formalized what Macleod had already indicated. . . .

Meanwhile in London things had moved very quickly. Macmillan had known that something was wrong very early that morning, before even the Cabinet meeting took place. Not having been able to sleep, and suffering from a familiar ailment, he had asked his staff to call a doctor at 4 a.m. Shortly before 5 a.m. Dr. Frederick King-Lewis (his son's doctor though not his own) drove round from his flat in Chester Street, Belgravia, to Admiralty House. He was with the Prime Minister for an hour and a half, but he at first regarded the matter as one calling for only routine treatment. After this visit the Prime Minister apparently felt better, and, though Edward Heath who called on him shortly after breakfast took away the distinct impression that he was not looking at all well, he had rallied a bit by the time the Cabinet met. The alert Sir Keith Joseph said later in the day that he had "rarely seen the old man in better form." This, however, was by no means the view of all the Cabinet—the Chancellor of the Exchequer (who traditionally sits opposite the Prime Minister in Cabinet meetings) even being heard to comment as the Ministers went out: "You know, this man is far too ill to make the journey to Blackpool."

In fact, of course, at the Cabinet Macmillan had made an oblique reference to what had occurred: his apparent (though not, in fact, specific) decision to soldier on was, he had emphasized, dependent on his getting a clearance from his doctors. Few of his colleagues, however, took this reservation very seriously. In every statement about his future intentions, from the time of the 1922 Committee luncheon right back in April, Macmillan had always included the saving clause "provided my health and strength remain." It had seemed a reasonable condition for a man of sixty-nine; but this time he had clearly given it more than its usual meaning. Just how much was shown later that evening when, after a consultation with two other doctors, including his own who had come back from the Lake District, Macmillan was driven from Downing Street to the King Edward VII Hospital for Officers in Marylebone to await an operation. He had meanwhile informed Lord Home as well as Butler.

It naturally took some time for the news of all this to get around in Blackpool. The original news-flash went out on television and radio just after 9.30 p.m., but at 10 p.m. in the bars of the headquarters hotel party officials were still unaware of what had occurred. Even when told, one group of area press officers stoically refused to believe it. But the bleak and grim-faced return of the ministerial guests from [an] agents' dinner soon put the matter beyond doubt. Within minutes, Iain Macleod had called his second press conference of the evening — this time anxiously explaining that when he had said earlier that the Prime Minister would make the position "absolutely clear" on Saturday he had, of course, no foreknowledge of what might occur. He added, somewhat pathetically, that he could not be expected to say anything about future arrangements as he did not yet know anything about them. . . .

Macleod's sense of numbed shock was by no means shared by the people who now gathered in bars and corridors. In contrast to the successive medical bulletins about Gaitskell nine months earlier, the news of Macmillan's illness was received by much of his own party with almost a sense of relief. For month after month the question mark had hung over this one man, and the party had come to accept that only he could decide the future. Now it looked very much as if the decision was going to be taken out of his hands; and after the ritual expressions of regret even the dedicated Conservatives came to realize that this might be good for the party. The drift and the uncertainty were over; now they were forced to act.

The talk in the conspiratorial groups that night was tough rather than sensitive, but it was also realistic. For the basic problem still remained: if not Macmillan, then who else? First, and most obviously, there was R. A. Butler.

The sixty-year-old First Secretary of State had remarked casually during a TV profile of himself only the night before, "I have had quite enough good luck to suit myself or anyone else." And for once it did indeed look as if Rab Butler's luck was in. It had, after all, always been said that if the Prime Minister were to be run over by a bus then Rab would have to be the automatic beneficiary. Now that — for the second time [Butler had been the heir-apparent when Sir Anthony Eden suddenly resigned in January 1957] — this seemed to have happened, it was hard even for Rab's opponents to see how his claims were going to be resisted. This time — even his enemies agreed that first night — Rab was not going to be easy to beat.

But whom should they run against him? In politics it is hopeless to match like against like: to win a victory against the odds it is imperative to gamble on contrast. For years, in the eyes of Tory constituency workers, Butler's polar opposite in the Tory Party had been fifty-six-year-old Quintin McGarel Hogg, 2nd Viscount Hailsham. Tempestuous where Rab was temperate, colourful where Rab was colourless, reckless where Rab was restrained — Hailsham was adored for having modelled his career on Churchill as Butler was despised for having followed the placid precedent set by his first mentor, Stanley Baldwin. Those who were ineradicably opposed to Butler's becoming Tory Party leader knew at once what they must do. Somehow or other Hailsham must be persuaded to set sail even though (as the shrewdest of them perceived) he might eventually end up as no more than a fire-ship. And Hailsham, who still regarded himself as Macmillan's own choice for successor, was eager to try for the job.

Other names were mentioned. The clear choice of the Conservative backbenchers in Parliament, the Chancellor of the Exchequer still remained a runner, but it soon became obvious that at least in the conference arena Round One was going to be fought out between Butler and Hailsham. The first shot was, in fact, fired by the Hailsham forces the next morning. Whether by accident or design Hailsham arrived on the Winter Gardens conference platform a tactical few minutes after the rest of his ministerial colleagues. Immediately there was a great shout and clapping of hands and banging of feet from the delegates. The conference was in no doubt of its favourite candidate. If the enthusiasm and ecstasy of the rank and file were the test of a Tory leader, Hailsham had made it. But they are not.

The real battle that first day did not take place in the conference hall. It was fought instead in a first-floor suite of the Imperial Hotel. In naming Butler to act as his deputy Macmillan had (some suspected deliberately) left one loose end untied. What was to happen about the annual mass rally — always traditionally addressed by the leader — due to be held on the Saturday afternoon? As he arrived in Blackpool from London at 6.15 p.m. on Wednesday October 9th Butler clearly believed that he must deliver this vital speech, or risk getting nudged out of the leadership contest. He was, therefore, relieved to learn that the executive of the National Union of Conservative and Unionist Associations — that strange, amorphous body that comes to life once a year to organize the annual Conservative conference — had just finished meeting and was proposing to invite him as acting Prime Minister to take over the speech at the annual rally. For once no victim of indecision, Butler immediately tried to get this proposal ratified by his Cabinet colleagues since the National Union had said that its invitation was conditional on Cabinet approval.

Having taken possession of the suite that had originally been booked for the Prime Minister, Butler summoned a meeting of all available Cabinet ministers. . . . Before Butler brought up the subject of Saturday's meeting he conveyed one piece of news to his colleagues that took them all badly by surprise. He understood, he said, that it was the Prime Minister's wish, in view of the uncertainty both about the length of his absence and his prospects of complete recovery, that "the normal processes of consultation" should now begin about the selection of a new Conservative leader. In fact at that stage Butler already knew that the Prime Minister's retirement was to be announced the next day, but he had been sworn to the strictest confidence which he did not break till the next afternoon when he warned in advance two of his closest supporters in the Cabinet.

It was bad luck for Butler that he had to pass on the Prime Minister's message at this moment. It meant that everyone present now knew that the question of who should speak at Saturday's rally was clearly involved with the question of choosing Macmillan's successor. Whoever got the job, got a head start in the race. The argument over the National Union's invitation was therefore a hard-fought one and the meeting dragged on for an hour and a half: Butler was not finding it easy to get what he plainly regarded as his right. The Cabinet Ministers present split up almost straight away into opposing camps. In favour of Butler's taking the rally were those like Henry Brooke, the Home Secretary, Enoch Powell, Minister of Health, and Keith Joseph, Minister of Housing, who were to be his supporters for the next ten days; against his doing it — or at least in favour of cancellation — were those who eventually were to cost him the leadership, Iain Macleod, Reggie Maudling, Frederick Erroll, as well as his own implacable personal opponents like John Hare, Christopher Soames and Ernest Marples. [But in the end Butler got his way.]. . .

Meanwhile the Hailsham supporters had not been idle. . . . That same evening the brash Conservative backbench television personality, Sir Gerald Nabarro, was announcing to a constituency meeting in Bolton: "Britain cannot be led and governed by a sick septuagenarian." Having dismissed Butler as "donnish, dignified and dull," damned Maudling as "manly, matey and money-wise," Sir Gerald went on to declare that the mantle of the Premiership "should fall on Lord Hailsham who has fire in his belly."

This was clearly an unauthorized one-man outburst—though it inevitably made its impact on the newspapers. The real work for the Hailsham candidature was being carried on more discreetly in the hotel corridors and the conference hall lobbies by a group of young Conservative M.P.s who had turned themselves almost overnight into a campaign staff. Prominent among them were the wealthy proprietor of the *Spectator*, Ian Gilmour, who had always up till then been associated with the progressive wing of the Conservative Party; Peter Walker, a young city tycoon, who had formerly been national chairman of the Young Conservative movement; and Anthony Royle, the rich and elegant Parliamentary Private Secretary to the Minister of Aviation, Julian Amery, who later emerged in his own right as the chief Hailsham campaign organizer. . . .

[The next afternoon at] 4.30 p.m. Lord Home appeared in the conference hall for the first time, and during the following half-hour the platform was seen to be filling up with Ministers who, the observant noted, seemed to be having some sort of note passed to them. As soon as John Boyd-Carpenter, the Chief Secretary, had finished a rambling dissertation on rates, Lord Home got to his feet. He had, he said, a message from the Prime Minister. In his flat, thin voice the Foreign Secretary then read out a 300-word letter in which Harold Macmillan explained that, whatever his previous feelings, it would not now be possible for him to carry the physical burdens of leading the party at the next general election. He therefore hoped it would "soon be possible for the customary processes of consultation to be carried on within the party about its future leadership," and he made it plain that once these were completed he would place his resig-

nation in the hands of the Queen. Lord Home added just one pious phrase of his own—that Mr Macmillan had "once more shown that his whole concern was for the nation and the party"—and immediately there was a great burst of applause from the entire hall.

Partly, no doubt, this was meant to underline Lord Home's tribute, but there was also relief at the end of uncertainty. In fact the decision had been taken over twenty-four hours earlier. On Wednesday afternoon Home and Poole (who had flown down specially to London) visited Macmillan, then still awaiting his operation in the King Edward VII Hospital. The original medical advice to the Prime Minister was that he must expect to be out of action for two or three months; and in face of that he recognized that he could scarcely carry on as an absentee Prime Minister in a period just before a general election. Macmillan's friends were later to say that had he been pressed to remain in office he would probably have done so, especially after he had learnt from his own surgeon (too late to stop the conference message) that he might, after all, expect to be back at his post in as little as six weeks. But, in fact, the reverse happened: far from being urged to stay, Macmillan was encouraged by Home and Poole to go. They grasped the sad fact that still eluded Macmillan: his illness provided the first cue for an honourable exit from office since the humiliating Profumo debate on June 17th.

Once Macmillan accepted that he must resign, he made Home and Poole promise to read out the announcement as soon as they reached Blackpool. He was afraid that if the announcement was left until later, people would say that his illness was only a sham. Unfortunately for the Conservative Party the time and place of Home's announcement meant that the curious "processes of consultation" would, for the first time, be carried out in the hurly-burly atmosphere of the annual conference. The quarrels and feuds would leak to the press; the devious Ottoman intrigues of the party would be changed into a kind of mass political beauty contest. . . .

Whether Macmillan had intended it or not—and the Hailsham supporters insisted right to the end that he had—the immediate beneficiary of the Prime Minister's letter was Lord Hailsham. Absent from the platform when the letter was read out—he was meeting his wife and one-year-old daughter at Preston station—he learnt of its existence . . . only when he arrived back at the Imperial Hotel shortly after 5 p.m. Once told, his reaction was instantaneous. He rushed upstairs and seized a copy of the letter from one of the Downing Street secretaries who had arrived in Blackpool. "This is it," he remarked a moment or two later, "it's now or never." It was obvious straight away—though strenuous efforts were made to dissuade him, especially by Lord Aldington—that his mood was "now"; and that night the big chance came.

Unlike the Labour Party, the Conservative conference does not go in for "fringe activities"—tea-meetings, brains trusts or evening rallies. But every year the Conservative Political Centre—a kind of intellectuals' pressure group within the party—holds one evening meeting that is complementary to the party conference without being part of it. This meeting is addressed annually by a Cabinet Minister and always provides an opportunity for the delivery of a testament of political faith. This year's speaker was Hailsham. . . .

Long before he arrived at the Pavilion Cinema to find 2,500 Conservatives packed inside and another 1,000 ticketless trying to storm the entrances, Hailsham had decided what he must do. He would go through with his prepared speech on the theme of "National Excellence" and then, at the end, when he came to reply to the vote of thanks, he would make a purely personal statement declaring his decision to renounce his peerage.

In the event the prepared speech was a flop. Hailsham stuck doggedly to his script, frequently fluffing his lines and often badly miscalculating his timing. After about an hour the audience grew restive; but in that gathering that evening Hailsham would have been a hero if he had simply read out the telephone directory. When eventually he sat down, the cheers rang boldly out. A few minutes later he was back at the front of the platform. This time there was no prepared text, and the nervousness and hesitation were part of the orator's equipment. "There is one other thing," he began with an unfamiliar diffidence, "that I feel I ought to say to you. I hope you will bear with me if I put it in my own words."

The rest followed inevitably. After a tumultuous demonstration (which put one outraged Conservative M.P. in mind of "the politics of the Nuremberg Rally") Hailsham—as befitted the first man ever in British politics publicly to place his own name in nomination to be Prime Minister—found himself at the centre of a volcanic eruption of emotion. It reached its peak when just after midnight he made a charismatic appearance at the Young Conservatives' Ball. Like Barry Goldwater at the Cow Palace in San Francisco nine months later this odd, emotional peer had become the party darling. But the Conservatives, unlike the Republican Party, do not elect their candidate by a convention.

For a few flickering hours Hailsham did indeed seem to have the light of star-dust, the strut of triumph, the throb of destiny. Yet that Thursday night he had taken the only initiative that was open to him, and its impact, though formidable, aroused an equally firm opposition. On radio and television that evening he was referred to in icily disapproving tones by Iain Macleod; later that night the forgotten man of the contest—Reggie Maudling—told everyone within ear-shot "You know, if you asked the Cabinet to raise their hands for Quintin I don't think a single hand would go up"; and the next morning that most orthodox and respectable of Conservative newspapers, the *Yorkshire Post*, wrote flatly that Butler would be the next Prime Minister, and dismissed Hailsham's promise to give up his peerage as "an unnecessary, a deplorable distraction." In the small hours of Friday morning even Hailsham himself confessed to Lord Aldington — the man who had most strongly advised him against taking such a melodramatic course — "You were quite right. It is all over. I am finished."

If he had failed to take the party by storm Hailsham had at least burst the whole contest wide open. Each of his rivals was now forced to follow his example, and they all suddenly started to fight for the prize. Butler gave a clumsy, self-promoting interview to the *Daily Express*; Maudling at last came out on television to say that he was willing to accept the Premiership; the wily Macleod hinted at a possible Home candidature in an effort to divert the Hailsham enthusiasm. That Friday, in fact, marked the first moment when Home as a candidate began to be taken seriously. It was partly due to Macleod and partly to that senior influential backbencher, Nigel Birch, who having destroyed the previous leader [see the selection beginning on page 147] now set himself the task of defeating both the front runners for the succession. Arriving in Blackpool that Friday afternoon he left no doubt as to how he intended to do it. To a journalist he remarked almost casually, "Oh, I'm an Alex Home man. There aren't any other possibilities. He's *going* to get it."

Only that morning the Foreign Secretary — always an idol of the annual conference — had enjoyed an oratorical triumph with his speech on foreign affairs. At that stage the delegates were probably all the more generous in their applause as they still looked upon Home as the one Olympian figure above the stresses and strains of mundane personal conflict; but whatever the motive, the fact now stood on the record that Home — in the midst of the parade of recognized candidates — had got almost as big an ovation as Hailsham. True, he had offered a prize "to any newspaperman who can find any clue in my speech that this is Lord Home's bid for the leadership," but in retrospect even that began to look not quite as innocent as it has sounded.

In any event the suspicions of Home's intentions increased that night when he gave an interview on B.B.C. television. For a prospective king-maker he showed a marked reluctance to take his own eyes off the crown. . . . The effect of all this was to leave the final day of the conference in a frayed state.

For one thing, the conference realized that by transforming itself into a political beauty contest, it had by no means established its right to a real or substantial voice in "the normal processes of consultation." Ministers and M.P.s were becoming convinced that the sooner the arena was transferred to the calmer, more rational atmosphere of London the better it would be for everyone. It was in that spirit that Butler came to make the final speech to the conference — the opportunity he had fought so hard to be given — on Saturday afternoon. This was Butler almost defiantly plain — making no concession at all to the hysterical atmosphere of heroes and hero-worship in which he found himself. As he wound his labyrinthine way through all the aspects of Government policy he appeared anxious to remind his audience of only one thing: that it was the Conservative Party's task not just to find a magnetic leader but rather to choose a Prime Minister who understood and grasped the whole reach and span of an already decided political programme. This was Butler's basic strength; and his speech, skilful if pedestrian, emphasized it.

It was not, however, what the 4,000 representatives had come to hear. His audience made that crudely obvious by reserving all its enthusiasm for the chairman of the meeting, Lord Home, and yielding Butler only the applause that politeness — perhaps guilty conscience — required. Yet Butler had made a deliberate decision. His sights when he sat down were plainly fixed on the coming — and as he believed — very different struggle that lay ahead in London. He had at least survived a week in which he had been forced to fight on his most vulnerable flank. In his own milieu of

Whitehall and the Cabinet Room he could begin to assert his claim. . . .

. . . The fact that the Prime Minister was still recovering from the sedative after-effects of his operation in King Edward VII Hospital necessarily meant that Butler was now the central public figure in the drama. It was he, having taken up day-time residence in Downing Street, who was now going to receive the other Ministers; and, more important even than that, he was surely bound to be the conduit pipe between the sick, retiring Premier and the rest of the Government. Significantly, though, Macmillan did not immediately summon Butler to his bedside. Instead, having held consultations with both the Government Chief Whip (Martin Redmayne) and the Lord Chancellor (Lord Dilhorne), he sent him a letter. In it the outgoing Prime Minister explained that in his present state of health it would be wrong for him personally to recommend any successor to the Queen; as an alternative he recommended that the Cabinet should agree to a procedure which in his view should establish which candidate really enjoyed the maximum support. At the time Butler saw nothing suspicious in this proposal. Indeed he cheerfully read Macmillan's letter to the assembled Cabinet the next morning and got them to agree to it.

Macmillan's suggestion had been that four official "straw" polls should be held as quickly as possible—one for the 350-odd Conservative members of the House of Commons, one for the roughly 200-strong active Unionist peers in the House of Lords, one for the 20 members of the Cabinet and one for the 150-odd officers and executive of the National Union to establish the feeling of the constituencies. . . . Once the evidence had been collected Macmillan undertook to present it to the Queen so that she might exercise her prerogative in the light of a demonstrated party preference. Now Butler had doubted from the beginning whether Macmillan would ever yield him any personal en-

dorsement; he himself had referred to Macmillan as "an ageing, foolish old man" in an interview with a journalist at the end of September. Therefore this proposal of an entirely novel method of giving advice to the monarch may well have come as a relief. He might not be markedly in the lead in any one of the four suggested polling areas, but he assumed that he was easily the strongest all-round candidate. Many Cabinet colleagues agreed with him.

What Butler overlooked was that with this one act of acquiescence he had forfeited his single solid asset. From now on, instead of being the tenant-in-possession, he was simply just another candidate for the succession. It was to Macmillan that the results of the various polls were to be presented and it was Macmillan who would weigh and evaluate them, put them together and present them to the Queen. . . .

. . . Each of the three challengers to Butler by now had his separate campaign staffs who knew that they had a job of work to do and that there was not much time in which to do it. In the Maudling camp the return to London had caused a considerable recovery of confidence. Admittedly their candidate had flopped badly at the conference but he himself was not too worried: "Now that we have returned to London it will be apparent that this is a matter which will be decided by deliberation and not by decibel meter." Maudling, in fact, started the week in a mood of jaunty confidence. Travelling back from Blackpool by train, Iain Macleod assured him once again of his personal allegiance and of his political conviction that in the end he must emerge victorious. Macleod's shrewd tactical brain had grasped the central point: that a right of veto was bound to operate against both Butler and Hailsham. It would be wielded by the intransigent opponents of each. The preservation of party unity must demand the emergence of a compromise candidate. To the last, Macleod had wanted Macmillan to stay. As soon as this became impossible, he plumped for Maudling. He was now certain that Maudling would get the job and nothing that happened at Blackpool—not even the glint in Home's eye—had altered Macleod's professional political appraisal of the situation.

But that Saturday afternoon in the railway carriage Macleod suffered a shock, which ought perhaps to have shown him the warning light. Slightly embarrassed, Maudling confessed to him that when he had been asked for his views at Blackpool by the Lord Chancellor (who was then conducting what afterwards passed into official terminology as "the poll of the Cabinet") he had replied that, although in no circumstances would he serve in a Government headed by Hailsham, he would accept office under Butler or, for that matter, under Home. The effect of the latter name upon Macleod was certainly electric: he launched into a tirade on the impossibility of a 14th Earl being a Tory leader in the second half of the twentieth century, basing his case largely on the damning, dispiriting effect that such an appointment would have on the people he really cared about in the party—the classless Young Conservatives and the working-class Tory trade unionists. The vision of Home leading the party would, he argued, make a mockery of everything that they had tried to achieve since 1945 in broadening the base of Conservative appeal. But though Macleod was angry he was not yet alarmed: to him the very notion of Home being Prime Minister was still inherently impossible. . . .

Macleod would certainly have taken Maudling's confession more seriously had he known one of the best-kept secrets of Blackpool. Some time after lunch on the Friday of his foreign affairs speech, Home had been waited upon in his hotel room by a deputation of four influential Conservative M.P.s. They were Selwyn Lloyd (Macmillan's sacked Chancellor), Martin Redmayne (the Government Chief Whip), Nigel Birch (Macmillan's arch-enemy) and Colonel Lancaster (a back-bench member of standing and seniority). They had one simple question to put to the Foreign Secretary. Although they quite recognized that he was not an active candidate for the succession, they asked him to give them an assurance that if a draft were forthcoming Home would not refuse it. Without too much hesitation Home gave them what they wanted: if the party genuinely desired him to lead it, he would step down from the Lords and become Prime Minister in the Commons. Indeed Home did more than that: later in the day he made arrangements to see his doctor in London on the following Monday so that he might have a complete medical check-up.

It is doubtful if any of the four recognized at the time quite what they had done. For (unknown to them) only three days earlier Home had given an assurance to all his Cabinet colleagues which most of them were to remember vividly and resentfully throughout the twelve months of his premiership. "I wish to make it clear," he had told his fellow-members in the Cabinet Room at the pre-Conference meeting on Tuesday October 8th, "that in no circumstances am I a candidate." It may not have been quite the famous Sherman statement of nineteenth-century American politics: "If nominated I will not accept, if drafted I will not run, if elected I will not serve." But for most of Home's colleagues it remained throughout the crisis the main basis for their belief that—whatever the pressures put upon him—the Foreign Secretary simply could not, without notice to them, slip his moorings as a non-starter. The only people who knew for certain that he had already done so were the four who had waited upon the Foreign Secretary that Friday afternoon; and it very much suited their purposes to keep this information to themselves. What they wanted—and what in the end they got—was a victory for their candidate with scarcely a shot being fired against him for the simple reason that nowhere until the very last moment was he definitely visible in any of his opponents' sights.

This was especially true of the Hailsham

camp. They were throughout the coming five days the most highly organized and the most noisy: but they did not suspect the danger from Home until much too late. . . .

. . . Indeed the amazing . . . thing about the Hailsham crusade for the leadership was how near it came to success. The timing and the setting for it had, of course, been exactly right. In no other week of the year could Hailsham have got his candidature off the ground: but at Blackpool, surrounded by his own public (the party militants), performing in his own natural arena (that of oratorical excess), and basking in the arc-lights of publicity (Hailsham was since the death of Aneurin Bevan the only natural-born "celebrity" in British politics) he had certainly succeeded in making his claim look a plausible one. Nor was it based entirely on publicity. Reggie Maudling, for example, was certainly wrong in declaring at Blackpool that Hailsham had no support in the Cabinet. In Conservative politics the blood-line is ever important. An excitable Hailsham lieutenant, Peter Walker, announced at one point: "We've got the Churchills and the Devonshires, now all we need is the Cecils." He may have been exaggerating but the remark reveals an important aspect of Tory thinking.

Astonishingly, in October 1963 a respectable proportion of the whole Tory "Establishment" was, in fact, working for Hailsham. In the Cabinet (quite apart from Macmillan himself, who characteristically abandoned his promotion of the Hailsham cause only when he became convinced that even in a new situation it could not succeed) there were originally both Sir Winston Churchill's sons-in-law, Duncan Sandys and Christopher Soames; outside it in the party organization there was Iain Macleod's opposite number as joint chairman, Lord Poole—whose wife at Blackpool had made no secret of the fact, even once in Mrs Butler's hearing—that "Oliver is breast high for Quintin"; while outside the Government and the party organization were virtually all those whom Maudling him-

self baptized "the blue-blood-and-thunder boys"—the buccaneering Tory "grandees" who traditionally meet together in the most neolithic of all London clubs, White's in St. James's. . . .

Strong-arm tactics, which tended to rebound soon, became characteristic of the approach of Hailsham's supporters. . . . Perhaps the person who suffered most from this kind of approach was Iain Macleod, whom for some reason the Hailshamites had expected to have in their camp along with the other joint chairman, Lord Poole. They found instead that he was doing his best to "wreck" their activities. At one stage Macleod was even stormed at in White's Club by the young and affluent Tory backbencher by whom he [was later] employed—Ian Gilmour, the proprietor of the *Spectator*. But despite the fact that many of his friends (and practically all his former most devoted supporters in the Commons like Gilmour himself) were involved in the Hailsham campaign, Macleod held out against all threats and blandishments with the uncompromising statement, "I'm not rowing in that crew."

The other potential supporter whom the Hailsham forces allowed to get away turned out in the end to be an even more vital figure. Prominent on the platform at the Hailsham declaration meeting at Blackpool had been Selwyn Lloyd, who bore no love for Butler or Maudling: the first he rightly suspected of helping to get him removed from the Chancellorship in July 1962; the second had actually taken over his old job. Selwyn Lloyd was therefore regarded as natural Hailsham campaign material. In fact at Blackpool he had already committed himself to Home; but throughout the early days back in London the former fallen Chancellor maintained contact with the Hailsham camp. He met Hailsham personally at least once, but normally communicated through a twenty-one-year-old undergraduate—the son of the then Conservative member for Bury St. Edmunds, Sir William Aitken. . . .

Throughout, the Hailshamites had the best intelligence service. . . . So it was fitting that in the end they should have been the first people to get the real news. At 10.25 p.m. on Wednesday October 16th the telephone rang in Randolph Churchill's home at East Bergholt, which had become the communications centre of the Hailsham campaign. On the line was a sad and disappointed Jonathan Aitken. Selwyn Lloyd, he reported, had just seen Home: he had committed himself irrevocably to Home's cause and had been told by him that he was now prepared to come downstairs from the House of Lords and accept the leadership. . . .

. . . [Meanwhile] those responsible for organizing the four "straw" polling stations — in the Cabinet, the Lords, the Commons and among the constituency parties — were reporting their returns to Macmillan in the King Edward VII Hospital. In the morning they had each separately visited the Prime Minister in his first-floor room at the hospital to tell him what their respective sounding had established; and in the afternoon Macmillan took the wise precaution, to avoid any suspicion of the books having been cooked, of having them repeat in front of each other what their various canvasses had shown. For this purpose Macmillan was brought downstairs from his room to the Matron's office where, still lying in bed, he received collectively the Lord Chancellor (Lord Dilhorne), the Chief Whip in the House of Lords (Lord St Aldwyn), the Chief Whip in the Commons (Martin Redmayne) and the joint chairman of the party (Lord Poole). One week later Redmayne was to lift the veil a little on what the Prime Minister had been told that afternoon by announcing in a public speech at Bournemouth that Home had been the common choice of all four polls — though he admitted that among Conservative M.P.s his lead had been "narrow."

But this was not the first occasion on which Redmayne released this information. At midnight on the same day that the results of the polls were presented to the Prime Minister he was using them for his

own purposes in argument with four Cabinet Ministers. Macleod's proposed meeting of "rebel" Ministers [Macleod and Maudling had learned, to their horror, only that afternoon that Home was emerging] had finally been arranged at the home of Enoch Powell (the Minister of Health) in South Eaton Place. There just before midnight — in addition to the host, Powell — assembled Iain Macleod (the joint chairman of the party and Leader of the House of Commons), Frederick Erroll (the President of the Board of Trade), Lord Aldington (Special Assistant to the joint chairmen in the Central Office) and . . . Reginald Maudling (the Chancellor of the Exchequer). To this gathering the Government Chief Whip was summoned by telephone. At the time he was naturally suspected of being part of the abortive conspiracy. But in fact, Redmayne had been a Home supporter since the previous Friday at Blackpool, and was present only as the official channel of communication to the Prime Minister.

Playing the traditional part of a Chief Whip with "rebels," Redmayne at once did his best to persuade them that their cause was hopeless. Without giving exact facts or figures he assured the five that Home had been the leading choice among all the segments of the party that had been consulted. He reminded them, too, that the procedure they were now disputing was one which only two days before (at the Tuesday Cabinet meeting) the four Ministers present had all endorsed. At last seeing the noose that the whole Cabinet had put its head into, Maudling and Macleod tried to cut free of it by asserting the overriding rights that any Cabinet must have in selecting a new Prime Minister. All right, they argued in effect, perhaps Home was the party's choice, but that did not necessarily mean that he was the ideal Prime Minister. If, even as the favourite, he could not unite the Cabinet, surely there was a case for re-examining the claims of the runner-up, who, they urged, could. Redmayne had only been summoned after Hailsham had on the telephone made it perfectly clear that he, too, was violently opposed to Home and was now ready—even eager—to serve in a Cabinet headed by Butler.

For the five men in Powell's house that night this change in Hailsham's attitude had naturally seemed decisive. There had been three public contenders for the leadership, and two of them had now agreed to serve under the third. What need, they kept pressing Redmayne, was there to take the matter any further? The crisis was surely over now that both Butler's main rivals had agreed to accept him as leader of the party and Prime Minister. . . .

. . . As the meeting broke up [Lord Aldington] offered a lift home to Redmayne, who had come round from the whips' office in Downing Street by taxi. The whole purpose of having Redmayne at the meeting had been to enable him to pass on the information he had learnt at it, both officially to the outgoing Prime Minister and informally to the Palace. But as Aldington drove down Whitehall, Redmayne said something that conveyed unmistakably that he did not seem to regard the situation as having been in any way changed by what happened. It was enough to alert Aldington's suspicions: early the next morning he himself telephoned Sir Michael Adeane, the Queen's private secretary, only to learn that no inkling of what had occurred had yet reached the Palace.

Getting the message through to Harold Macmillan mattered rather less, though Butler was by no means the only man to suspect that the outgoing Premier was never told the real importance of the meeting in Powell's house. Yet if Macmillan was never made aware that both Maudling and Hailsham had withdrawn their claims in Butler's favour he at least knew from newspaper headlines like "Cabinet Revolt" or "Midnight Cabinet Drama" that something had gone wrong. Far from giving him pause, the effect was to make him more determined than ever to press ahead. From his hospital bed he had a telephone call put through to Home. The Foreign Secretary was uneasy: "Well I thought I was coming in to heal, not to wound?" But Macmillan pressed him to keep up his courage: "Look, we can't change our view now; all the troops are on the starting-line. Everything is arranged. It will just cause ghastly confusion if we delay." Just after 9 a.m. Macmillan sent his formal letter of resignation round to the Palace.

Right at the beginning, before his operation, Macmillan had let it be known that he wanted, if possible, to delay his actual formal resignation so as to go to the Palace in person to deliver up the seals of office. The growing tensions of the week, and the vision of the Tory Party publicly tearing itself to bits, made it clear that this would not be practicable. But, so far as Macmillan's regard for constitutional protocol was concerned, the next best thing happened. As he could not go to the Queen, she came to him. At 11.30 a.m. in spite of the fact that a month before she had cancelled all public engagements on the ground of her pregnancy, Queen Elizabeth arrived at the hospital and was ushered into the Matron's office where her Prime Minister of the last seven years was lying propped up in bed. While declining to give formal advice on his successor Macmillan then read her a long memorandum which he had prepared the previous night after hearing the results of the polls, and offered her a copy to take away with her. The Queen accepted it, but she had already made up her mind. On returning to the Palace at noon she immediately sent for the 14th Earl of Home who drove out of the Foreign Office at 12.15 p.m. and was back home having lunch in Carlton Gardens by one o'clock with the royal invitation to form a government in his pocket. . . .

[*Further efforts were made to prevent Lord Home from becoming Prime Minister but without avail. Iain Macleod and Enoch Powell ultimately refused to serve in Home's government. Later, in February 1965, the Conservatives adopted a new, elective method for choosing the party leader. See Appendix.*]

Roy Jenkins

4. HUGH GAITSKELL

Hugh Gaitskell preceded Harold Wilson as leader of the Labour Party. On his death in January 1963, the House of Commons adjourned for a day—a tribute normally reserved for former Prime Ministers. But, as this portrait shows, Gaitskell while he lived was surrounded by controversy. Roy Jenkins, a member of Parliament, became minister of aviation in the 1964 Labour government.

My friendship with Hugh Gaitskell, although it arose out of politics, was not primarily a political one. To a substantial extent it could, I think, have survived prolonged political disagreement or even complete separation. Yet the Gaitskell I knew was always a leading politician. When I first saw him he was already a departmental Minister. I have no clear recollection of speaking to him before he was Chancellor of the Exchequer. And during the years when I knew him best and saw him most frequently he was a highly dominant leader of the Opposition, living under the constant pressure of public events.

I did not see Gaitskell develop from obscurity to fame. When I knew him he was always in the centre of events, and most of his triumphs and failures were political ones. But not all of them. At times he dominated politics. But he was rarely dominated by them. This was not primarily because of the range of his interests, although that was considerable, and not at all because he had any peculiar quality of unconcern; on the contrary he was easily emotionally involved. The true reason was the immensely high priority which he always gave to matters of personal relationship. He cared desperately about his friends, and the small change of social intercourse assumed an unusual importance in his life. In the midst of a period of high success he could be temporarily but deeply cast down by the unexpected failure of some small private event to which he had been looking forward. As a result, he conspicuously lacked that quality of cool, tough, detachment from individual affections which is often considered essential for a leading politician. He could be blind to the faults of those whom he liked and equally blind to the virtues of those he did not—and in neither case was he in the least influenced by a calculation of who could be useful to him. He would sometimes throw away political allies with an extraordinary recklessness, yet he clung to personal friendship with a persistent loyalty.

All this sounds like a recipe for careless and attractive failure in politics. Yet Gaitskell was cheated of the highest achievement only by the tragedy of his illness and death. Even without its natural fulfilment, however, his life in politics was one of outstanding success. At forty-nine he achieved the leadership of a major party, and did so at a time when formidable rivals were thicker on the ground than they are today. During the seven years for which he held this office he consistently opted for strong leadership. This was not a question of the force of his personality, or of any desire to dominate. It was simply that he be-

From Roy Jenkins, "Leader of the Opposition" in *Hugh Gaitskell 1906–1963*, ed. W.T. Rodgers (London, 1964) pp. 115–131. Reprinted by permission of Thames & Hudson, Ltd. and the author.

lieved it was his duty to make up his mind before rather than after his followers. He always pointed the way and asked them to follow. . . . Mild-mannered ex-don though he may have appeared at the date of election, he became better known to the general public than any former leader of the opposition who had never been Prime Minister.

Both at the higher level of influencing events and at the lower one of household fame, therefore, Gaitskell, in spite of his lack of professionalism and his privately, rather than publicly, orientated personality, was a successful, even a memorable leader. What were the qualities which made him this, and how did they develop during the last decade of his life?

His first break-through to fame was when he became Chancellor of the Exchequer at the age of forty-four. This promotion came unexpectedly, almost casually. Previously he had been a quietly competent departmental minister and assistant to Cripps at the Treasury. His sudden elevation to one of the first three positions in the Government owed everything to the confidence of those with whom he had worked closely and almost nothing to his public standing. . . .

While he was at the Exchequer luck ran steadily against him. The government as a whole was tired. Its majority was tiny. The Korean War and the rearmament programme which followed from it brought vast economic difficulties. Aneurin Bevan, the most popular minister with the Labour Party activists, was restless and looking to the years of opposition which seemed to lie inevitably ahead. In these circumstances a young Chancellor, without any particular following of his own, might have been expected to play for safety. Instead, Gaitskell showed a determination verging on stubbornness. He emerged as the one strong man of the Labour Government's last year. He made enemies, but a public reputation as well.

When the Government went out, however, it looked as though his position might not hold. Nearly all the other leading figures in the Labour Party had experience in opposition. Gaitskell had none. Before the war he had been a don and during the war a Civil Servant. As a minister he might be very good, but surely he, more than most, worked best with the smooth support of the Whitehall machine and would be lost without it.

This prognosis proved to be the reverse of the truth. In office everything came easily to him and he was a moderate success. In opposition he had to fight a long, often disagreeable battle to establish his position, but he eventually stood out as the dominant politician of his generation.

First, he had to take the decision to compete. In Parliament this was easy enough. For a time, at any rate, his rôle there was secure. But it needed to be buttressed by a position in the party outside which he did not at that stage possess. That meant that he had to make a place for himself as a Labour Party conference figure. The temptation not to try for this—at any rate for a time—would for many people have been overwhelming. In 1952, the first year of opposition, with Bevanism firmly in the constituency saddle, the conference was much more a demonstration against the Right of the party than a deliberative assembly. In theory, Gaitskell could easily have stood aside. There have frequently been Labour ministers almost but not quite of the first rank, who have been active in Parliament, but have steered clear of the rougher arena of the party conference.

Gaitskell, however, was prevented from following this course by two factors. First, he could never bear to contract out of conflict. Perhaps surprisingly for a man of gentle manners and quiet charm, he was fascinated by it. He did not positively like rough interchanges and political in-fighting, as Ernest Bevin or Aneurin Bevan appeared to do, but he could not keep away from them. Morally, he was in the bravest of all categories: he flinched, but he always went on. He disliked the noise, but he never kept away from the place where the guns were firing loudest.

Second, he had a shrewd sense of power and realized that, without establishing a position in the conference, he could never achieve the commanding rôle in the Labour Party to which his other talents seemed to entitle him. Accordingly, in 1952, in the dismal resort of Morecambe and at the most bitter and snarling of all such assemblies, there began the curious love-hate relationship between Gaitskell and the Labour conference which was to dominate much of the rest of his life.

That year he was heavily defeated for the National Executive Committee. He followed this up by the challenge of his Stalybridge speech. This was delivered on his way back from Morecambe and seemed at the time to be an act of almost foolhardy defiance. Many were muttering that the Labour Party was slipping into an irresponsible extremism which would condemn it to a long period of sterility, and that Communist infiltration was doing much to stir up this mood. Gaitskell said in public these things which others were merely whispering. By so doing he made himself the most exposed man in the party, who looked for the moment as though he could never again be acceptable to the bulk of its opinion. Exposed, as prominences always are, he had certainly become, but he had also taken a big step towards becoming the recognized leader of that moderate section of the party, which, particularly as elections approach, almost always triumphs. . . .

In the meantime, Gaitskell was rapidly increasing his parliamentary stature. Butler was at the Exchequer and he was Shadow Chancellor. Although they were both accused of the besetting party sin of "Butskellism," economic debates during this period were conducted at a higher level and with more interest on both sides than in any other period since the war. Gaitskell's annual reply to the Budget became a regular parliamentary *tour de force*, listened to with rapt attention by a packed House. For the first time in these speeches there was shown to the full those qualities which became characteristic of his parliamentary oratory at its best: a very full knowledge of the subject, presented with a relentless logic, which avoided aridity because of the emotional force, never shrill or bitter, which lay behind it. . . .

Outside Parliament, Gaitskell's position remained uncertain until the autumn of 1954. In 1953 he was again defeated for the party executive. It began to look as though he and Aneurin Bevan had settled down to the boring attrition of trench warfare. From his emplacement with the constituency parties Bevan kept up a fairly constant bombardment of Gaitskell's equally well dug-in position with the parliamentary party; and vice versa. But it was not an exchange which seemed likely to produce a decisive result. Then the Treasurership of the Labour Party fell vacant. For this post, unimportant in itself, the whole conference, trades unions as well as constituency parties, elects. Both contestants were given an opportunity to get out of their trenches and they both responded with alacrity. The result was a clear victory for Gaitskell. The majority of the big trade union leaders had decided that Gaitskell, despite his utterly dissimilar background from their own, was a man with whom they could work, and that Bevan was not. The decision came at a most important stage in his career.

After this result there was a gradual ebbing of the ideological conflict within the party. The General Election of 1955 contributed towards this, but even when it had been lost, there was no return to the full bitterness of the preceding years. . . .

That year Attlee was clearly near to relinquishing his twenty-year-old leadership. Gaitskell came only gradually and reluctantly to accept the view that he ought to be a candidate. This was not out of mock modesty. I do not think he doubted, at that stage, that he would one day be party leader. But, at forty-nine, he believed that Herbert Morrison, with whom he had worked closely over the preceding five years, should have a turn first. In June 1955, he argued most determinedly in favour of this course. Over the summer, however, he was persuaded that the desire of the Labour MPs was for a much younger leader than Morrison. If he allowed him to be the only "moderate" candidate, Bevan might conceivably still snatch a victory; and even if he did not, a short Morrison tenure might lead to a subsequent reaction in favour of the Left.

Once he was convinced of the force of these arguments Gaitskell went forward unhesitatingly. He told Morrison of his decision at the earliest possible moment in October, choosing a luncheon with no one else present — not perhaps the easiest occasion — for breaking the news. He certainly did not look forward to doing so, and when it was over he was greatly relieved. Morrison had taken the information remarkably well. Perhaps at this stage it was natural tolerance. Perhaps he underestimated the force of Gaitskell's challenge. If the latter was the case, he was greatly mistaken. When the contest came, in December, Gaitskell swept the field. He was elected on the first ballot, with nearly twice as many votes as the combined total of Morrison and Bevan. He was the youngest leader of any party for sixty years.

Suez was Gaitskell's first crisis in his new position. At first he seemed to hesitate, but as soon as he saw that Lord Avon [then Sir Anthony Eden, the Prime Minister] intended to seek a solution through force, Gaitskell mounted an impassioned denunciation of his actions. He carried most of the Labour Party — and many others — enthusiastically with him on this course. But there were a few Labour MPs who stood more or less quietly aside, and it was noticeable — a piquant situation — that Aneurin Bevan was much less wholehearted in his condemnation of the Government's adventure. . . .

Gaitskell's vehemence on this issue, widely criticized though it was, even by some who were themselves opposed to the Government's action, probably did him no harm in the country. It helped to imprint his personality upon the public, and it be-

gan a period in which the Labour Party bounded ahead of the Conservatives in the public opinion polls. Where it did do him some harm was in the House of Commons. For some months afterwards he had difficulty in getting a good hearing from the Government benches. Their occupants paid him back with mocking noise for his part in the destruction of Eden. It was an experience to which he was most unused and which was peculiarly upsetting to his style of oratory. . . .

With his principal rivals within the Labour Party, however, Gaitskell's relations improved rapidly in the period after Suez. Wilson had already succeeded him as Shadow Chancellor. Bevan was at first a little more recalcitrant. But at the Brighton conference of 1957 his "naked into the conference chamber" speech led both to a rupture with his old friends of the unilateralist Left and to a reconciliation with Gaitskell. Shortly afterwards Gaitskell asked him to become Shadow Foreign Secretary and the relationship between the two men became amicable and moderately close. It reached its high-water mark during their joint visit to Russia immediately preceding the 1959 General Election. . . .

This important partnership was first made less relevant by the election defeat, and then destroyed by Bevan's sudden illness and subsequent death. The election campaign, on the whole skilfully fought by Gaitskell (although he was subsequently critical of himself for one major mistake), was hard throughout and at the end cruelly disappointing. . . .

Looking back, this defeat was unavoidable. No radical leader could have carried the country in its 1959 mood. Gaitskell did at least as well as anyone else would have done. But the inevitability was not so obvious at the time. The whole Labour Party began to cast about for the causes of the setback. From the moment of his return to London, Gaitskell was active in the search. Perhaps mistakenly, he allowed himself no period of recuperation. Without doubt, he and those of us who were close to him, made serious tactical mistakes during the ensuing weeks. We over-estimated the rationality of political movements. Equally without doubt, however, the battle which then began, and continued, in different phases, for two years, had to be fought. Broadly the Labour Party was divided into two camps. On the one side stood those who wished to react to defeat by giving the party a more modern appearance and a stronger appeal to the uncommitted voter. They saw its essential role as that of providing an effective alternative government to the Conservatives. It must therefore appeal to the marginal members of the Leftward thinking half of the country.

On the other side stood those whose primary concern was to defend the ideological citadel. If the citadel became increasingly cut off from the surrounding countryside and unpopular with the inhabitants that could not be helped. Elections were not of primary importance. One prominent socialist thinker wrote cheerfully of another ten years of Conservative government.

Some members of the party stood a little apart from both the camps, and it would have been theoretically possible for Gaitskell to have joined them. But it would have been utterly out of keeping with both his character and his convictions. He was incapable of equating a leader's rôle with that of a chairman.

The first phase of the battle — that over Clause 4 — was far from an immediate success. Gaitskell and those who were with him tried to move an injured party into a more comfortable position, and were rewarded for their efforts with some sharp and angry cries. Even so they got it a little way, before the attempt had to be abandoned. Yet, after this abandonment and the shifting of attention away from the issue, the party began quietly and almost imperceptibly to move itself in the direction indicated. No one looking at the programme, outlook and assumptions of the Labour Party today could doubt that Gaitskell, in a long-term sense, had won his battle. The party is incomparably closer to what he wanted than to what his opponents wanted. It would not go the whole way at his bidding. But it would not have gone at all had he not taken the risk of pointing the way.

After the Clause 4 stalemate came the counter-attack. It was on another front, that of unilateralism and neutralism *versus* the commitment to the Atlantic alliance and the defence policy which this entailed. But basically it was the same issue — whether the Labour Party's rôle was to be primarily that of a party of power or a party of protest. During the spring and summer of 1960 the unilateralist forces built up with frightening speed. Union after union toppled almost casually into their camp. Gaitskell's position became more exposed than that of any party leader since Baldwin in 1930.

At the Scarborough conference that autumn the almost unthinkable happened. On the central policy issue of the year the leadership was defeated. It had nearly — but not quite — occurred over German rearmament in 1954, and everyone had then assumed that an adverse vote would be an intolerable humiliation for Lord Attlee, rendering his continuance in office almost impossible. Yet he was less committed on that issue than his successor was on unilateralism.

What, then, would Scarborough mean for Gaitskell? Would it force his resignation, or would it leave him with the possibility of carrying on only as the prisoner of a section of his "followers," a figure shown to be so weak that he could not hope to command respect in the House or in the country? In fact, by one of the odd quirks of history, Gaitskell avoided both these alternatives by the widest possible margin. Even the conference itself was far from being a humiliation for him, although it was a great emotional strain. A majority of the delegates was committed to vote against him, but by the time the crucial debate took place many of them were regretting their mandates.

Gaitskell, in his own speech, had both to capitalize this mood and to raise a banner around which men would fight, if necessary risking their political positions in the process. Typically, he chose to do this in the least equivocal way possible. There was no doubt about his banner; the doubt was whether the men with uneasy minds would follow it.

This last doubt was soon removed. His old bastion of the Parliamentary Labour Party remained reasonably secure. When Harold Wilson hesitantly decided to run against him for the leadership his majority was more than two-to-one. And as the contest was fought on the clear understanding that Gaitskell, if successful, would lead against the Scarborough decision, the result struck a great blow, not only against the decision, but against the whole principle of conference authority. Yet he could not rest on this victory. Throughout that winter of 1960–1, Gaitskell "fought, fought and fought again" on innumerable platforms up and down the country. Nearly every week-end he would make three or four full-length speeches. His physical resilience appeared as high as ever, and he would often fortify himself with a late evening of relaxed conversation before setting out on these grinding expeditions; but, in fact, he was near the margin of his strength.

Sometimes at these meetings the reception would be hostile and even noisy. In these circumstances one of Gaitskell's greatest strengths was his stubborn faith in the power of reasoned argument. What he prided himself upon being was a rational man. The superiority of the multi-lateralist case was to him so obvious that intelligent people of good-will must surely see it. He would go on patiently explaining what he believed until others believed it too. And this approach, combined with his immense agreeableness of manner in friendly intercourse, succeeded in shifting a good deal of opinion within the party. But was it shifting fast enough? As the Easter union conferences approached this looked extremely uncertain. Gaitskell suddenly began to foresee the prospect of a second defeat, and to recognize that this might be fatal. For a

party leader to defy a single conference aberration was one thing. For him to attempt to ignore a series of adverse decisions, amounting to the expression of a settled point of view, was something quite different.

At this stage, more I think than at Scarborough, Gaitskell faced in his own mind the distinct likelihood that in six months' time he might have to go—probably to retire completely from politics. It was a discouraging prospect. It would mean that his period as a party leader, which had begun under such bright auspices just over five years before, would end in complete failure. He would be remembered only as the man who led his party to its third successive electoral defeat and was then rejected by his own followers. Once he had assimilated this possibility in his mind, he faced it with complete equanimity.

Then, with bewildering rapidity, the outlook changed. When it was least expected an avalanche movement began. The unions followed each other back into the Gaitskell camp as quickly as, the year before, they had moved the other way. Many of the constituency parties did the same. All the hard persuasive work of the winter began to bear simultaneous fruit.

The victory which this made certain was ratified at Blackpool in October 1961. It left Gaitskell in a far stronger position than he had been before Scarborough. He was dominant in the Labour Party, and he had impressed the public outside as a leader of force, wisdom and courage. No one foresaw that he had only fifteen months of leadership ahead. By his efforts he seemed to have secured for himself a long tenure of the leadership on conditions of tolerable authority. But what in fact he had done was to bequeath this easement to his successor, and to give Harold Wilson the elbow-room which has helped him to look like a Prime Minister. If Gaitskell had lost, not only himself but any other Labour leader for years to come would have paid part of the price.

The use to which Gaitskell himself put the new room for manoeuvre was, ironically, a most unwelcome one to many of his closest supporters on previous issues. He swung the Labour Party into a posture of general hostility towards Britain joining the Common Market. The merits of this issue need not be argued here. I would merely record that while his attitude here seemed to me not wholly consistent with his previous general outlook on world affairs, it was in no way the result of a sudden lurch, taken with electoral considerations heavily in mind. I had seen his opposition growing for a year or more before it finally revealed its full force to the public. Like all his political positions it was fixed partly by logic and partly by emotion. And once fixed, he held to it with great tenacity.

I then had the opportunity (although it was a small consolation at the time) to see his political qualities and defects through, as it were, the other end of the telescope. Broadly, they looked much the same as I had previously thought them to be, although I inevitably felt a little more sympathy with those who had so often differed from him in the past. Courage could be interpreted as inflexibility and an aggressive respect for rationality as a tendency to equate little points and big ones. Yet, by and large, he appeared just as impressive as a temporary opponent as he had so long done as an ally and leader. The warm persuasiveness of his manner and the absolute honesty of his purpose were formidable weapons, on whichever side of them one stood.

Nor did this difference make close personal relations with him impossible. At first I thought it would, but that was under the shock of a sudden break in a long habit of agreement. But then he made it clear that he was still faithful to his old rule of the primacy of private relations. For the last few weeks of his active life we were back on terms of the closest friendship.

What did he leave to English politics? First, the promise of being a great Prime Minister, not because he would necessarily have avoided mistakes, but because he would have infused the whole Government with a sense of loyalty and purpose, and made men of widely differing gifts and character proud to serve under him. Second, a Labour Party with both the will and the capacity for victory, two qualities of which, without him, it might only too easily have deprived itself. And third, a memory which is a standing contradiction to those who wish to believe that only men with cold hearts and twisted tongues can succeed in politics.

V. Elections and Electioneering

David Butler and Anthony King

1. THE MAKING OF TORY STRATEGY

Britain's major political parties are in many ways much more highly developed than their American counterparts. This fact emerges particularly strikingly in connection with elections. The Democratic and Republican parties in the United States often act as little more than national holding companies; it is the candidates and the state parties who carry on the active work of electioneering. The British parties, by contrast, have large headquarters staffs and elaborate policy-making machinery. Pre-election planning has become a highly coordinated activity, beginning months, even years, before polling day itself. As this selection shows, the problem is complicated for British politicians by the fact that there is no fixed election date.

The outlook for the Conservatives in the months immediately after October 1959 could hardly have been more buoyant. The party had just won its third successive electoral victory, and had a leader whose standing with the public showed every sign of continuing to rise. The economy was expanding rapidly and, despite the summit debacle of May 1961, Britain continued to exert substantial influence in world affairs. The 1959 intake of new Conservative M.P.s included many able younger men whose presence on the back benches boded well for the future. By contrast, the Labour party—divided, demoralised and increasingly absorbed in abstruse questions of party doctrine—seemed bent on self-destruction. It was in this mood that Mr.

Macleod addressed the 1960 Conservative conference:

> The Socialists can scheme their schemes and the Liberals can dream their dreams; but we at least have work to do.

In 1960 it was possible to believe that the Conservatives could count on governing Britain for the next generation.

Even then, however, many in the party did not lose sight of the difficulty of winning a fourth successive victory. No party had ever won four times in a row, and the wrangling on the Labour side was certain to subside eventually. As the government's term of office lengthened, the number of people in the country disgruntled in one way or another with its actions seemed

From D. E. Butler and Anthony King, *The British General Election of 1964* (New York, 1965), pp. 77–97. Reprinted by permission of Macmillan & Co., Ltd.

bound to grow; the government would increasingly be blamed for anything that went wrong. By 1963 or 1964 Mr. Macmillan and his colleagues would have a long record to justify and inevitably less room for manoeuvre than the opposition; fresh promises could scarcely be made at the last moment. In the meantime the party was in danger of becoming over-confident and inflexible, and of losing touch with the public. The Prime Minister himself perceived this danger particularly clearly. He was also conscious of the need to keep the Conservative party united by constantly renewing its idealism and corporate sense of purpose. The latent differences among Conservatives, which had erupted during the Suez crisis, might come to the surface again if the government ever lost its forward momentum. In 1960, too, Mr. Macmillan and others in the party sensed that Britain was entering a period of profound international change, and that the country would have to adapt itself rapidly merely in order to survive.

Their response to this challenge was twofold. First, the government decided to apply for membership in the European Economic Community. Although taken primarily for other reasons, the decision had a political aspect. . . . The Conservatives suspected that Labour would either split over Europe or come out in opposition; whichever happened, the government would have something new to counter the slogan "time for a change." Second, the government in 1960 and 1961 launched a series of enquiries—Beeching [on the railways], Robbins [on higher education], Buchanan [on urban transport]—whose reports were intended two or three years later to form the basis of the Conservative domestic programme. The enquiries had as their overall aim "the modernisation of Britain" and in conception were closely linked to the European challenge. . . .

Despite the government's mounting difficulties during 1961 and 1962, the move into Europe remained the major premise of Conservative forward thinking. Modern-

isation was no more than its necessary corollary. But then, in January 1963, with President de Gaulle's veto, the entire edifice collapsed in ruins. As a senior party official later put it:

Europe was to be our *deus ex machina*; it was to create a new, contemporary political argument with insular Socialism; dish the Liberals by stealing their clothes; give us something *new* after 12–13 years; act as the catalyst of modernisation; give us a new place in the international sun. It was Macmillan's ace, and de Gaulle trumped it. The Conservatives never really recovered.

At the time many Conservatives were privately relieved; the traditionalists had never welcomed Europe, and even many pro-Europeans disliked the internal tensions which the policy produced. But the problem of thinking forward to the election at once assumed new, and altogether more ominous, proportions. The Conservatives needed a period of calm in which to evolve new policies. Instead, the first nine months of 1963 were devoted to the struggle over the leadership. . . .

Thus, it was not until Sir Alec Douglas-Home became premier in October 1963 that the Conservatives were able to concentrate in earnest on the problem of retaining power. The problem had a number of related aspects. First, consideration had to be given to the timing of the election. Second, the Conservative party had to be pulled together. Third, the party had to develop its policies to the point where they could be convincingly presented to the country. Fourth, a consistent propaganda and publicity theme had to be evolved. And, fifth, it had to be decided what role Sir Alec himself should play in the pre-campaign period—as well as how Mr. Wilson should be dealt with.

The first problem—timing—had already been postponed. On September 26th Mr. Macleod, then still party Chairman, remarked: "The general election will be in 1964; I am sure of that." After the leadership struggle, the possibility of an early election seemed even more remote. There remained three options: March, May—June or the autumn. March had certain attractions; the new government would still be fresh and the April budget would probably have to be tough; moreover, Conservatives feared that poor local government results in April and May would further depress party morale. In fact, the possibility of a March election was not finally ruled out till mid-February. But it had never been a probability. . . . Most Conservatives accepted that Sir Alec Douglas-Home needed time to establish his position in the House of Commons and to make an impact on the country. The party also needed time to recover its morale. If the opinion polls had shown a marked Conservative revival, Sir Alec might have opted for March, even at the last moment. When they did not, he decided to wait.

The choice between May—June and October proved far more difficult. The Prime Minister himself inclined towards an early election, believing that, once the electors had to face the real alternatives, they would quickly leave Labour. He also apparently had considerable faith in his own capacity for meeting and impressing the country face-to-face. Mr. Maudling, Mr. Selwyn Lloyd and a number of other ministers shared Sir Alec's preference for May—June, though for somewhat different reasons. They feared that continuing political uncertainty might in time damage the economy and possibly lead to a run on sterling. It would become increasingly difficult for the government to govern. If the voters were bored with the government and determined on a change, they would be even more bored and more determined by the end of the summer; if the government still had a chance, it was because the voters feared Labour—and this fear would manifest itself whenever the election came. . . .

The arguments for October, advanced chiefly by Mr. Butler, Mr. Hogg and Mr. Macmillan, were at least as powerful. October had traditionally been a favourable month for the Conservatives, and the gov-

ernment could hope to gain from a good summer, with parliament in recess and Labour deprived of its main sounding board. Labour had completed its planned pre-election campaign, was short of funds, and would be caught badly off balance. Economic difficulties might cause trouble by the end of the year, but with luck no deflationary measures would be required before Christmas. Above all, the "Octobrists" insisted on the need for time—time for people to forget Profumo; time for Sir Alec to make an impact on the country and for Mr. Wilson to begin to pall; time for the Conservative party to recover its fighting spirit; time for prosperity to recover its hold. . . .

The final decision did not have to be taken at once. . . . Late in March it was tentatively decided to make an announcement shortly after the Easter recess. Mr. Maudling needed to know roughly when the election would come for budgetary purposes, and the continuing uncertainty undoubtedly contributed to the agitation on the Conservative back benches; Mr. Selwyn Lloyd said publicly that people should be put out of their misery. Sir Alec consulted his senior colleagues in London on March 26th before retiring to Scotland for Easter. On April 7th, two days after his return, he saw most of the cabinet in his room at the House of Commons; the *Daily Telegraph* commented that he clearly wished to reassure M.P.s that he was "taking full account of opinions other than his own." The cabinet appears to have been evenly divided, but the weight of Central Office and the Research Department in the end came down on the side of October. Lord Blakenham, the party's Chairman since the previous October, told Sir Alec simply that the government had at least a chance of being returned in the autumn but none at all in June. Finally on April 9th the Prime Minister announced that the election would be deferred. The Octobrists had won.

The second problem—pulling the party together—took some nine months to solve and continually distracted the Conservative leaders from the central business of winning the election. Neither policy planning nor propaganda, much less the successful projection of the Prime Minister, could proceed smoothly as long as the party continued to bicker. In January 1964, 48% of a Gallup sample thought Labour more united than the Conservatives; only 22% thought the reverse. A poll of leading Conservatives would probably have produced a remarkably similar result. . . . Newspaper headlines continually contained phrases like "Tories in Turmoil" and "When Tory Bites Tory." A party official remarked in mid-January:

It's terrible. I've been bitchier about other members of my party than I ever thought I could be—a most unpleasant atmosphere to work in.

Reviving morale among party workers in the country proved the easiest task. They desperately wanted unity and quickly responded to Sir Alec Douglas-Home's personal charm and buoyancy. By January, Conservative area agents were agreeing that the party had never had a more popular leader and that morale among the rank and file had almost completely recovered. One area agent recalled:

When Sir Alec was here in November, he made a wonderfully favourable impression. Everybody commented on how genuinely friendly he was, and how he seemed interested in what people were saying. As far as our people are concerned, he's the best leader we've had in a long time—since Baldwin really.

The back benchers in parliament proved more intractable. With Labour's lead in the opinion polls holding steady at between eight and ten per cent, one-third to a half of the Conservative parliamentary party were in danger of losing their seats. They seemed increasingly inclined to take matters into their own hands. Mr. Martin Redmayne, the Chief Whip, had lost the confidence of some Conservatives over his handling of the Profumo affair, and neither he nor Mr. John Morrison, chairman of the

1922 Committee, could exert the requisite authority. Mr. Macleod's *Spectator* article roused many back bench M.P.s to fury, and Mr. Heath's bill to abolish resale price maintenance touched off the most prolonged Conservative revolt since Suez. "They've gone berserk," a senior party official observed. Gradually, however, in May and June calm was restored. Sir Alec's own optimism began to permeate the back benchers, who were also reassured by his growing authority in the House of Commons. . . .

The third problem confronting the Conservatives from October 1963 onwards concerned the development of party policy. Their room for manoeuvre in this area was not large. After thirteen years in office, the Conservatives knew they would be forced to fight mainly on their own record, and on issues chosen by Labour. Radical new policies could not be introduced at the last moment; the Conservatives themselves would not believe in them, and the public would scorn them as blatant electioneering. The party had to take care to do little that could be interpreted as criticism of its own past record. As the party of government, the Conservatives were inevitably more inhibited than Labour in advancing new proposals; ministers knew better than their opposite numbers the practical objections to particular ideas and could hardly avoid being conscious of civil service objections in the background.

To an extent not generally realised outside the party, the Conservatives focus their election planning on the preparation of the formal manifesto. The party's best brains devote much of their time to it, and elaborate manifesto machinery has been established. The practice probably grew up for fortuitous historical reasons, but it now has a heavy weight of tradition behind it. It has a number of virtues. Consciousness of the need to produce a manifesto helps ensure a constant stream of forward policy thinking. This is particularly important when the Conservatives are in power and liable to lose sight of long-term problems in the midst of day-to-day policy making. Preparing the manifesto also enables senior M.P.s to keep in touch with party officials outside and encourages them not to neglect electoral considerations entirely. . . .

Forward planning had begun very shortly after the 1959 election. The Research Department conducted an informal enquiry into publicity, organisation and so on, and the Advisory Committee on Policy, chaired by Mr. Butler, established a number of *ad hoc* committees on subjects like monopolies and mergers, consumer protection, and industrial relations. Sir Michael Fraser, director of the Research Department, and Mr. Peter Goldman, director of the Conservative Political Centre, continued to be looked to for new ideas. It was during this period that the twin themes of Europe and modernisation began to be developed. In 1961 Mr. Macleod formed a small committee to discuss the manifesto consisting of ministers, M.P.s, business men and others. It met irregularly until Mr. Macleod left the government two years later. . . .

The committee's main function was to provide ideas and working papers for the body which would eventually draft the manifesto—the "steering committee." This was an innovation of the 1959 election, which Mr. Macmillan revived shortly after the Common Market collapse. Chaired by the Prime Minister himself, it included the most senior members of the cabinet and the party Chairman, together with Lord Poole [a senior party official] Sir Michael Fraser, and Mr. Goldman. Sir Michael Fraser and Mr. Goldman acted as links with the party's policy apparatus outside Parliament and with the Macleod committee. The steering committee suspended operations during the Profumo period and did not begin work again until after the change of leadership. Thereafter, it met regularly until the final draft of the manifesto was ready in 1964.

Between January and October 1963, the Conservative plan—in broad outline—had been to await the results of the various enquiries launched in 1960 and 1961 and then

to fight the election on modernisation. But, with the advent of Sir Alec Douglas-Home, a new problem arose. The party had always relied electorally on an alliance between "the right" and "the centre"; but Sir Alec looked and sounded rather old-fashioned, and even Conservative papers like the *Sunday Times* suspected him of strongly traditionalist leanings. If the centre was not to be alienated, action had to be taken at once to make the new government appear progressive and up-to-date. Similar action was required to reassure the progressives in the party. Accordingly, many of the plans and proposals which would normally have found a place in the manifesto were made public prematurely. . . . The hastily prepared Queen's Speech in November committed the government to twenty-four specific bills; the theme again was "modernisation of Britain, covering many of the economic and social aspects of our national life." In December the government published for the first time its five-year advance estimate of public expenditure.

A great deal of work on the manifesto, however, remained to be done—on two problems in particular, the social services and land. Influential figures in the party, notably Mr. Macleod, Mr. Powell and Mr. Goldman, had felt for some years that the social services must sooner or later be completely overhauled; the Beveridge principle of flat-rate contributions and benefits had outlived its usefulness. The 1959 manifesto spoke of concentrating "Exchequer help on those with the lowest earnings," and a graduated retirement scheme had been enacted in 1961. Mr. Goldman and others wished more radical reforms to form the centre-piece of the 1964 manifesto; at one stage consideration was given to the possibility of presenting some legislation to parliament before the election. But detailed proposals could not be agreed upon in time to be included in the manifesto, which confined itself to enunciating the principle of relating benefits to earnings and to proposing "a full review of social security arrangements." "I've led the horses to water, but it's not easy to make them drink," commented one party official. . . .

The impetus behind the discussions on land and land prices was more obviously electoral. Shortages of land around London and other big cities slowed down house building, and rising prices hit both local councils and prospective owner-occupiers; Labour seemed to be making substantial headway with its proposals for a land commission. Various proposals were advanced earlier in the year, but by August 1964 the issue had been narrowed to whether or not the government should propose the imposition of a betterment tax on development land. According to newspaper reports, Sir Keith Joseph, the Minister of Housing and Local Government, regarded the proposal favourably; but the Prime Minister and Mr. Maudling demurred. The manifesto stated only that "in considering any further measure to tax land transactions, the test must be that it should not adversely affect the price or supply of land." A number of Conservatives complained after the election that the failure to advance more stringent proposals had been a serious blunder. But one influential figure remarked:

I was against doing anything. The party was naked on land and everybody knew it. If we tried to cover our nakedness at the last moment, we would look ridiculous and we couldn't help but produce a half-baked scheme.

Throughout this period, the problem of policy shaded imperceptibly into the fourth problem — the problem of presentation. . . .

The party began by emphasising modernisation. Ministerial speeches during the winter of 1963–64 dealt with little else; Conservative progress in the fields of industry, science and technology was described, and it was explained how developments in these fields would be hindered by Labour. The first three party television broadcasts after the change of leadership dealt with these topics. But somehow the theme never caught on. Audiences seemed uninterested in modernisation and were perhaps even a little frightened by it. . . . Nor was it always clear what the word implied; it was vague and easily misunderstood.

The modernisation theme never disappeared entirely; a large portion of the cabinet was identified with it, and a large section of the manifesto dealt with it. Gradually, however, during the spring and early summer, the party's publicity reverted to what were essentially the themes of 1959 — prosperity, and the threat to it if Labour won. From March onwards Conservative speakers laid increasing stress on the country's material progress and on the dangers to it implicit in nationalisation, bureaucracy and higher taxation. Two of the three party broadcasts from May to August were mainly concerned with attacking Labour. . . . The party's advertisements also sought to reproduce the spirit of the pre-1959 campaign, though without copying exactly its form. "We fought it like "59," a senior Conservative said afterwards, "not because we wanted to, but by default: we didn't know what else to do."

All this assumed that the election would be fought chiefly on domestic affairs. The available evidence indicated that a substantial majority of voters followed the Conservatives in wishing Britain to retain the independent deterrent, just as they preferred Conservative to Labour policies on nationalisation; but the evidence also made it clear that few electors were interested in either subject. The Conservatives accordingly left it to their industrial allies to carry the burden of anti-nationalisation propaganda, and themselves made less of the deterrent than they would otherwise have done. . . . Only Sir Alec Douglas-Home insisted on keeping the deterrent continuously to the fore. He believed it to be of supreme importance and saw it as his duty to make the public aware of its significance. As one of his senior colleagues put it:

Every P.M. has one issue he cares more about than anything else. Alec's is the bomb. He'd even be prepared to lose an election on it.

Moreover, Sir Alec himself felt most comfortable in his accustomed field of foreign and defence affairs. Long before the formal campaign began, observers had noted that his speeches tended to acquire a new confidence and authority the moment he moved away from domestic matters.

The new Prime Minister's relative inexperience in domestic affairs conditioned the way the Conservatives approached their fifth problem—making Sir Alec known to the British public. Although a cabinet minister since 1957, Sir Alec had never headed a home department and, even as Foreign Secretary, had made less public impact than his immediate predecessors. The whistle-stop tours which began early in 1964 and continued until the eve of poll were intended to make him a more generally familiar figure; they were also designed to offset the somewhat strained appearance which Sir Alec presented on television. . . .

One publicity theme Sir Alec inherited from Mr. Macmillan—the image of "the team." In press advertisements in the winter of 1963–64, Sir Alec often appeared together with other, often younger cabinet ministers. Later on Mr. Butler referred to "an administration of all the talents." By emphasising the "team," the Conservatives sought to contrast their own wealth of talent with Labour's "one-man band." Mr. Wilson had been attacked on first becoming leader for his left-wing views. Later the Conservatives attempted to show that Mr.

Wilson had no colleagues of anything like comparable ability; many Conservatives believed, and thought they could convince the electorate, that Labour "could not form a government." Many in the party also thought they could convey to the public their own sense of Mr. Wilson's deviousness and unreliability—hence the attacks on him early in 1964 as a "slick salesman of synthetic science." This approach also misfired, however, and by March it was apparent that Conservative attacks on Mr. Wilson were only serving to increase his public stature. Thereafter government speeches left Mr. Wilson himself largely alone, though they continued to warn of the Labour party's "inexperience" and "lack of talent." Conservatives feared that over-violent attacks on either Mr. Wilson or Labour might lead to a reaction in their favour. But many of them were also quietly confident that Sir Alec Douglas-Home's virtues and Mr. Wilson's limitations would impress themselves in time on the voting public. . . .

On the eve of battle the Conservative mood could be characterised as one of heavily qualified optimism. The party believed it could win; it was not convinced that it would win. Many electors clearly felt that it was time for a change. Everything hinged on the Conservatives' ability to dissuade them from acting on that feeling.

David Butler and Anthony King

2. THE 1964 CAMPAIGN

Despite the prominent role played by the two major party leaders, general elections in Britain are not presidential elections. The leaders' personalities are important, but not quite as important as in the United States. The parties reflect this fact (as well as taking account of the personal interests of politicians other than the party leaders) in the way they organize their campaigns. Coordination is usually emphasized rather than individual enterprise. In 1964 the campaign promised to be particularly gruelling, with the Conservatives and Labour running neck-and-neck in the opinion polls in the early days of September.

At 4 p.m. on September 15th, after the Prime Minister had paid a flying visit to the Queen at Balmoral, it was announced from 10 Downing Street that Parliament would be dissolved on September 25th and that polling day would be Thursday, October 15th. . . . [The date had] been confidently tipped ever since the spring. Indeed, in early September there was almost more speculation on when the announcement would be made than on what it would be.

The parties certainly were already acting as though the date was fixed. They rushed to use up their allocations of party political broadcasts, and the week-end of September 5th saw the Conservatives holding briefing meetings in London, the Liberals gathered for an abbreviated assembly, and the Labour party taking advantage of the annual Trades Union Congress. The Prime Minister told 200 prospective candidates that "the trend of opinion was running strongly the Conservative way" and cabinet colleagues joined him in setting out the government's record. The Liberals, in the sombre setting of Central Hall, Westminster, seemed to be giving themselves an unjubilant send-off until Mr. Grimond wound up with a rousing call to go out and capture the floating vote: "If it is floating, it can be pushed. Push it."

The TUC at Blackpool proved a less sympathetic launching pad than it had been five years before. Mr. Wilson, in a much heralded speech on Monday, September 7th, failed (perhaps deliberately) to rouse his audience as Mr. Gaitskell had done in the same hall in 1959. He did make a categorical promise to restore trade-union law to the status quo before *Rookes v. Barnard*: he promised consultation on restrictive practices and other union problems—and he delivered a long lecture on the economic situation in general. At the end of the week, after an unusually tranquil Congress, the trade unions passed a vehement declaration of support for the Labour cause. . . .

The main party news of the next few days was provided by the publication of Labour's 7,000-word manifesto. *The New Britain* was launched with a press conference and a television broadcast on September 11th. . . . Its emphasis on the need for growth, innovation and efficiency won it the most sympathetic press reception a Labour manifesto has ever had.

September 12th really marked the beginning of the campaign. Labour held a giant

From D. E. Butler and Anthony King, *The British General Election of 1964* (New York, 1965), pp. 109–126. Reprinted by permission of Macmillan & Co., Ltd.

rally at the Empire Pool, Wembley, with a protracted pageant as a prelude to Mr. Wilson's Kennedy-like clarion call:

> Those who are satisfied should stay with the Tories. We need men with fire in their bellies and humanity in their hearts. The choice we offer, starting today, is between standing still, clinging to the tired philosophy of a day that is gone, or moving forward in partnership and unity to a just society, to a dynamic, expanding, confident, and, above all, purposive new Britain.

At the same moment, the Conservatives held rallies in twelve regional centres, each addressed by cabinet ministers. Sir Alec speaking in London gave his followers a somewhat muted send-off although he did coin his only widely quoted phrase, dubbing the Labour manifesto "a menu without prices."

> There is not a word on where the money is coming from or what the price of the article will be. Without these details the prospectus is void.

At the outset the [opinion] polls showed the parties almost level but the events of the last years had conditioned the Labour leaders to the idea they would win and many denied that they had seen any evidence of Conservative recovery. The Conservatives had no doubt about the recovery, but, although they all believed that they now had a chance of victory, their confidence did not match Labour's. The Liberals were discounted by their major rivals but they did go into the campaign confident that their fortunes had not slumped as badly as the polls suggested. Launching the 4,000 word Liberal manifesto *Think for Yourself—Vote Liberal* on September 15th, Mr. Byers said flatly that the Liberals sought, if not the balance of power, "a decisive position" in the House: he also stressed the need for a really massive Liberal vote—a theme used more and more explicitly as the campaign advanced.

On September 14th Sir Alec rushed across Kent on the first of his whistle-stop tours and the following day Mr. Wilson started campaigning in his own constituency of Huyton and in Liverpool nearby.

On September 16th, at Stevenage, he made the first of his twenty set-piece speeches —an appeal to housewives. . . .

The Conservatives unveiled their 7,000 word manifesto *Prosperity with a Purpose* on September 18th. It contained few surprises, inevitably, and its detailed but undramatic proposals received a tepid press welcome. Its impact was still further muted by Mr. Wilson's challenge to Sir Alec to debate the cost of the two parties' programmes on television. The challenge was probably not meant to be accepted: but it was adroitly timed to steal the headlines in the next morning's press.

Mr. Wilson's challenge not only diminished the impact of the Conservative manifesto, but also provoked some protracted exchanges on TV confrontations. Sir Alec never replied formally but Mr. Grimond volunteered to take his place and demanded a role in any future television encounter. Several meetings at lower levels were proposed by the broadcasting authorities; Sir Keith Joseph did debate housing with Mr. Stewart but all other clashes at the ministerial level were somehow vetoed, usually by the Conservatives. Nevertheless, television did provide the most important events of the week preceding the dissolution. In the BBC's *Election Forum* programmes Mr. Grimond, Mr. Wilson and Sir Alec were subjected on successive nights to tough interrogation by professional interviewers, pressing home questions chosen from those sent in by more than 18,000 viewers. It was generally agreed that Mr. Grimond and Mr. Wilson acquitted themselves with distinction. Sir Alec's performance was more uneven: he seemed ill at ease, and by referring to the proposed supplement for older pensioners as a "donation," presented Labour spokesmen with a phrase which they exploited throughout the campaign to illustrate the Conservatives' patrician attitude.

The battle intensified sharply on Friday, September 25th. Parliament was dissolved. Mr. Wilson, at the first of his daily campaign press conferences, developed, with characteristic edge, several challenges to the Conservatives. Where would they draw the age line for their "donation" to pensioners? Why had production not increased at all in 1964? Further challenges followed on Saturday but on Monday, September 28th, Mr. Maudling reversed the process in the first of the Conservative press conferences. Two days before, in one of the most publicised *obiter dicta* of the campaign, Mr. George Brown had suggested that interest on mortgages might be cut to 3%. Mr. Maudling enquired whether this was a promise and how much it would cost. The Labour party denied that Mr. Brown had named a specific figure but emphasised that they wished to bring down the cost of housing. Conservatives were eager to take advantage of Mr. Brown's indiscretion but they soon found that they did not wish to appear as advocates of dearer housing. After a day or two the issue was allowed to subside. Many partisans felt that on balance neither side had gained from it.

Mr. Wilson continued with his series of speeches on set topics. He spoke in Cardiff on September 27th of the economic situation; alluding to the popular TV series *Steptoe and Son* he re-named Sir Alec and Mr. Selwyn Lloyd "Stop-Go and Son"; if the Conservatives won, the brakes would be applied to expansion again within six weeks. In Plymouth the next day he turned to the need to expand the navy and all conventional forces. In Hammersmith the following night he dealt with housing and land prices, guaranteeing security to owner-occupiers after the promised land commission came into being. Meanwhile, in Scotland, Sir Alec was campaigning busily but drawing less publicity; this pattern continued throughout the following weeks partly because his phraseology and his themes were less varied and less newsworthy and partly because he was more often cut off from the main body of political reporters, who tended to hover round the Smith Square press conferences.

Wednesday, September 30th, stands out as the most exciting day in the whole campaign. That morning the National Opinion Poll in the *Daily Mail* showed the Conservatives with a 2.9% lead — the previous Sunday the Gallup poll had put the Conservatives just ahead for the first time in three years. If the trend continued Labour was heading for heavy defeat; even to those who were sceptical about the polls, it was plain that the boost to Labour which had been generally expected to follow the start of the campaign had not yet materialised.

Anxiety over this may have contributed to Mr. Wilson's only serious lapse in the campaign. After a sleepless night he said at his press conference that a case could be made out for an enquiry into whether strikes at election time were deliberately fomented on behalf of the Conservative party. He alluded to an unofficial stoppage at the Hardy Spicer component firm which threatened the whole motor industry with shutdowns. . . . Mr. Wilson recalled the British Oxygen strikes in 1955 and 1959: "In 1959 I think it was demonstrated conclusively that there was a political motivation in that dispute." Mr. Maudling immediately and with characteristic casualness fielded the accusation at his press conference:

I must say that's a rum one — Tory shop stewards going round sabotaging Mr. Wilson's election! Really!

Mr. Wilson's accusation attracted wide ridicule the following day. But he was unexpectedly released from his difficulties by Mr. Herbert Hill, the chairman of Hardy Spicers. By issuing a libel writ Mr. Hill made the whole matter *sub judice* and his arrogant description of his workers as "poor dears . . . of pretty poor mentality . . . with a pretty poor level of intelligence" made Conservatives only too anxious to forget all reference to Hardy Spicer. . . .

But September 30th was notable in another way. The balance of payments figures for the second quarter of 1964 were issued showing a deficit of £73m. That evening at Norwich, Mr. Wilson, who had already talked of a balance of payments crisis, accused the Prime Minister in stinging terms of deceiving the public, likening him to John Bloom (the tycoon whose companies had just collapsed so spectacularly).

When Sir Alec Douglas Home spoke here [on September 29] he already knew that this morning the government were being forced to put out trade and balance of payments figures which would blow sky-high the carefully fostered myth on which the Tories were hoping to win the election — the myth of gently rising prosperity based on a sound economy which would guarantee that it could continue. The figures are far worse than those which forced Mr. Selwyn Lloyd [in 1961] to bring the economy to a standstill and to introduce the pay pause.

When Mr. Maudling maintained that there was no crisis, he was asked about Mr. Selwyn Lloyd's speech two days earlier demanding that Labour should promise not to devalue as they had done in 1949 when "faced by a similar crisis."

But the announcement on October 2nd of increasing borrowing powers for Britain made Mr. Maudling's case harder to argue. . . . That evening, in perhaps the hardest hitting of all television broadcasts, Mr. Brown rubbed the point home:

There's no point in beating about the bush any longer. We have got to face the facts now. This country is lurching towards the biggest economic crisis since the war. If the present trend continues it will mean that our jobs, our wages, our hire purchase payments, our mortgage rates are all in jeopardy.

In the remaining days of the campaign, the economic crisis seldom achieved headlines but it played a part in many Labour speeches and was an obvious embarrassment to Conservatives.

The Conservative counter-attack concentrated on the cost of Labour's domestic proposals. On October 2nd Mr. Maudling estimated them at £900 million. He invited Labour to elaborate on how they would find the money, and promised to give an answer if they failed to. The Prime Minister meanwhile was travelling the country, drawing warm applause at his country whistle-stops, but having an increasingly rough passage in the towns. Each night the television news showed him on the stump, stressing his repeated themes — the need to safeguard our growing prosperity and the need to maintain Britain's voice in world affairs. He always spoke more assuredly on foreign and defence issues than on domestic matters.

Sunday, October 4th, represents a landmark in the campaign — at least in the frantic atmosphere of Smith Square. The serious Sunday papers dwelt on Labour errors in the past week and its failure to get its campaign off the ground. But the press that day produced what one Conservative strategist called "a symmetry of nonsense." For the gloomy editorial comment appeared simultaneously with two *Sunday Telegraph* Gallup polls showing Labour now well ahead; one poll suggested a lead of 4½%, the other one of 6½%. This followed a NOP report two days earlier showing a 4½% swing to Labour in the marginal seat of Coventry South. Advance news of the Gallup poll may have led Mr. Butler, at his one appearance at the Conservative press conference, to speak of a "strong undercurrent of [sic] Labour" — a much quoted phrase which led to accusations of defeatism. Advance news of the polls was also said by those present to have had a marked effect on Mr. Wilson, who on the Saturday night gave one of his best performances at Newcastle. . . .

The immigration issue had been simmering in the background, with press reports on affected constituencies, while Sir Alec and others managed to avoid challenges to repudiate explicitly the Conservative campaign in Smethwick*. The Prime Minister at last brought the issue to the headlines with his speech in Bradford on October 6th. He claimed that Britain would have been flooded with immigrants but for the passage of the 1961 Act which the Labour and Liberal parties had heatedly opposed. But Sir Alec's speech was not the prelude to a wider exploitation of the issue.

* A Labour-held constituency near Birmingham where the Tory candidate was alleged to be exploiting racial tension. [Editor's note]

Indeed his words were somewhat drowned by Mr. Hogg's next explosion. At Plymouth that evening Mr. Hogg accused Mr. Wilson of saying that Mr. Macmillan had "debauched" the country's public life. When a heckler shouted "What about Profumo?" Mr. Hogg retorted

If you can tell me there are no adulterers on the front bench of the Labour party you can talk to me about Profumo.

Not content with one reminder of the name of Profumo, Mr. Hogg returned to the subject the next night, with a lengthy attack on the *Daily Mirror* for its reporting of his first speech. The *Mirror* delightedly printed his attack in full and the issue was given a further lease of life. Mr. Wilson cheerfully refused to comment saying that it was for Sir Alec to do so. Conservative Central Office was visibly embarrassed. . . .

The Conservatives undoubtedly felt that the campaign was going badly. Their NOP lead on October 7th showed a drop from 2.9% to 0.9%. On October 9th another NOP poll showed that Mr. Barber, the Minister of Health, would lose his seat at Doncaster on an 8% swing, and the stock market, which had reached a new peak on October 1st, had its worst day for two years. The bookmakers who had quoted level odds a week earlier now reported a rush of money on Labour, who became 3–1 on favourites.

The Liberals had stolen few headlines during the campaign, though Mr. Grimond's far-flung travels by plane and helicopter had been duly reported and some of Mr. Byers's remarks at his daily press conferences received notice. The party's television efforts were well praised and publicised. They began to receive more attention as the polls showed that Liberal strength, instead of declining as the two major parties drew level, was increasing. . . .

The election had not seemed to stimulate great public excitement, although the leaders' speeches were well attended. But after Mr. Hogg's outburst, he had some very rough meetings at which he was virtually shouted down. Sir Alec encountered in-

creasing and often very boorish heckling. At Leeds on October 6th he was provoked into suggesting that the hecklers were "hired" by Labour, an accusation from which he and Lord Blakenham had to retreat some distance. The heckling reached its climax at the Bull Ring in Birmingham on October 8th when his last set speech —his only one to a non-ticket audience —was rendered completely inaudible by continuous chants of "Tories out," "No Polaris," and "We want Wilson.". . . The heckling was ugly and may have attracted some sympathy to the Conservatives. On the other hand the spectacle of the Prime Minister doggedly plodding on with an unheard speech hardly left an image of command. . . .

A *sotto voce* story that appeared only in a late edition of the *Daily Express* (and on an inner page) caused a mild stir. Mr. R. A. Butler, interviewed by Mr. George Gale in the train up to Darlington . . . was reported as saying that the result looked like being very close.

We're running neck and neck. I'll be very surprised if there's much in it—say 20 seats either way. But things might start slipping in the last few days. . . . They won't slip towards us.

He was reported as commenting on the Prime Minister

Alec has done very well. Possibly he has spent too much time outside London. . . . He's a bit bored with Ted [Heath].

and on Mr. Hogg's outburst

A great pity. It brings up the past. It reminds people of the last year of the Macmillan government. I don't think talking about adultery on any Front Bench is helpful. And anyway the adultery of Profumo's wasn't the point. It was the lies. . . .

On Sunday October 11th the last phase of the campaign began. The day's Gallup poll had confirmed the Labour advantage of a week before. The time for a really vigorous counter-attack had come. Sir Alec had had a fairly easy passage on his only appearance at the Conservative press conference the day before (though he did describe the party's morale as being "as good as can be expected") but it was left to his chairman, Lord Blakenham, hitherto little in the limelight, to speak out on the Sunday in the most vigorous terms yet used at any of the press conferences:

The return of a Labour government would reduce the safety of Britain and its status in international affairs. The return of a Labour government would spell financial crisis and economic disaster for this country, as it did on every other occasion when the Labour party has been entrusted with power. . . . They are still a socialist party, and are led by an avowed man of the left. A majority of the parliamentary Labour party, led by Hugh Gaitskell, supported a Conservative government over the nuclear deterrent. . . . At Scarborough after the last election, Mr. Gaitskell wanted to divorce the Labour party from the commitments on nationalisation.

The Conservative counter-attack was . . . pressed home on the following day when Mr. Maudling at last produced his long heralded estimate of the taxes needed to pay for Labour's programme—9*d*. on the income tax, 6*d*. on a gallon of petrol, 4*d*. on 20 cigarettes, a penny a pint on beer, and 3/- a bottle on spirits, as well as 6/- on the weekly national insurance contribution. "If this is the price of Harold Wilson, it is too high a price to pay." . . .

Mr. Wilson to the dismay of some of his party decided to spend the last five days of his campaign in Liverpool, staying close to his own constituency; he did, however, make forays on both sides of the Pennines and he received an extraordinarily warm welcome. The Prime Minister devoted the beginning of the week to his final broadcasts and to a quick tour of Essex before rushing up to Scotland for the eve of poll. . . .

The final television appeals of the parties reached more people than anything else in the campaign. Mr. Grimond on October 10th rounded off the successful and distinctive Liberal TV series with yet another demonstration of his exceptionally sympathetic television personality.

It is no wonder that this general election is now boring a great many people. They are fed up with the endless bickering between the Tory and Labour parties. They want attention to the things that matter to them. You must have some touch of idealism in politics. Without that politics wither and are dead. . . . You should send back to the House of Commons people who will speak for you and not merely for the party machines. In practical terms that means again sending back Liberal members with a massive Liberal vote behind them.

Mr. Wilson's final appeal on October 12th was prefaced by Lord Attlee, looking very old, but conjuring up the authority of an ex-Prime Minister to deny that Britain's weight in the world depended upon her nuclear weapons. Mr. Wilson, in his speech, spoke resonantly and unusually sympathetically of the need for Britain to modernise herself and push ahead economically while caring for the old.

. . . We seek to create an open society in which all have a vital and vigorous part to play. If you want to see Britain moving ahead and getting ahead, if you want to sweep away outmoded ideas, the old-boy network that has condemned so many of our ablest young people to frustration, then you feel with us the sense of challenge, of excitement and adventure. For if the past belongs to the Tories the future belongs to us, all of us.

The Prime Minister's final appeal was a reasoned attack on Labour's policies, less skilled and convincingly delivered in its domestic passages than in its climactic assault on the folly of relinquishing the British bomb:

. . . It is just at this moment, when France and China are becoming nuclear powers, that the Socialists would propose to discard all control by a British government over Britain's nuclear arm. . . . I must be sure that each of you recognises the consequences of such a Socialist decision. It would mean that we should surrender all our authority in world affairs and hand over the decision about the life and future of Britain to another country. This I am quite sure you cannot allow. When you are faced with these questions, you cannot answer "I do not know." The answer must be "yes" or "no." Plainly, then, I have told you my point of view. The responsibility and the choice are now yours.

[Labour, with 44.1 per cent of the vote and 317 seats in the House of Commons, won the election. The Conservatives polled 43.4 per cent of the popular vote and won 304 seats.

The Liberals, with 11.2 per cent, won 9 seats. Harold Wilson succeeded Sir Alec Douglas-Home as Prime Minister on October 16.]

Kenneth O. Morgan

3. SWANSEA WEST

General elections in Britain are decided on a national basis. Although regional disparities in voting appeared in both 1959 and 1964, most constituencies tend to move with the national tide. Indeed, it is a rule of thumb in Britain that few individual candidates for Parliament are worth more than about five hundred votes. Much local electioneering thus has little more than ritual significance. But in some constituencies five hundred votes can spell the difference between victory and defeat. Such a constituency in recent years has been Swansea West.

Swansea West was the most marginal seat in South Wales. First formed in 1918, it had returned on different occasions Liberal, National Liberal, Conservative and Labour members. In 1959 it was the only seat in Wales to change hands, Mr. Hugh Rees winning it for the Conservatives from Mr. Percy Morris, the Labour member since 1945. But Mr. Rees's majority was only 403 and Labour would recapture the seat with a swing of under 0.5%. Early in 1964 both major parties brought their leaders to Swansea. Sir Alec Douglas-Home opened his pre-election campaign in the Brangwyn Hall on January 20th, and Mr. Wilson followed a few days later. In May, Mr. George Brown addressed local party workers.

The constituency formed part of a prosperous town, whose economy had been largely transformed since the war. Light manufacturing industries, partly based on a trading estate in the north, had replaced the old metallurgical works, while the need to restore bomb damage had contributed to a substantial building boom. The docks continued to thrive, especially on the import of oil. Work for women could be found in the expanding professional and shopping services. Thousands of Swansea men, however, found employment outside the town and commuted to work; the massive steel works at Margam employed 2,000 men and the new Trostre and Velindre tinplate works a further 1,000. In early 1964 the dispute which closed down the Margam works seriously affected Swansea's working population. More ominous still, in May the closure of the Prestcold refrigerator factory threw 1,500 men out of work. But in general the town bore an unmistakable air of affluence and satisfaction. During August an enormously successful National Eisteddfod in Singleton Park coincided with the Glamorgan cricket team's first-ever victory over the touring Australians.

For an urban division, Swansea West was unusually scattered. Set in the narrow coastal plain along the curve of Swansea Bay, it extended from the docks in central Swansea to Mumbles Head five miles away. It covered an area of nearly 10,000 acres and, with many open green spaces, seemed

From Kenneth O. Morgan, "Swansea West" in D. E. Butler and Anthony King, *The British General Election of 1964* (New York, 1965), pp. 265–275. Reprinted by permission of Macmillan & Co., Ltd.

less like a community than a network of urban villages. All three parties found difficulty in assessing its basic character. Nevertheless, the social division between East and West had become increasingly marked since the war. East of the docks and the river Tawe, Swansea survived as an old Welsh industrial settlement; in the west, the growth of private suburban housing accompanied the rise of a very different type of society. It was in Swansea West that most of the symbols of the new expansion could be seen, notably the University College with over 2,300 students. For forty years Swansea's population had tended to move westwards, as families migrated from their old neighbourhoods to the more desirable areas along Mumbles Road and towards the Gower peninsula. In many ways, the difference in class structure and outlook between Swansea East and West symbolised the great divide between two generations in South Wales.

This social division was faithfully reflected in politics. Swansea East was an impregnable Labour fortress; at a by-election in 1963 the Conservative candidate finished fourth and lost her deposit. But in Swansea West the political balance was finely poised. Of its eight wards, three — Brynmelin, Townhill and Fforestfach — voted overwhelmingly Labour and returned Labour candidates to the borough council; all were typical Welsh industrial communities. A fourth, Victoria, returned Independent councillors but voted predominantly Labour at parliamentary elections. The other wards — St. Helen's, Ffynnone, Mumbles and Sketty — mostly returned Ratepayer councillors and the Conservatives had had little success in challenging them despite the wards' middle-class character. In practice, the party conflict in Swansea West took the form of a clash between the old industrial centre and the expanding residential fringe. Prior to the election, Labour supporters noted anxiously that their own solid wards were losing population, much of it to council estates in the East; Sketty, by contrast, swelled in population after

1959 from 7,000 to 10,000. But these changes were less unfavourable to Labour than at first appeared. The increase in Sketty included a massive sky-scraper council estate, one of the first municipal projects in the constituency for many years.

Labour had dominated the Swansea council for a generation or more. By 1964 it was Labour that had to contend with the feeling that "it was time for a change." The council's housing and comprehensive school programme both came under heavy fire. In both divisions, Labour's affairs were managed by the executive of the Swansea Labour Association, whose offices, next door to a cinema near the High Street railway station, were reminiscent of the old cloth-cap days of the movement. Two full-time agents were maintained: in the East, Mr. J. G. Davies, a remarkable patriarchal figure who had acted as secretary of the Association since 1916; in the West, Mrs. Peggy England Jones, an experienced and able campaigner who had served in Swansea East from 1950 to 1959. Active branches or "ward councils" existed in all eight wards in Swansea West, and it was their relative autonomy which had partly led to the defeat of 1959. Until then Labour's organisation had had the edge, but in 1959 the "grass-roots" methods used in the strongest Labour areas broke down under the impact of re-housing. Few postal votes went to Labour, and at some polling stations in Labour wards turnout was under 60%. Since then immense efforts had been made to rectify the faults. Although financially the party still relied heavily on voluntary activities and contributions (the candidate was unsponsored by a trade union), paid canvassers were imported from Neath and Aberavon during the summer of 1964. Postal votes were processed (more than 500 by the end), removals traced, and new efforts made to persuade all ward councils to prepare marked registers. By polling day there had undoubtedly been an improvement since 1959.

The Conservatives had steadily improved their organisation during the

1950s. . . . Conservative branches operated in each ward, along with fourteen women's branches and three of the Young Conservatives. The women mainly manned committee rooms; the Young Conservatives predominated as canvassers and stewards (though they seemed less conspicuous than in 1959 when Mr. Rees's youth and bachelor status inspired eager feminine assistance, and a profusion of "Hugh for me" rosettes.) The Conservative agent, Mr. F. C. Jones, active in the constituency since 1953, hid force and tenacity beneath a genial exterior. Largely through his efforts, 1,200 of the 2,000 postal vote applications in 1964 had been processed in the Conservative offices. The premises themselves were new, while their structural repairs led visitors to joke incessantly about "modernisation." . . . .

The Liberals were a new element. As the "Mecca of nonconformity" (it still contained 142 chapels in 1964), Swansea had once been a Liberal stronghold, but no Liberal had fought Swansea West since 1929 and the local party had disappeared in the National Liberal split of 1931. A new association, however, was formed in 1961 and by 1964 it had over 150 members. Some were older chapel-goers who had once cheered Lloyd George and voted for Sir Alfred Mond; others were younger suburban Liberals of the Orpington school. The local executive of 18, headed by a university economics professor, had an average age of 35. Although in the 1963 local elections the Liberals polled over 800 votes in the Labour ward of Townhill, the party concentrated its canvassing efforts mainly in the Conservative wards of St. Helen's, Ffynnone and Sketty. They gave the impression throughout of conducting a predominantly anti-Conservative campaign. The Conservatives complained bitterly that the Liberals were fighting Swansea West only because the Conservatives had decided to fight Carmarthen, a seat where the Liberals hoped to do well. The Liberals retorted that they would get between 5,000 and 7,000 votes in Swansea West. From the outset, the Liberals appeared amateurish, short of workers and short of funds, but their enthusiasm was infectious. It was personified by the agent, Mr. Robert Morgan, a vigorous young works manager in a timber firm who had himself been a local government candidate in Ffynnone. . . .

The Conservative, Labour and Liberal candidates were all able young Welshmen. Mr. Rees, the sitting Conservative, was 36 years old; he had been born in Swansea and educated partly at a local grammar school, and was by profession a chartered surveyor in the town. Much was made of his local connections during the campaign, and in his speeches he referred naturally to local places and issues. A diligent constituency member, he had suffered somewhat since 1962 from the silence imposed on him as a junior whip. He spoke easily without notes, in an attractive Swansea accent, and proved the most accomplished platform performer of the three. Only at question time did he tend to become a little belligerent.

Mr. Alan Williams, the Labour candidate, was even younger, the 33-year-old son of a Caerphilly miner, a graduate of London and Oxford universities, and now lecturer in economics at the Welsh College of Advanced Technology, Cardiff. He had fought Poole in 1959. Despite frequent television and radio appearances, he was less well known in Swansea than Mr. Rees, though this may have had its advantages since Mr. Morris in 1959 was believed to have suffered from being a prominent figure on the local council. Mr. Williams spoke less fluently than his Conservative opponent but gained confidence as the campaign went on; he seemed most comfortable answering questions which he did with friendliness and good humour.

Mr. Owain Glyn Williams, 41, the Liberal, was fighting his first campaign. An Ammanford solicitor and law graduate of the University College, Aberystwyth, he was the most identifiably Welsh of the three candidates; he spoke Welsh fluently, his accent still betraying his native Merioneth. Like his Labour namesake, he was little known despite several television appearances. During his campaign, he sought publicity in the local press with aggressive letters which insisted that the truly "wasted" votes would be the ones for Mr. Rees. His platform appearances made up in evident sincerity what they sometimes lacked in precision; his great personal charm showed itself at question time. Throughout, he displayed energy and resourcefulness.

With the election date announced, all three parties swung immediately into action. The Liberals adopted Mr. Williams on September 16th, dubbing him "the rose between two thorns." Their flamboyant headquarters in Walter Road (only four doors from that of the Conservatives) owed much to the inspiration of a former member of the Rank organisation. The Conservatives set out to overwhelm the opposition with a well-advertised adoption meeting in the Dragon Hotel, eye-catching press advertisements, and innumerable posters, window bills and car stickers. . . . Labour moved quietly at first, but with a more purposeful air than in 1959. Close supervision of the constituency was maintained by the regional office in Cardiff. Canvassers were numerous and better distributed than five years before, and the number of car stickers was much higher. Thirty thousand copies of "Points from Labour's Plan" were issued from the Labour Association offices, together with literature on issues such as pensions and leasehold reform. None of the three election addresses was outstanding; only the Liberals listed proposals specifically for Swansea itself.

The strategy of each candidate soon became obvious. Mr. Rees sought to turn Labour's flank by attacking the Swansea Corporation. He criticised their failure to repair corporation housing and to permit leasehold enfranchisement of council property, and their decision to abolish the 11-plus examination. He praised the government's financial "good housekeeping" and its success in transforming the industrial pattern of South Wales. In general, Mr. Rees dwelt more on Welsh issues than did either of his opponents. Some of his best speeches came late in the campaign, when he ranged far and wide over both domestic and foreign questions. He was especially effective on housing, where he could exploit his professional knowledge as a surveyor. Like Mr. Keith Flynn in Cardiff West, however, Mr. Rees ran into some difficulty over leasehold reform; in the last week, the Conservatives published "Swansea Election News," a newsletter which pointed out that Mr. Rees had introduced a Leasehold Tenure Bill in 1962, though without receiving government support. Attendance at the seventeen Conservative meetings exceeded the totals of either of the other parties; about 2,000 people turned up in all. Mr. Rees alone addressed fourteen meetings, being joined for the other three by Sir Keith Joseph, Lord Brecon and Mr. Selwyn Lloyd. The last named met with persistent heckling from university students, not all of them intoxicated by Mr. Lloyd's eloquence alone.

For Labour, Mr. Alan Williams declined to be drawn into local controversies. He derided Mr. Rees for appearing to campaign for the local council instead of for parliament, and accused him of "looking around for a parish pump handle to shake." In his thirteen meetings, and in two joint meetings with the Liberals, Mr. Williams dwelt almost exclusively on domestic issues, notably pensions, housing, leasehold reform, and education. Although an economist, he devoted less time to analysing the country's economic weaknesses than to explaining how newly-created wealth should be shared throughout society. He seldom used local analogies, illustrating the evils of the Rent Act, for instance, with examples drawn from London. Mr. Williams alone thought it worth while to address the University College students; they rewarded him on polling day when student canvassers abounded. At his meetings, he usually spoke for about twenty-five minutes, and his speeches varied little from ward to ward; his average audience numbered around seventy. The main outside speakers were Mr. Douglas Jay, who drew about two hundred to a large cinema in the centre of the town, and Sir Frank Soskice, who addressed a smaller audience in a Sketty grammar school.

Mr. Owain Glyn Williams relied less on meetings, holding only seven. He deplored the other parties' ties to vested interests, and depicted the Liberals as the only force for new ideas in British politics. Like his Labour opponent, he dwelt almost wholly on domestic issues. On leasehold, he quoted Lloyd George's "Yellow Book" to support the claim that the Liberals had the best record. Mr. Williams looked forward to a Welsh parliament, but generally paid less attention to Welsh affairs than might have been expected. Although he attacked the other parties with equal enthusiasm, Mr. Williams gave the impression of regarding the Tories as his main target. No doubt, this was partly because a Conservative held the seat; but also the Swansea Liberals believed their long-term destiny lay in ousting the Conservatives as the main opposition to Labour. The impression of an anti-Tory front was reinforced by the holding of two lively Liberal-Labour meetings. Mr. Rees declined to appear at either, and his written replies to questions were greeted with some derision.

Questions at meetings almost all concerned domestic affairs, especially housing, the cost of living and social security. Defence, foreign policy, and nationalisation were hardly mentioned. The issue that caused all three candidates most trouble was old age pensions. Mr. Rees had to explain the government's inability to raise pensions to higher levels, and to explain away the Prime Minister's "donation" remark (this being one of the few instances when the national campaign impinged on Swansea). Mr. Alan Williams was pressed on Labour's refusal to promise to abolish the earnings rule, and also on why Labour's pensions plan would take so long to implement. A lady in her seventies taxed Mr. Owain Glyn Williams's ingenuity by pointing out, with chapter and verse, that the highest pension the Liberals promised her would still not cover her rent and food and fuel bills. Among the questioners were a few hardy regulars: the earnest lady preoccupied with the under-developed countries, the student with incessant queries on Ferranti, the avuncular stalwart of the Socialist Party of Great Britain whose class war rhetoric seemed somehow out of character. . . .

On October 15th, it was clear from early morning that the poll would be heavy. In some polling districts, one elector in four had voted long before mid-day, and by 5 p.m. the Conservatives estimated that 70% of their supporters had turned out. The day began fine, but heavy showers after tea caused momentary anxiety to Labour. By 6 p.m., however, Labour's forecasts of their victory margin were edging upwards. Both major parties used fully marked registers everywhere, and all their committee rooms appeared fully manned. The Conservatives had as many cars as they could use; Labour, with nearly a hundred, had never had more. Transport presented a particular problem to Labour, so many of whose supporters had moved within the town; in the Labour Association offices, a transport officer worked all day regulating vehicles. No help, however, was received from the Swansea East Labour organisation, now cruising home to a 23,000 majority. The Liberals, though hampered by a shortage of workers, managed to man fifteen committee rooms at least part-time; the drivers of cars, however, were sometimes wastefully used. Quite unexpectedly, all three parties had occasion to complain of the local returning officer's organisation. In Dunvant and Brynmelin, nearly 1,500 voters were directed to the wrong polling stations; in Brynmelin they were told to go to a building which had been torn down four years before. . . .

Shortly after midnight, the result was declared. It had been awaited with considerable anxiety, not least by Mr. Harold

Wilson who had personally enquired of Swansea West from Mr. Cliff Prothero, the party's Welsh regional organiser, during the day. But any Labour fears proved groundless. On an 81.7% poll, Mr. Alan Williams gained the seat from Mr. Rees with a majority of 2,637. Mr. Owain Glyn Williams, with 4,672 votes, lost his deposit. . . . As Mr. Rees sportingly conceded, 2,637 was "a good, proper majority," the largest in the division since 1950.

VI. *Pressure Politics*

Samuel H. Beer

1. PRESSURE GROUPS IN BRITAIN

In 1956 it was possible for Samuel H. Beer to write: "When an American looks at British politics, one of his first questions is likely to be, 'Where are your pressure groups?'" At that time hardly any scholarly work on the subject had been published. Since then, however, several general works on British pressure groups have appeared, and a number of case studies. Professor Beer's article of 1956 nevertheless remains one of the most perceptive contributions. The following passages deal mainly with the scope and methods of group activity. But, as Professor Beer points out, pressure groups cannot be understood if they are studied in isolation: "their aims, methods, and effectiveness are profoundly affected by the context within which they act." In recent years, the acceptance by both the Conservatives and Labour of the welfare state and the need for a managed economy has led most pressure groups to become rather more independent of the parties. The development in both parties of a "quasi-corporatist" approach to government has also meant that British pressure groups operate in an unusually sympathetic environment.

If we had some way of measuring political power, we could quite possibly demonstrate that at the present time pressure groups are more powerful in Britain than in the United States. That at any rate is the impression of the present writer after making some preliminary inquiries in this largely uncharted field. Looking at the process of policymaking of the recent Churchill Government, for example, one finds hardly a field of domestic policy in which the effects of organized pressure are not profoundly marked. This is true, for instance, of policy toward agriculture, labor, veterans' pensions, old age pensions, teachers' salaries, equal pay for women, commercial television, and—to bring in an important "sectional" interest—the Lancashire textile industry. Nor have the demands of groups been reflected only in the policy of the Government and the party in power. The Opposition—whether Labour or Conservative—also has been affected and the competition between parties for the votes of the same group is often so intense as to modify profoundly what one

From Samuel H. Beer, "Pressure Groups and Parties in Britain" in *American Political Science Review*, vol. L, no. 1 (March 1956), pp. 1–23. Reprinted by permission of the author and the American Political Science Association.

might regard as "conservative" or "socialist" principles.

The old age pensioners, for instance, are a large and growing group, whose members, although not as effectively organized as they might be, are nevertheless sharply aware of their interest, of which the competition between the parties continually serves to remind them. If the Tories were to follow what they call their "net and ladder" principle of social policy—i.e., aid for those most in need, the opportunity to rise for the others—they might well prefer to put additional funds into an increase in public assistance, rather than spread them among various types of benefits, some of which are inevitably paid out to persons not greatly in need. They have chosen, however, to meet Labour's promise to restore all benefits to the level of purchasing power which they had in 1948, proposing indeed to make good the rise in prices since 1946. In 1954, as an election year drew near, both party conferences put the raising of old age pensions in the forefront "and," tartly commented the *Manchester Guardian,* "on the domestic side, not much else besides." Opportunely, the Government's increases came into effect only a short time before the General Election of 1955.

At the present time, British parties avoid pitched battles of opposing social philosophies and carry on the political fight through small raids, designed to capture votes from particular interest groups. In general, this tactic, which makes party programs and government policy vulnerable to pressure from organized groups, resembles the present pattern of pressure politics in the United States. And in the past, as in the present, one finds similarities as well as striking differences in the ways in which interests have brought influence to bear on government in the two political systems.

In British history, pressure groups go back at least to the 18th century—witness the various organizations which agitated for parliamentary reform from the 1760's to the 1790's—and the great period of reform in the first half of the 19th century provides many examples of highly effective pressure politics. There was the National Political Union of Francis Place, who, in Bernard Shaw's words, founded "the science of putting pressure on Parliament from outside," Wilberforce's Anti-Slavery Society, Thomas Attwood's political unions, O'Connell's Catholic Association, and that model of successful pressure groups, the Anti-Corn Law League. Yet in Britain as in the United States such organizations, founded primarily for the purpose of putting pressure on government and usually concerned with only a single piece of legislation, need to be distinguished from another type of organization which in both countries in recent generations has become far more important and effective. The latter is best represented by the organizations of the great interest groups of the modern economy—for example, trade unions, trade associations, farmers' groups, and professional associations—although their methods and form of organization may be adopted by other groups, such as war veterans. These organizations commonly have a large dues-paying membership and a considerable private bureaucracy. More important, they normally have other functions than their political ones—for instance, the internal regulation of their members or constituent organizations—and their concern with government policy does not come to an end with the passage of some particular act, but continues and indeed may be heightened as policies favorable to them are adopted. In spite of the earlier development of industrial capitalism in Britain, organizations of this type seem to have come into existence in about the same period in both Britain and the United States, beginning in the latter part of the 19th century. Once the pattern of the permanent bureaucratic organization did emerge in Britain, however, it developed farther than in the United States, British organizations of this type today showing a greater degree of concentration and including a far larger fraction of their potential members.

Pressure groups, whether of the special

purpose or the permanent bureaucratic type, have flourished in both Britain and the United States. Going back far into British history, but rarely found in the United States, is another device by which interests have been linked with the political process. This is the M.P. who "represents" a particular interest in the legislature, not covertly or illicitly, but openly and with general acceptance. For in spite of Burke's speech to the electors of Bristol, British custom has always been far more tolerant than American of the legislator who is intimately connected with outside interests. One may doubt that the subsidy for political expenses which Richard Nixon received from his well-to-do supporters would cause much excitement in Britain where not only the M.P.s. sponsored by trade unions but also quite a few others receive help from interested organizations in the form of contributions to election expenses and even to personal income. . . .

The M.P. who acts as the acknowledged spokesman for an interest in Parliament has been very important in the past. But although he will still be found today, he has greatly declined in importance as a means of interest representation in comparison with that more modern figure, the private bureaucrat of the permanent, large-scale pressure group. Indeed, when we compare the pattern of interest representation of the Victorian period with that of today, the most significant change is the shift of power from the older to the newer type, from the "interested" M.P. to the private bureaucrat. Yet even in the new pattern there are elements of continuity with the old. In contrast with American theory and practice, the "interested" M. P. was a more "legitimate," a more closely integrated part of the representative system. Similarly, today the massive pressure groups of Britain are, in comparison with the American pattern, far more intimately linked with the apparatus of government, especially of government administration.

During the war this association was even closer than at present, many trade associations being at least in part virtually embodied in the administration. In spite of the relaxation of control since the war, there remains a system of "quasi-corporatism" which leaves no important organized group without a channel of influence and a real share in the making of decisions. The main substance of this system is continual, day-to-day contacts between public bureaucrats in the government departments and private bureaucrats in the offices of the great pressure groups — the Farmers' Union, the British Legion, the National Union of Teachers, the Federation of British Industries, the British Medical Association, and countless trade unions and trade associations. A great deal can be done at the "civil service" level, especially in view of the opportunities for discretion which must be left to civil servants by the vast network of rules and orders under which Britain's welfare state is run. As an official of one organization put it, "Very much can be done which is in effect policy-making — what you try to do is to create an opinion among officials which is favorable to stretching the regulations."

Sometimes this connection is formalized by the inclusion of representatives of the pressure group in government committees. The Federation of British Industries, for instance, has representatives on some 70 government committees and similar bodies; the Trades Union Congress has representatives on 60 government committees. The old practice of a formal deputation to a minister is also still used, the classic example being the bodies of dignitaries and officials from various pressure groups which call upon the Chancellor of the Exchequer or Financial Secretary in the early months of the year to present their views on what ought to be done in the Budget.

The formal deputation is less important than it once was, but meetings with ministers are, of course, indispensable for major action. (Even then, as one pressure group official pointed out, you are likely to be successful only if you have prepared the way by winning over the permanent secretary of the department and other key officials). The annual determination of the prices for agricultural products which will be guaranteed by the government provides such occasions. In these prolonged negotiations, on which depend the expenditure of hundreds of millions of pounds, civil servants from the Ministry of Agriculture and certain other departments deal with experts from the National Farmers' Union. The delegation from the N.F.U. will be led by its president, Sir James Turner, who, probably attended by other higher officials of the Union, at critical points will carry the negotiations up to the Minister of Agriculture. At this level, not only the technical arguments—of which Sir James happens to be a master—will be deployed, but also suggestions of electoral retaliation and, so it is said, hints of the withdrawal of farmers' cooperation from certain administrative tasks in which their help is virtually indispensable, in particular the county agricultural committees. Since money is involved, the Chancellor of the Exchequer will at some time be brought in, on which occasion it will make a difference to the outcome if he believes—as a recent Chancellor is reported to have said—that "the farmers are the swing vote."

Confrontations of ministers, however, normally develop out of the immense mass of daily informal contacts at the civil service level. Again and again officials of pressure groups will mention that they continually ring up their "opposite numbers" in the departments and discuss a problem with them on a first name basis—an informality of contact often made easier by the fact that the private bureaucrat worked with the public bureaucrat in the same ministry during the war. Nor is the initiative confined to the pressure groups. For instance, quite commonly when the Ministry of Education has to draw up a new regulation (which may or may not have ultimately to be submitted to Parliament), it will send its draft of the regulation to the headquarters of the National Union of Teachers to get their comments and criticism. It is understandable that the Union finds it hardly worthwhile any longer to send a formal deputation to the minister, although not many years ago, before it had won its present "recognition," it fought strenuously for the right to such audiences.

A recent summary of certain aspects of the work of the Federation of British Industries by its Director-General in its general outlines also applies to many other pressure groups:

There are . . . many consultative committees consisting of official and industrial representatives; and almost every day the F.B.I. is approached by one or another Government Department for advice. But consultation is not really effective unless it takes place before rather than after the event. On the Government side, the process may be a nuisance, but it generally saves a lot of trouble in the long run. So we are constantly impressing on Government Departments the need for them to consult and to consult early. . . .

Of course the great bulk of the work of Government is administration, not policy; and most of what I have called the F.B.I.'s policy work lies in the field of administration. Let me put it another way. Parliament may decide upon a line of policy. . . . Industry may or may not like the policy; and the F.B.I. will say so on its behalf. But when the issue is decided, it may make a world of difference to industry how the policy is implemented and translated through administration into action.

In the representation of interests, the M.P.'s role has declined, but not disappeared. How old and new methods may be combined is illustrated by the successful campaign by the National Union of Teachers in 1954 to defeat the proposed increase in teachers' contributions to their superannuation fund. Having won a modest victory when the Minister of Education accepted the recommendations for an increase in teachers' salaries presented by an advisory committee—on which the Union has a majority of the teachers' representatives—the Union set out to defeat the Minister's announced intention of raising the superannuation contributions. Possibly, as the Union said, the proposed increase had not been discussed at the committee level although it hardly seems likely that the teachers' representatives did not know about it. At any rate, being unable to win its point in dealings with the Ministry, the Union turned to more public methods. With 20 M.P.s as members — four of them "sponsored" candidates — the N.U.T. had a fair basis in Parliament to work from. Although all but one of these were on the Labour side, in this instance the Union picked up considerable support from Conservatives, led by a forceful and frequent rebel, Sir Robert Boothby. Within a week or so of the introduction into the House of the bill to raise contributions, branches of the N.U.T. were sending protests to the M.P.s from their constituencies. Within the House of Commons and within the parliamentary parties — the education committees in each party being used — protests were made by M.P.s. Early in February the parliamentary Labor party officially took a stand in opposition to the bill. Later that month the second reading was postponed and after at least two cabinet meetings at which the question was discussed it was put off until autumn. In October the Minister of Education was obliged to resign, and shortly afterwards the new Minister announced the withdrawal of the bill.

Contrasts of this system of "quasi-corporatism" with the relations of pressure groups and government in the United States, if not sharp, are at least suggestive. For obvious reasons, the individual legislator, and the legislature generally, under cabinet government occupy a less important position. While "rebel" groups and party committees from time to time have influence, there are, for instance, no organs, formal or informal, comparable in power with our legislative committees. Not only do interest groups enjoy a greater degree of concentration, but the government with which they deal also is more highly centralized than ours: greater power to exert pressure is linked up with greater power to act. . . . Usually — this is the point to stress — if you can bring over the Minister and the Chancellor of the Exchequer you have not much else to worry about. Compare the position of the American pressure group which, if it wants positive action, must win its battle at many different points — committees in both houses, the presidency, the secretary , the bureau chief. It is no wonder that our pressure politics is so much noisier and less tidy than Britain's.

The pattern of pressure group relations with the administration, however, in broad outline is not unfamiliar to an American. There is perhaps better articulation in Britain resulting from the fact that normally only one rather than several major pressure groups represents each interest and that more effective contact with the members of the interest group results from its usually including a larger fraction of its potential membership. Perhaps also relations are to a greater degree formalized and institutionalized in Britain than in the United States, although, of course, our national government is clustered with advisory committees and many pressure groups have continual relations with departments and bureaus. . . .

A further principal difference from the American pattern is obvious: it is that the amount of "business" transacted between pressure groups and departments is larger and more important. This results not only from the differences between a unitary and a federal system — compare the importance of educational policy at Westminster and in Washington — but also from the fact that Britain has a welfare state and a controlled economy. Perhaps there was a time when most pressure groups wanted government to stop doing things. But today in Britain as in the United States nearly all want — apart from tax matters — positive action: subsidies, benefit payments, services, favorable regulation such as tariffs. The more positive the state, the larger the amount of business transacted between government and pressure groups is likely to be. Quite naturally, it has been the programs of the welfare state and of the controlled economy around which pressure activity has tended to cluster, giving rise to the system of "quasi-corporatism.". . .

Reginald Bevins

2. POSTMASTER-GENERAL

Most studies of British pressure groups lay stress on the importance of the informal consultations which link the groups with government ministers and civil servants. In some studies the relationship is made to seem not only highly respectable but even a trifle cozy. Reginald Bevins's account of his conflict with the commercial television companies conveys a somewhat different impression. Written in a racier style than is usual among ministers of the Crown, it is also remarkable for having been published so soon after the event. The Postmaster-General in Britain is responsible for preparing the legislation governing both commercial and B.B.C. television. Mr. Bevins was appointed to the office (which is outside the cabinet) in October 1959.

When Harold Macmillan asked me to go to the Post Office he did not even mention television. I soon learned, however, that the Television Act was due to expire in 1964 and within a year of my appointment the Cabinet decided to set up an independent committee to examine the future of television and broadcasting. Eventually Sir Harry Pilkington, the glass manufacturer and a director of the Bank of England, accepted the Chairmanship and I appointed a politically broadly based committee. . . .

I realised, however, that if I waited for the Pilkington Report it might be impossible to take the decisions on it and to pilot a bill through Parliament before the end of the present Parliament. I therefore suggested to the Prime Minister that he should set up a Committee of Ministers to consider the main issues in advance. He agreed and he appointed R. A. Butler as Chairman. . . .

On the two questions which will figure prominently here — the rentals .paid by the programme companies and a second commercial programme — my colleagues in the Government supported me first in the view that the Independent Television Authority should charge commercial rentals, and, secondly, in the view that we should take our time before taking a firm decision about a second commercial programme. . . .

What I hoped for and worked for was a solution which would be fair to the taxpayer: which would give the public better television and would give the companies a fair crack of the whip. . . .

Towards the end of 1962 I had the Bill ready. Then the fun started. Of course, there was no hyperbole about Lord Thomson's remark that commercial television is "a licence to print money." Indeed the companies paid literally nothing for the public concession to enjoy the revenues of an advertising monopoly in television. Granada, for example, had an advertising income of about £16 million a year. The rental it paid to I.T.A. was £750,000 but that paid only for the I.T.A.'s transmitting services. . . .

How had the companies been prospering?. . . Collectively, [they] had been earning a return of at least 75 per cent per annum on capital: some more than 100 per cent per annum.

The Government's original intention had

From Reginald Bevins, *The Greasy Pole; a Personal Account of the Realities of British Politics* (London, 1965), pp. 85–114. Reprinted by permission of the author and Hodder & Stoughton, Ltd.

been to secure economic rentals by applying a special levy to the companies' profits before normal taxation applied. This has been widely criticised on the ground that it gave excessive and arbitrary powers to me. It probably did. In addition, however, the I.T.A. had pleaded with me to persuade the Chancellor of the Exchequer to abolish the television advertising duty which was said to be putting the smaller regional companies in peril.

And both the Inland Revenue and the Post Office who had been making detailed studies of how the levy would work, were becoming increasingly disturbed at the scope it allowed for perfectly legal and legitimate avoidance. . . .

For these and other reasons the Chancellor of the Exchequer agreed to abolish the television advertising duty provided I would agree to switch the basis of the levy from profits to turnover. To this I agreed and so did my colleagues in the Government. I explained this change to a meeting of Conservative back-benchers in late January. They seemed to prefer it. Certainly at that point no one criticised it. But whether the back-benchers preferred it or not, it soon became clear that others disliked it.

Most politicians develop a sixth sense; an instinct that warns them of rough seas ahead. I sensed this during early February [1963]. Although I was acting on Government decisions my instinct told me that I was moving out on a limb. . . . Hostile items started to appear in some of the newspapers. . . . The National Broadcasting Development Committee, under the chairmanship of a former junior minister and friend of mine, Sir Harmar Nicholls, was also at work. I was being constantly lobbied by a small group of Conservative M.P.s who were now hostile to the Government's proposals. Soon I was to learn that there was also lobbying of more influential ministers, not always ineffectually. . . .

In early February I heard a rumour that the second reading of the Bill was to be delayed until after Easter. I at once saw Iain Macleod, then Leader of the House, who was responsible for Parliamentary business. He told me that the Bill was unpopular "with Government back-benchers" (which was far from true) and heartily disliked by the big four companies (A.T.V., Associated Rediffusion, A.B.C. and Granada). I told Iain that the Bill was right and would be accepted by the House of Commons and public opinion. I insisted there should be no delay and I got my way.

So we had the second reading on 25th February 1963 and I announced the change in the basis of the levy. The House of Commons accepted the second reading without a division. Not a solitary voice was raised against the main principles of the Bill in the House. Not one M.P. voted against it. I was not, however, deceived by this delightful show of unanimity.

During the following week pressure behind the scenes mounted. The broad strategy was by now becoming clear. Some of the larger companies intended to use their influence to obtain the support of the press and especially the financial columns to ridicule the levy and its authors. They already had friends and allies in the House. Whether they had financial interests or not, I never at any time questioned the integrity of their motives.

And of course attempts were made to influence uncommitted Government supporters. At this time there was a steady stream of visitors to the Conservative Party Broadcasting Committee at the House of Commons. Many were representatives of the larger companies who came to indulge in extreme special pleading. Of course they did not take in everyone by a long chalk, for the Party includes some very shrewd men and women.

The influence of some of the leading figures in commercial television upon the upper reaches of the Conservative Party will soon emerge. These were the most difficult people to counter. I only learned of their influence when pressures were applied to me from above. . . .

[Their tactics were] becoming clear. They had already tried to secure a second commercial programme and that had not come off. Now they would try to force the Government either to abandon the levy or to emasculate it. They were confident they could do this, but I do not think they understood me. If, however, this frontal attack failed they would once again press for a second commercial programme, by say 1965. They calculated to exploit the anti-B.B.C. sentiments of the Conservative Party. If this succeeded they would then ask "What is the point of the levy for it does not apply until 1964 and by that time the big profits will have been drastically reduced by competition for advertising revenue." This would have put me in a dilemma and given an impression of Government cowardice.

But, again, if this failed they would threaten to withdraw from television altogether. And if that failed they would try various stratagems to postpone the progress of the Bill so that it simply did not become law. . . .

At about this time the *Daily Express* sought me out for a talk. . . . Knowing what was brewing behind the scenes I was feeling rather intransigent. The Irish in me sometimes gets the better of the inhibited Englishman in me. It did this time. I suppose I spoke too freely, certainly too freely or offensively for some Conservative backbenchers, though not all. I made it clear that in my judgement the Government had hitherto failed in its duty to the taxpayer and I spoke critically about pressure groups. . . .

Within hours [of the report's appearing] a Conservative M.P. — who I do not know — had circulated photostatic copies throughout the House of Commons to other members. Naturally my opponents were furious at the press report. Several people including one or two "friends" were putting it about that the Prime Minister should ask for my resignation. I went through the division lobby twice that evening. I was completely cold-shouldered. Not a soul spoke to me. . . .

That evening I saw the Chief Whip,

Martin Redmayne, and the Chairman of the 1922 Committee, John Morrison at their request. I readily agreed to attend the 1922 Committee on the following day. There I explained the circumstances in which the interview took place. I justified many of the statements in the article, but added that I had been under the impression that the interview was largely for background purposes. I ended by emphasising that my one wish was to hack my way through the television jungle and to emerge for the party's sake with an honest solution. The meeting accepted my explanation. . . .

I suppose the calculation was that I was off-balance. I was not. For approaches were made by certain interests to the Prime Minister and to R. A. Butler. I was urged to see the spokesmen of the Big Four [i.e. the television companies]. It so happened that I had already asked for this since I was genuinely anxious to know how they reached the conclusion that my proposals would put them out of business. . . .

These gentlemen had already seen my Director General and others at the Post Office on several occasions and failed to convince them that the companies' figures were correct. According to Sir Edwin Herbert [of Associated Rediffusion], the companies estimated that had the levy been in operation during 1962–3 the companies' profits before tax would have been reduced from nearly £24 million to just over £6 million, whereas, according to Post Office and Treasury calculations, the reduced figure would have been nearly £14 million. This was an extraordinary discrepancy amongst civilised business people. I was anxious to clear it up. The reasons for these differences soon became clear. First the companies had assumed that the levy would be payable on discounts remitted to advertisers. I said this was not so and that if it was felt that there was any ambiguity I would gladly remove it. Secondly, the companies had omitted income from the *TV Times*, income which clearly derived from their television concessions and nothing else. This was agreed. Finally, and most important, they had produced figures on the assumption that when the television advertisement duty was abolished they would not be able to recover its equivalent from advertisers and would be so much worse off. This was palpable nonsense. I pointed out that the companies had in fact succeeded in passing on the duty to advertisers who were free to place their business with newspapers or television and must regard the existing advertising rate plus the duty as good commercial value. . . .

But I made it clear that, whoever was right, this was a red herring since the amount of the levy and the prosperity of the companies would depend mainly on future advertising revenues. On that all the experts in the advertising world were agreed that this would increase. I was in no doubt then, and I am in no doubt now, that the Government's figures were accurate. . . .

Still, the Prime Minister was unhappy with all this and discussed it with the Chancellor of the Exchequer and other ministers and myself. He felt we ought to make yet another attempt to reconcile the two sets of figures. So the Chancellor of the Exchequer and I saw the companies' representative once more. We were totally unimpressed and said so in no uncertain terms.

On 24th April I attended another Party Committee and explained in great detail where I disagreed with the companies' memorandum. This meeting was attended by a broad cross-section of the Party and what I said was very well received. This, I should explain, was the prelude to taking the Bill in Standing Committee. . .

Our first sitting took place on 7th March and our final sitting on 9th May. We sat for about six hours a week and had twenty-two sittings. The official report ran to 1,040 printed pages. . . .

I was down at Chequers on Sunday, 28th April, to take part in discussions on future Conservative policy with Harold Macmillan and his colleagues. On the preceding Friday I received a private message through a friend that the higher echelons in the Government, but not the Chancellor, were weakening to pressures on television. . . .

At lunch a very curious thing occurred. I was seated at the main table beside the Chief Whip. I admired Martin Redmayne very much but I would not have his job for all the profits of the television tycoons. It really is a hell of a job. He at once got on to television. I tried to change the subject. Had the food and drink been good this might have been easy, but it wasn't. It was very inferior mutton. So he got back to television and he was clearly unhappy about it. He said I must reduce the amount of the levy by about £4 million. I said No. I also said that the Chancellor would say no. "But he has already agreed," came the reply.

Directly lunch was over I tackled Maudling [the Chancellor]. He was reticent and apologetic. It was clear he had agreed. I found this incredible because at every stage Maudling and I had acted in concert. Indeed at an earlier point John Boyd-Carpenter, the Chief Secretary to the Treasury whose judgement I had long admired, had insisted on increasing the scale of the levy. This was very sad. I was not sure whether I was more sorry for myself or for Reggie Maudling. . . .

Monday, 29th April, was hectic. I first had to join the Chancellor of the Exchequer in a meeting with the companies' accountant on the tedious question of the figures. The Chancellor was on my side.

When the accountant had gone, Maudling wanted to talk. We had a "Scotch on the rocks" and then another. I knew what he was up to. He was watching me. I was watching him. He said, "Now look, Reg." "No," I said. We both laughed. He said it was difficult and I said I knew that and got away quickly and walked into the sunshine and across the square to the House.

At five o'clock the Chancellor of the Exchequer, Leader of the House, the Chief Whip and I were due to meet the dissidents. But I had been asked to see my fellow ministers for further talks both before and after this meeting. At the first meeting Iain Macleod and the Chief Whip pleaded with me to give way. I said no, but let us listen to what they had to say. They presently trooped in — my talkative friend Sir Harmar Nicholls, David James, Wavell Wakefield and Frank Bishop, both eminently reasonable, and Ernest Partridge, looking at me as though he could kill me — I don't know why. Anyway they had nothing new to say. Several of them said they would have to vote against the Government on the financial clauses, at which the Chief Whip naturally squirmed. I judged that the Chancellor was getting near to saying he was prepared to reduce the levy. I wrote on a bit of paper, "You must *not* give way" and put it under his nose. He took my advice.

When the meeting broke up my colleagues once again started to work on me. They argued that to carry it through with the support of the Labour Party in defiance of a minority of our own Party would be politically damaging to the Government. I said it would be even more damaging to the Party in the public mind if the Government surrendered to pressure. In the end I said I would think it over. This was dreadful. . . .

We finished the committee stage on 9th May. This was a relief, however shortlived. Within a few days the lobbying had started all over again. I decided to attend the Party Committee during the following week to explain the minor concessions on which I had decided. Two significant things occurred at this meeting. The demand for a second commercial channel was revived, although only the A.T.V. Company had expressed a wish for one. And my friend, Selwyn Lloyd* turned up. This was the first occasion he had been present and he alleged that no serious attempt had been made to reconcile the figures of the companies with those of the Government. There was also a demand that the final stages of the Bill in the House should be postponed. This did not surprise me. . . .

The final stages of the Bill were due to be

*At this time a backbench M.P. [Editor's note.]

taken in the House on the following Wednesday. On the pretext of [another] debate the Television Bill was postponed until after the Whit recess. This pretext may have been genuine.

On the 20th May I was again asked to have a conference with the Chancellor of the Exchequer, the Leader of the House and the Chief Whip. The Chief Whip said, "Selwyn insists on your writing a second commercial channel into the Bill." I explained that if I conceded this demand it would at once be argued that the levy on turnover could not stand; that we should have to revert to a levy on profits and that could be partially avoided. I turned to the Chancellor for support. I reminded him that the Treasury had wanted £18 million from commercial television. He gave me the impression that he was tired of it all and didn't give a damn. I could understand why the Chancellor was tired of it. I wasn't. This meeting ended without any firm decision. . . .

Now, however, I realised I was battling against time. I had to finish the Bill in the House and give the Lords one month, with the Whitsuntide recess of two weeks supervening. Therefore any further delay would put the whole thing in peril. Yet it was delayed again from the third to the fourth week in June. On hearing of this I at once saw the Chief Whip. He assured me there was no intention of dropping the Bill through shortage of time, but spoke of meeting yet another Party Committee immediately after the recess.

I warned him of the dangers of abandoning the Bill. If the General Election did not take place until 1964 the Government could extend the present contracts on the existing financial terms for two years. This would rightly be used against us at the Election. If, on the other hand, the Election were to come in October, there could be no Bill until after the election. If a Labour Government were then in power it must not be assumed that their goodwill for commercial television would remain. . . .

At this time I received a letter from R. A.

Butler forwarding further papers, asking me what I proposed to do and adding in his own hand "I think there is a good deal in this. We really can't whack them any more." I also had more talks with the Chief Whip. I was insistent on taking the Bill during the following week. The response was that it was a "bloody awful Bill and nobody liked it." He said he was not prepared to risk further Government unpopularity by a hostile demonstration by our back-benchers in the House. He felt that as many as 40 or 50 might vote against the Government. I said this was nonsense —there might be half a dozen but no more. A minister in charge of a Bill can stand five or six of his own side going against him, but twenty or more means resignation.

I said that if the Government proposed to break the Bill or to hack it about then it ought to go back to Cabinet. The Chief Whip agreed and said he would arrange for it to be mentioned at Thursday's Cabinet. I said that if it was and Cabinet reversed their earlier decisions he would have my resignation. He then said he was only joking and that he would see the Bill was fitted into the following week's business.

That the Chief Whip understood my mood became obvious when the Leader of the House announced in the House on the following day that the Bill would be taken on the following Monday. On the Thursday I attended yet another meeting of the Party Committee and spoke against an early go-ahead for a second commercial programme. Some members were not very pleased. Once more a biased report, slanted against me, was given to the press. . . .

The final stages of the Bill were to be taken in the House on Monday, 24th June and if not concluded then late on Thursday, 27th June. There is tactical significance in "late on Thursday" because many provincial members, especially Labour members, leave for their trains at about 11 p.m. and the Labour benches then become very thin.

On the Monday matters went very smoothly. The levy was approved. Throughout there was a good sprinkling of my friends on the Government side, supporting me morally and in speeches. At about 11 p.m. the Chief Whip suggested we should call it a day and leave the debate on the second I.T.A. programme until Thursday.

Much can happen in three days, and it did. On the Tuesday I was again pressed to accept the lobby amendment to write not later than October 1965 for the start of the second programme as a firm commitment, hoping no doubt, to bind the next Government. I once more explained why not and wrote two letters on the following morning confirming it. At six o'clock on the Wednesday I was again pressed. At seven Selwyn [Lloyd] came in and we had a somewhat animated talk which was ended by the division bell. I then went off to a Party dinner at St. Stephen's Club and got home at about midnight.

At one o'clock in the morning I was awakened by the telephone ringing. It was my loyal Parliamentary private secretary, Gordon Matthews, who told me the Chief Whip wished to see me at once at the House. I said I was going back to bed and that he could tell the Chief Whip anything or nothing. He did what any wise P.P.S. would do—he went into hiding.

At 11 a.m. on the Thursday the Chief Whip phoned me at St. Martin's-le-Grand. He had come out of Cabinet specially. He put the same old question to me, adding the suggestion that if I refused I should probably lose the Bill altogether through lack of time. I refused. At this he suggested putting the question back to Cabinet that morning and asked if I would accept their decision if it went against me. I said no. "Then there's no point in going to Cabinet is there?" For once I agreed. There wasn't.

At seven o'clock that evening we started on the last lap in the Commons. John Rogers and Selwyn Lloyd spoke for an immediate start on the second channel. Martin Redmayne and Iain Macleod who were sitting on my right on the Treasury Bench were openly applauding these speeches. Now, significantly, the Opposition benches were almost empty although it was not yet ten o'clock. I heard reliably that they had all gone home. They might have felt that in their absence "the Lobby" could defeat or at least seriously embarrass the Government.

The Government benches now filled up, mostly with men who were against my line. I made what the *Financial Times* referred to as a closely argued speech which would have convinced any fair minded audience—as it may have done—that I was right. I said that we should see how things went and that if in 1965 it seemed we could have a successful second programme the Government would then issue a licence so that the programme could be on the air in 1966. But no commitment to be written into the Bill. This represented a slight concession, but only slight. The amendment was then withdrawn and there was no vote. Reading the next day's papers it was pretty clear that some of our people were crowing victory amongst themselves and to the press.

By midnight the House had finished the Bill. My Post Office people and I went downstairs. . . for a drink. The Chief Whip came down and congratulated me. He said "they" were jubilant, "they think they've got what they asked for. No harm in letting them think it." Martin Redmayne was quite an operator. . . .

James B. Christoph

3. A CAMPAIGN IS LAUNCHED

As Professor Beer pointed out in his article, the tightness of party discipline in the House of Commons causes British pressure groups normally to concentrate their energies on ministers and civil servants. Pressure may be exerted through members of Parliament, but the votes of members can seldom be solicited successfully. The case is different, however, when the issue is one such as capital punishment on which a "free vote" is normally allowed.

For the capital punishment issue the period from 1949 to 1955 was a fairly quiescent interval between major Parliamentary crises. The chief events of this period—the activities of the Royal Commission [on Capital Punishment] and [a series of] notable murder cases—took place outside Westminster and only indirectly and sporadically affected the mood of Parliament. The tides of public sentiment may have been moving in the direction of abolition, but they were moving rather sluggishly, and their impact upon those who make policy in this area was slight. From the viewpoint of the abolitionists, what had to be created most was a groundswell of public support, effective organization and suitable Parliamentary opportunities. By the end of 1955 the abolitionists believed that events were running in their favour and these conditions now existed and could be turned to their advantage.

That theirs was still an up-hill struggle was clear to the abolitionist leaders. Although they took encouragement from some of the public reaction to the Bentley, Evans-Christie and Ellis cases, they were aware that the majority of Britons still re-

Reprinted from *Capital Punishment and British Politics* by James B. Christoph by permission of the University of Chicago Press, pp. 109–116. © 1962 by the University of Chicago. Reprinted also by permission of the author and George Allen & Unwin, Ltd.

mained staunch supporters of the death penalty. Public opinion polls taken during this period, for instance, showed continued majority support for the retention of capital punishment, despite perceptible movement away from *overwhelming* acceptance of it.

TABLE 1

PERCENTAGE OF PERSONS SUPPORTING VARIOUS POSITIONS ON THE DEATH PENALTY

	Retain	Abolish	Don't Know
October 1953	73	15	12
July 1955	50	37	13
December 1955	61	25	14

Nor was Parliamentary opinion disposed to welcome much change during the life of the 1951 Parliament. Time and again Government spokesmen refused requests that they bring in new legislation affecting capital punishment or give facilities to abolitionist bills proffered by members of the Opposition. For example, the Royal Commission on Capital Punishment reported in 1953, but for over a year no debate took place on its recommendations, despite a fairly steady barrage of questions laid down by Labour abolitionist M.P.s. Finally, in December, 1954, the Leader of the House of Commons announced that the Government would find time for a debate on the Commission's findings as soon as Parliament convened in the new year. It was clear also that the Government did not plan to introduce any of the legislation proposed by the Commission but wanted simply a *pro forma* debate which would "take note of the Royal Commission Report." A free vote was to be permitted on the government's motion.

The Howard League [for Penal Reform] and certain abolitionist M.P.s might have preferred some less controversial figure than Sydney Silverman [a left-wing Labour M.P.] to introduce an amendment to the resolution to the effect that the death penalty should be suspended. But when Silverman did introduce such an amendment, all abolitionists supported him. . . .

The Commons debate, which took place on February 10, 1955, followed predictable lines. The Conservative Home Secretary, Major Gwilym Lloyd-George, moved that the House do no more than "take note of" the recommendations of the Gowers Commission. He rejected all of that group's chief proposals . . . but promised that the Government would re-examine the remainder of the recommendations in the light of the present debate. He then turned his attention to the Silverman abolition amendment (now bearing the names of three Conservatives as well as three Labour members). In opposing it, Lloyd-George used the three reasons that had been relied upon by Home Secretary Ede in 1948: that (1) capital punishment still serves as an effective deterrent to potential murderers, (2) prolonged imprisonment is not a satisfactory alternative to the death penalty, and (3) there is clearly no overwhelming public sentiment in favour of change. . . .

The remainder of the debate was disappointing, especially to those who had looked forward to an informed examination of the Royal Commission's proposals. Most of the speakers addressed themselves to the time-worn arguments for and against capital punishment, and the Royal Commission's efforts faded farther and farther from sight. The Silverman amendment was rejected in a division 245 – 214, and the Government motion subsequently agreed to.

Analysis of the vote reveals that, including tellers, 463 of the 625 House members took part in the division, an unusually high percentage for a free vote. Among those voting for the abolition amendment were 194 Labourites, 17 Conservatives, and 3 Liberals, while numbered among the successful opponents of the amendment were 239 Conservatives, 5 Labourites, and one Liberal. Nearly 160 M.P.s did not vote, chiefly because they were absent from the Chamber; and 90 of them were Labour. Had the absentees been present and voted along the party lines revealed in the actual vote, however, the amendment would still have been defeated. A comparison between this division and the free vote in 1948 on Silverman's original amendment to the Criminal Justice Bill is illuminating:

	1948	1955
Labour		
Abolitionists	215	194
Retentionists	74	5
Conservatives		
Abolitionists	14	17
Retentionists	134	239
Liberal		
Abolitionists	7	3
Retentionists	0	1

These figures reveal two things. First, they confirm the suspicion that despite its supposed non-partisan character, the capital punishment question generally divided Parliament fairly closely along party lines. Labour continued to supply the abolitionists with the bulk of their supporters and had fewer defectors to the "improper" lobby than did the Conservatives. The second item to be noted is the strengthening of abolitionist support among Labour Members. . . . Abolitionists learned from this vote that they could now rely upon an almost solid phalanx of supporters on the Labour side of the House. They saw that their chances of success depended upon two possibilities: either that Labour would be returned with a parliamentary majority at the forthcoming General Election, or, if not, that they could induce enough Conservative M.P.s to desert the traditional Tory position on hanging to make up a bipartisan abolitionist majority.

The first possibility was eliminated by the results of the General Election of May, 1955. The Eden Government was returned to power with a fairly comfortable Parliamentary majority of 59. Contrary to the impression that was conveyed at the time, the new Tory contingent was not younger than its predecessor in the 1951 Parliament. However, many of the new men had come up through Young Conservative organiza-

tions that had been influenced by the "new Toryism" reflected in the political attitudes of leaders such as R. A. Butler and Iain Macleod. Their views on capital punishment were not generally known, but hopes rose among abolitionists that a sufficient number of them might be broken away from the solid battalion of retentionist Tories. Thus the abolitionists faced the twin task of holding together their forces on the Labour and Liberal side of the House and at the same time wooing more than thirty Conservative M.P.s to the cause.

The advent of a new Parliament and the impact of the Ellis case [in which a woman was hanged for a crime of passion] convinced many abolitionists that the time was ripe for another large campaign directed at both public and Parliament. Except for occasional flurries set off by individual cases and the quiet activities of the Howard League, there had been no large organized effort to propagate the abolitionist case since the demise of the National Council for the Abolition of the Death Penalty in 1948. This time the initiative was taken neither by the Howard League nor by the abolitionists in Parliament but by persons connected with the world of letters.

Victor Gollancz, the controversial Left-wing publisher, is generally credited with having initiated the new movement, along with the noted writer Arthur Koestler and the prominent ecclesiastical radical, Canon L. John Collins of St. Paul's Cathedral. Gollancz brought to the abolitionist movement not only his usual fiery moral passion, but also long experience with organizing and conducting campaigns to aid the underdog. For example, though a Jew and a fervent anti-Nazi, at the end of the war Gollancz campaigned against the idea of revenge against the Germans and organized the Save Europe Now Committee to collect funds and supplies for the devastated German people. Again, at the time of the war between Israel and its Arab neighbours, he founded the Jewish Society for Human Service, the first aim of which was relief for displaced Arabs. An *Observer* profile once described "V.G." as "not just a man of vague goodwill but a passionate moralist, an ardent non-denominational Christian and a socialist of ethical rather than utilitarian enthusiasm," an aspirant saint with a flair for personal publicity, "sometimes too noisy, too wilful, too insensitive for the absolute comfort of his associates." For better or worse, the large-scale public campaign of 1955 and 1956 came to be associated with the personality of Gollancz more than any other person.

Several weeks after the hanging of Ruth Ellis, Gollancz approached the secretary of the Howard League with the suggestion that together they organize a comparatively short and intensive campaign for abolition, making use of massive public meetings and all the publicity they could get. Although they were in agreement with the purpose of the Gollancz group, officials of the League felt that it was wiser not to affiliate formally with Gollancz and his friends. . . . The League was sensitive about its relationship with Home Office officials and was somewhat fearful that too much publicity for its abolitionist activities might jeopardize the progress it was making in other areas of penal reform. The League did nothing to stifle the campaign, however, and several of its officers and many of its members later joined as private persons. In addition, it made available to the new group many of its resources, including its library, files, and contacts with penal officials in Britain and abroad. Thus by the middle of 1955 there were in existence two different but related groups working for abolition: one an established, multiple-purpose, rather demure reform organization, the other a new, single-purpose, publicity-conscious band of impassioned crusaders. The leaders of the two groups could hardly be more different personalities; Viscount Templewood, Sir George Benson, M.P., and Hugh Klare on one side; Gollancz, Koestler and Canon Collins on the other. Yet their aims in this case were identical, and their activities were to be complementary rather than competitive.

In August of 1955 there came into being the National Campaign for the Abolition of Capital Punishment, "with the object of bringing capital punishment to an end at the earliest possible moment." Gollancz was chairman, and the Executive Committee was composed of Koestler, Canon Collins, Gerald Gardiner (a prominent liberal barrister who was Treasurer of the Howard League), and three persons associated with each of the major political parties: Christopher Hollis, Reginald Paget and Frank Owen. In addition, the Campaign indicated that it was forming a Committee of Honour, which was to be widely representative of national life. Among the first to be included in this group were Benjamin Britten, Professor C. Day Lewis, the Earl of Listowel, Henry Moore, Lord Pakenham, J. B. Priestley, Canon Raven, Moira Shearer and Dr Donald Soper. It was apparent that part of the campaign would be the search for the endorsement of prominent and respected Britons.

In the first six months of its life, the Campaign had few Parliamentary contacts and no Parliamentary opportunities. Its chief target was the larger public, which it hoped to influence in such a manner that when the next abolitionist motion came before the House of Commons that body would be faced, for the first time in modern history, with the prospect of a nation thoroughly alarmed over the perpetuation of hanging. To achieve this the campaign planned to use not only the traditional educational campaign with its meetings, speakers, books and pamphlets, but also symbolic gestures calculated to make a special stir. It was suggested, for example, that abolitionists abstain from attending any place of entertainment or party on the eve of an execution, close their shops or places of business for an hour the day before an execution, and attend vigil-meetings at places of worship and assembly. At the same time, sympathizers were discouraged from taking part in disruptive or sensational action, such as demonstrations outside prisons, which might identify the Campaign with hyper-emotional elements in the community. As things turned out, the Campaign leaders found little use for these gestures, partly because they were coolly received and could not be easily organized but chiefly because from its inception until the passage of the Homicide Act in 1957 there were no hangings in Britain. . . .

Most of the Campaign's activities took place during the 1955–56 session of Parliament. . . . The first four months of the Campaign were important, nonetheless, because this was the period in which the most active members were recruited, ammunition for the anticipated struggle in the forth-coming Parliamentary session gathered, and contacts with the principal organs of opinion strengthened. For example, Arthur Koestler and Frank Owen covered Fleet Street to make sure that the press gave publicity to the actions of the Campaign and, if possible, showed sympathy for its aims. Members of the Committee of Honour were stimulated to write to their local papers, particularly in the provinces, where press sentiment for abolition was rare. Circulars were sent to members of the Howard League, Christian Action, the Clerks of the Friends Meetings, to Labour and Co-operative Parties, and to selected members of the Bar. Gerald Gardiner revised the old Notes for Speakers of the defunct National Council for the Abolition of the Death Penalty for the use of speakers before local groups. Several of the leaders of the Campaign wrote books on capital punishment, each from a particular standpoint and aimed at different kinds of audiences. Unlike its predecessor in the late '40's, the Campaign had money to spend and, because its promoters were fond of short, intense campaigns, did not hesitate to spend it in a way calculated to draw maximum public attention.

Encouraging signs of support spurred on the group. Its first public meeting in No-

vember, 1955, filled Central Hall, Westminster, and overflowed into Church House. A collection of nearly £1,100 was raised in twenty minutes. An organizing secretary was hired. In addition to its London headquarters in the publishing offices of Victor Gollancz Ltd., the Campaign opened a Scottish office and set up local committees in Birmingham, Sheffield, Leeds, Bristol, Cardiff, Swansea and elsewhere. By the end of 1955 it had collected the names of sixteen thousand active supporters and had asked all of them to contact their M.P.s early in the new year. A substantial body of sympathisers was now in hopeful readiness for action when Parliament chose to take up the death penalty issue once again.

The National Campaign was not the only group to be vocally demonstrative on the question. Its members strove to get other groups to declare their views, as well as to create a sense of urgency that would call forth debate and resolution among individual Britons. A Howard League petition signed by 112 public opinion leaders begged the Home Secretary to reconsider implementing the "admirable recommendations" of the Royal Commission on Capital Punishment. Major Lloyd George remained unmoved by both pleas, however, and in November announced the government's total rejection of all the Royal Commission's proposals that would involve legislation. In September the Liberal Party Council passed a resolution urging the Parliamentary Liberal Party to do everything in its power to secure the early removal of the death penalty.

By late 1955 several signs appeared that gave a fillip to the organizers of the campaign. The results of an Oxford Union debate before a standing-room-only crowd of students showed 378 in favour of the motion "that the Death Penalty should be abolished forthwith" and 161 opposed. Two years earlier when the same subject was debated, the majority for abolition had been only 40. The polls, too, began to show a rather significant movement of public opinion away from the absolute retention of the death penalty and toward either abolition or some experimental middle ground. . . . At no time were the abolitionists able to claim a majority for their position, but instead they had to base their case upon evidence that opinion was

moving in that direction in a rather remarkable way. . . .

[*Capital punishment was finally abolished in Britain in 1965.*]

Ian Waller

4. M.P.s AND P.R.O.s

Pressure groups lobby members of Parliament for a variety of reasons. They hope to create a climate of opinion in favor of their cause. They wish to exploit opportunities for bringing indirect pressure to bear on the administration. They often wish to take advantage of their connections with M.P.s for business purposes. In this selection, Ian Waller describes a number of recent exercises in political public relations. Mr. Waller is political correspondent for the London *Sunday Telegraph* and writes as an avowed critic of some types of pressure group activity. His article first appeared in 1962.

During the past year there has been mounting awareness and uneasiness about the activities of commercial and political pressure groups at Westminster. And there can be little doubt that it is well justified. In the political field the government of the Central African Federation has openly adopted new techniques of persuasion and the East German government have, in a different and far more sinister way, been equally active. The ever widening range of governmental influence over the economy naturally increases the desire of business interests to ensure that their position is either protected or given scope for expansion; and a new class of skilled professional operators has come on the scene to assist them, mostly in the guise of "public relations consultants."

Pressure groups are not, of course, a new phenomenon. Parliament is the natural and proper focal point for any interest with an axe to grind and they will naturally seek to

ensure either the election of Members sympathetic to their point of view or hope by the force of their arguments to convert others. . . .

In criticising what is now developing one does not condemn the desire of interested groups to make their views known or seek to suggest that the Commons could be — or should be — a collection of men and women utterly detached from every outside interest. One cannot talk in black-and-white terms. No doubt abuses have existed at all times. . . .

It is the methods now being used rather than the desire to influence that are open to criticism and about which more should certainly be known and, where necessary, safeguarded against. Equally important, awareness is the best safeguard against the insidious growth of undesirable practices to the point where they become the accepted norm.

It is, for example, no longer unusual for

From Ian Waller, "Pressure Politics" in *Encounter*, no. 107 (August 1962), pp. 3–15. Reprinted by permission of the author and *Encounter*.

M.P.s to be paid retainers to represent or advise special interests. The acceptance of lavish hospitality or agreeable and costly foreign tours can easily be justified by the individual on grounds of gaining practical experience, "of seeing for himself," but can also all too often end either in him gaining a completely one-sided picture or in feeling a sense of obligation to the host authority. Again, I wonder whether Sir Winston Churchill or Lord Attlee, with their Victorian standards of rectitude in public life, would have tolerated a situation in which Members in the semi-privileged (and, at least to the outside world, important) role of Parliamentary Private Secretaries were openly representing public relations firms and acting as "go between" for the firm's clients and M.P.s.

One cannot of course separate these developments from the changing pattern of social and professional standards generally. The morality of the "expense-account society" cannot be expected to leave Westminster untouched. . . .

But however important these elements may be, the first and most vital fact is that the prizes for a successful pressure-group operation can be very great indeed. The classic example is, of course, the one so ably analysed and documented by Professor H. H. Wilson in his book *Pressure Group: the Campaign for Commercial Television* (1960). The story he unfolds, thanks partly to the shameless pride of the main campaigners, is quite breathtaking—the capture of the Conservative Party, the capitulation of a basically hostile Cabinet, and the defeat of the Establishment by a handful of determined men, well placed on the Conservative benches, in the Cabinet, and the Conservative Central Office. Parallel to it went a skilfully planned campaign in the country, the address-feeding of so-called "news items" and bogus letters "to the Editor": (Professor Wilson traced 22 similarly worded ones in provincial papers over different signatures, but all from the same address), and what I regard as the cynical cultivation of every conceivable interest from Roman Catholicism to the Hallé Orchestra. By playing on a general desire for an alternative programme, a synthetic but irresistible public opinion was created which gave a handful, in the words of Mr. Roy Thomson, "a licence to print your own banknotes.". . .

Another interesting campaign was recently run by *"Aims of Industry"* against the North of Scotland Hydro-Electric Board, a body whose work in bringing power to the Highlands has won the praise of Scottish M.P.s and local authorities of all parties.

Initiating a debate on this campaign on December 21, 1960, Mr. George Thomson, Labour M.P. for Dundee East, alleged that its origins lay in the fears of some Scottish landowners that their land might be taken over for further schemes. There is, of course, no reason why they should not protest about any particular scheme. But the campaign was not limited to this but was directed against the whole concept of hydro-generation, the efficiency of the Board, etc., and is widely credited in Scotland with having led the Scottish Secretary to order an inquiry into the Board and to delay further developments. Whether or not this is justified is irrelevant. The interesting thing is how the campaign is alleged to have been run. Mr. Thomson described it in these words:

How is *"Aims of Industry"* conducting its campaign? First, it had to find out where the Highlands were, so it sent an emissary—I am told a Mr. T. A. Cutbill, who describes himself as editorial director of *"Aims of Industry,"* from Fetter Lane, London. Mr. Cutbill visited Inverness. According to my information, his purpose was to discover and whip up pockets of dissatisfaction with the Hydro Board. . . .

Then the *"Aims of Industry"* organisation went into that operation at which it is particularly expert. These hidden persuaders started their campaign to brainwash the citizens of Scotland. Since midsummer, they have been supplying the Press with ready-made articles and so-called editorial comments, which have been used in whole or in part by local papers in the area of the Hydro Board. There can be no doubt that very few of the letters which have appeared in the Press supporting the attack on the Board have come from within the Board's area. There is reason to believe that some of the letters which have come from within the Board's area were not written by the individuals who signed them but were passed on to them from outside the area of the Board by friends who asked for signatures.

There was a need on the part of "Aims of Industry" for some sort of Scottish façade, what we know in political jargon as a front organisation, so "Aims of Industry" set up what is called the Scottish Power Investigation Committee. . . .

Whether Mr. Thomson's allegations are justified or not, I cannot say. But in preparing a TV programme on the issue last year, I found that they were certainly widely believed in Scotland among those interested in the Hydro Board's work. Unfortunately "Aims of Industry" refused to take part in the programme to enable the charges to be answered—an unusual display of modesty on the part of a P.R. organisation.

The second new development is the emergence of professional advisers or "fixers," so-called public relations consultants anxious to assist others—and themselves—to squeeze every conceivable drop of commercial or political advantage out of Whitehall and Parliament. Gone is the crude and petty squalor revealed by the Lynskey Tribunal in 1948 with its miserable tale of sausages, suit lengths, and bottles of whisky; of a spiv and a weak gullible junior minister. Today's operators are bland; they belong to the right clubs and entertain in the best restaurants; they bandy first names; they trade on knowing the right people. How far they succeed is difficult to assess; certainly they enrich themselves, thanks largely to the remarkable naïveté of so many business men, and some of them, I know, are a pest to ministers and senior civil servants. . . .

The three aspects of pressure-group operations that I want to examine in some detail are: (1) representation of outside interests by Members of Parliament both directly and also indirectly through public relations firms; (2) the general activities of public relations firms; (3) finally, and most important, the efforts of overseas governments to influence Parliament.

Representation of outside interests by Members is undoubtedly growing. Sometimes it is open; for example, accepting directorships—and this obviously is most common in the Conservative party and is certainly not new. Some professional associations also have representatives. I am thinking in particular of the Police Federation for which Mr. James Callaghan has acted as spokesman; and the Educational Institute for Scotland (the Scottish N.U.T.) who have had the services of two Scottish M.P.s, a Socialist, Mr. George Thomson, and a Conservative, Commander C. E. Donaldson. There are no doubt other examples.

Let me hasten to say I see nothing to criticise in the activities of these three Members. They are absolutely open about their connections and Mr. Callaghan's is included in Who's Who. The House knows whom they are speaking for, and the organisations are clearly of a different nature from commercial pressure groups. . . .

Nor, for the purposes of this article, am I going to discuss at length the question of open representation of commercial interest except to say that the rate at which it is increasing is interesting. The Roth analysis of The Business Interests of Members of Parliament reveals the following facts about the composition of the House of Commons in 1961.

Over 330 M.P.s hold a business connection of the order of a company directorship or better; this includes no less than 280 out of 365 Conservative M.P.s (or 7 out of 9) and 50 of 258 Labour Members (one in five).

According to Mr. Roth at least a score of M.P.s became directors in the two years after the 1959 general election; the 330 M.P.s hold a total of 490 directorships, an increase of 70 since 1959. And there are 280 positions such as chairman, partner, managing director, etc., an increase of 80. . . .

But in addition to this large element of open representation there is a widening range of indirect or concealed representation, that is as advisers. How wide it is impossible to say. Very often (and this is the most serious aspect) it is undisclosed, and one keeps on coming across the most unexpected people either acting for a particular firm or being retained by a public relations firm to look after the interests of their clients. . . .

An instructive example . . . was published a year ago in the *Sunday Telegraph* (June 18, 1961). Mr. Francis Noel Baker told me that after he had made some comments in the Commons on the proposal to run "Minicabs" in London, he was approached by another M.P. and invited to a dinner in one of the Commons private dining rooms. The purpose of the dinner was to meet Mr. Michael Gotla, Managing Director of Welbeck Motors, the firm responsible for "Minicabs."

The M.P. was Mr. Ronald Bell, Conservative member for South Bucks., and the dinner was, it transpired, backed by a public relations firm, Michael Clarke-Hall and Associates, who were running Welbeck Motors' P.R. campaign. Mr. Bell, who is listed in *Who's Who* as a barrister, is also what he described to me as an "advisory director" of Michael Clarke-Hall's. He explained the dinner party in the following words:

Welbeck Motors are seeking to introduce a service which is controversial and a live political issue. The directors wanted to meet M.P.s who were interested in the subject. I was asked if I could help them to meet politicians of both parties to discuss the problems involved. I asked a few Members who I knew were interested if they would like to meet Mr. Gotla.

There were several Labour and Conservative M.P.s and peers at the dinner and we had an amicable discussion. Many controversial questions were put to Mr. Gotla and his fellow directors. I believe that it helped both sides to see the problems involved.

An even more noteworthy example because of the blandishments offered, the fact that a foreign firm was involved and that it was interested in British Government contracts, was the visit to Lockheeds, the American aircraft manufacturers, eighteen months ago. Assisting in the arrangements

for this were a firm of business consultants, Michael Parker, Ltd., and Dr. Reginald Bennett, the Conservative M.P. for Fareham. I am not sure what Dr. Bennett's connection with this firm was but it was close enough for him to seek me out at the Commons to explain the whole business within a few hours of my first contacting Michael Parker's. The trip itself was certainly conducted on a lavish scale—not only were the M.P.s invited, but their wives as well—and must have cost the firm thousands of pounds, an investment which they presumably thought would reap rich dividends.

Two M.P.s who turned down invitations, both for the same very proper reasons, were Sir Arthur Vere Harvey and Colonel George Wigg, the former invited presumably because of his intimate knowledge of the aircraft industry, the latter for his interest in defence. Their attitude, which seems to me to be the only possible one, was summed up by Sir Arthur in a debate on the aircraft industry on March 22, 1962, when, referring to the trip, he said:

I would not dream of accepting. I was asked, but I think that one puts oneself under an obligation if one accepts such invitations. I do not say this because some hon. Members went. I mention it merely to show the extent to which the Americans will go to influence foreign Parliaments. It is going on all over the world. . . .

The activities of P.R. firms at Westminster take a variety of forms. Generally they aim, as in the instances I have cited, at putting their client's views before interested M.P.s, or building up a pressure group, or creating (in the jargon of the trade) "a favourable image" for their client; to secure, one way or another, favourable legislative or administrative treatment; or to combat political hostility.

But Parliament can have a variety of other uses too. A dinner party in one of the dining-rooms, even if there is no particular motive behind it, provides an agreeable background for a P.R. man to impress his clients that he moves in influential circles—and there's never any difficulty in finding a few Members willing to fill in time before a division by eating a free meal. Parliament can also provide a useful publicity forum for the promotion of a commodity, as a famous frozen food firm tried in 1960; it is also very useful on occasions to be able to make use of the House of Commons address for business purposes. . . .

A fundamental precept of Public Relations is that some bait must be provided to arouse interest, to create a favourable impression, to impose a sense of obligation, however tenuous. The whole loathsome round of P.R. parties, lunches, dinners, trips, gifts, and gimmicks is based on this fundamentally immoral assessment of human nature, and every journalist sees only too much of the endless outpouring of invitations all outbidding each other in the lavishness of their entertainment and their would-be "smartness.". . .

Most P.R. activities are aimed primarily at journalists, the immediate aim being to get a mention in the news columns. Pressure on M.P.s is a more sophisticated business. Not the least of P.R. successes has been to convince businessmen that "dealing with" and "understanding" journalists or politicians is a specialised task. On the political front their great strength is their supposed knowledge of the way around Whitehall, of how to get in touch with "the right person," of being able to ensure a view-point is understood. Hence the psychological importance of being able to take a client to dinner in the House and of "name-dropping," the efforts to get Ministers and Civil Servants to accept invitations to intimate little parties or lunches. Many industrialists are astonishingly innocent, particularly about politics, and are sitting ducks for this sort of confidence trick. It is, in this context, interesting how many P.R. men have come from government P.R. service or have worked in the Conservative Central Office and so can be presumed to know the political ropes. . . .

The P.R. Campaign for the Central African Federation is particularly noteworthy as the most skilful and probably the first professionally-planned pressure-group exercise on behalf of an overseas government. The P.R. firm is of course *Voice & Vision*, a subsidiary of Colman, Prentis & Varley who ran the Conservative party general election campaign. Their task has not been purely confined to organising the now well-known trips of M.P.s to Rhodesia, but also includes purely professional advice on improving P.R. and advertising methods both in Salisbury and in the High Commission offices in London.

It is widely believed that *Voice & Vision* were chosen by Sir Roy Welensky on the advice of Mr. Macmillan and Mr. Iain Macleod — something the latter, at least, must have rued, as the skill of *V. & V.'s* campaign played no small part in building up hostility to him last year and culminated in a damaging backbench revolt. He was certainly showing no enthusiasm last June. When asked about the attempts to influence policies by commercial or P.R. people on the B.B.C. programme *Gallery* (June 15, 1961) Mr. Macleod replied:

Yes, I think that inevitable with Africa playing such a dominant part in the world scene. One does get a little worried about the influence of some firms who have particular interests in Africa, public relations firms.

Voice & Vision's main activity has been to take groups of M.P.s out to the Federation for a fortnight's tour. Forty in all have gone so far; 19 Conservative, 20 Labour, and one Liberal. There have also been some journalists, two Church of Scotland ministers, and representatives of the Federation of British Industry and the National Farmers' Union. The man actually organising this aspect and responsible for choosing the Members is Mr. McWhinnie, formerly Lobby Correspondent of the *Daily Herald*, who naturally has an intimate knowledge of Westminster.

One striking feature of the list of M.P.s selected is that it does not include a single Labour party specialist in colonial affairs nor conspicuous critics of the Federation. The great majority of Labour M.P.s are trade union members who had not previously shown any great interest in colonial affairs. Only two—Mr. Richard Marsh and Dr. Dickson Mabon—turned out to be critical, yet the majority opinion in the Party is overwhelmingly hostile to Sir Roy Welensky. The Labour Members in fact represented a small minority. But minority opinion in the Conservative party—the small left-wing group who share Labour's criticisms of the Federation—was quite unrepresented. Surely a very strange balance.

The Conservative list certainly contains more members with a specialised knowledge, but all I think sympathetic to Sir Roy. This lack of members with an expert knowledge is very important, and must obviously reduce the value of the offer to let members meet whomever they wish. Unless a Member is an expert, is he likely to know whom to ask for or will he fall in with the organised programme? Mr. Marsh and Dr. Mabon took the precaution of first being briefed by experts as to who and what to see. They certainly met everyone they asked to see although Mr. Marsh says this inevitably involved overcoming natural inhibitions about asking one's host to go to trouble and possible expense to satisfy an individual wish.

Again, how representative were the organised tours? I cannot possibly judge. The African nationalists were very critical and at one time refused to co-operate with *Voice & Vision*. As Mr. Marsh put it to me, "You can meet a Liberal-minded European and a violently extremist nationalist. It can be said you have met 'both sides.' But have you really?"

It is difficult to say what effect this campaign has had. It looks as though it has failed to save the Federation or sway, this year at least, Government policy over Northern Rhodesia. But, as I have already said, I don't think there is much doubt that it played a big part in whipping up opposition to Mr. Macleod in the Conservative party last year. . . .

Finally, the most controversial pressure group of the lot—the East Germans. In addition to the desire, in common with other Eastern bloc countries, to win ideological support from Western Parliamentarians, they have the particular aims of securing diplomatic recognition and creating, both at home and abroad, the impression that they have sympathetic support in the West.

I am not concerned with the question whether East Germany should be recognised, or of the nature of Herr Ulbricht's régime. Neither are directly relevant to the specific question of the existence of the pressure group and the behaviour of some M.P.s—except in so far as one would have thought that the highly charged political atmosphere surrounding the régime behoved politicians to behave with some restraint and sense of responsibility, particularly when they are in the country, and to have some regard for national policy even if they do not agree with it. . . .

Unfortunately, as the controversy surrounding the last two years of the Leipzig Trade Fair shows all too clearly, some M.P.s have failed to show any realisation of the extent to which their presence is welcomed for political reasons by the East German Communists and skilfully exploited to give the impression that they belong to an official parliamentary delegation. Indeed, some of the Members have themselves done a good deal to encourage this particularly last year. This spring the unprecedented warning of the dangers of visits being exploited given by Mr. Heath in the House had, I think, some effect.

But last year, for example, two of the main figures, Mr. Burnaby Drayson and Brigadier Terence Clarke (both Conservative M.P.s) sent out invitations for a party at Leipzig decorated with the Union Jack and the House of Commons crest. Mr. John Woollam was quoted on the East German radio as referring to "the British delegation"—although he subsequently told me that this was used out of its context. This year about half a dozen M.P.s were there at one time, some under the auspices of Mr. Rudi Sternberg, an astute British naturalised businessman who controls a big share of East German-British trade. They were photographed in a group talking to Herr Walter Ulbricht; they toured the fair together (earning the nickname "Sternberg's circus" from critical British exhibitors). . . .

There is no doubt that it has been a lucrative business. A relative (and unexpected) newcomer to the world of big business is Mr. Arthur Lewis, the Labour M.P. for East Ham North, who first made news by lying down outside the Savoy Hotel to stop blacklegs during the Savoy strike some years ago; at Leipzig this year he was a prominent figure in its leading hotel, the Astoria.

Business interests in East Europe among politicians crosses party boundaries. There is Ian Mikardo on the Left of the Labour Party; staunch Conservatives like Brigadier Clarke, Mr. Drayson, specialising in East Germany as directors of Mr. Rudi Sternberg's group of companies (Mr. Sternberg controls a major share in the trade through his £3,500,000 contract for export of potash from East Germany); Conservative Peer, Lord Boothby, and Socialist M.P., Sir Leslie Plummer, joined forces years ago for a tour of East Europe to study trade prospects. They have both recently joined the board of Consolidated Foundry Plant, Ltd., a big export consortium doing extensive engineering business in East Europe. The ramifications seem endless. The East German Chamber of Foreign Trade employs a Public Relations firm, Notley Advertising, Ltd., to promote its interests here and, until last summer, Mr. Drayson was its adviser on East Germany, and Brigadier Clarke was certainly then associated with them; Brigadier Clarke and Mr. Drayson are both members of the rather obscure Conservative backbenchers' 1962 Committee formed last year, whose principal founder members were backbenchers who had been to Leipzig; Mr. Drayson is secretary of the all-party East-West Trade Committee of which Lord Boothby is chairman and Sir Leslie Plummer is vice-chairman.

After this year's Leipzig Fair, I wrote (*Sunday Telegraph*, March 11):

I have no doubt that the reason Mr. Sternberg and Mr. Drayson are so anxious to bring M.P.s out (to Leipzig) is to build up a pressure group at Westminster sympathetic to East Germany.

Neither has challenged this statement. . . .

VII. *Members of Parliament*

Nigel Nicolson

1. AN M.P. AND HIS CONSTITUENTS

A member of Parliament normally seeks to cultivate good relations in a number of different directions. His hopes for promotion depend in large part on his relationship with the party leaders and whips. His life will be made easier if he is on good terms with the majority of his parliamentary colleagues. He will try to cultivate the ordinary voters in his constituency. But most M.P.s would probably agree that they are especially conscious of their relations with their constituency party or association. At the very least, cordiality between a member and his supporters is desirable for its own sake. At most, the M.P. may depend for his political survival on his local association, if in a crisis he rebels against the national leadership. Constituency associations seldom repudiate sitting members of Parliament, but the Suez crisis of 1956, which strained to the utmost the unity of both major parties, led to several such cases. The most celebrated was that of Nigel Nicolson at Bournemouth East and Christchurch.

My abstention from the vote of confidence on the Government's Suez policy led to the biggest political upheaval which Bournemouth has ever known. I will attempt to give a full and honest account of what happened: full, because if it is to be of any value as an illustration of the mechanism of constituency politics and the power of a local Conservative Association, it must not skimp essential facts; honest, because it would be doing a great injustice to my constituents to present a one-sided case, or to hold them up to ridicule for my own advantage.

I give this account as an example of what can occur when a Member and his constituency supporters disagree on a policy matter of the utmost gravity. I do not say that the Bournemouth incident is more important than several other controversies which took place at the same time and for much the same reasons. . . . I write about my own experience because I know most about it, and because it would be presumptuous for me to comment in detail upon the experiences of other Members about which I obviously cannot know all the facts.

The constituency of Bournemouth East and Christchurch, which I have repre-

From Nigel Nicolson, *People and Parliament* (London, 1958), pp. 135–153. Reprinted by permission of the author and Weidenfeld & Nicolson, Ltd.

sented in Parliament since February 1952, was created in 1948 by boundary changes which divided Bournemouth into two unequal halves. The larger half, Bournemouth West, was allotted the centre of the town, together with the main hotels, shopping centres, and the wealthier suburbs; Bournemouth East included the big residential districts of Boscombe and Southbourne, to which was added, for parliamentary purposes, the neighbouring borough of Christchurch. It is an almost wholly urban constituency, "one of the most agreeable," as my predecessor, Brendan Bracken, wrote to me when he accepted a peerage in 1952, "in the entire country." . . .

If you walk down Christchurch High Street, or along the quiet curving roads of Southbourne, you will realize at once that this constituency could never be anything else but Conservative. . . . The Conservative majorities are enormous. My own increased from 14,000 in the by-election of 1952 to 18,500 in 1955. This solid majority is made up of three types of people: the shop-keepers, proprietors of boarding-houses and small hotels, and the professional men; secondly, many of the workers in the two local aircraft factories and Ministry of Supply establishments; and thirdly, the retired, the widowed, and the single. This last category is of particular importance in local Conservative life. The women provide a large part of the Association's membership of some five thousand, and do most of the work. The men, who in their retirement have come to live in Bournemouth, bring with them a combined experience ranging over the whole field of business, the Church, medicine, law, the civil and colonial services, and the armed forces. Most of them were only able to join a political party late in their lives, and they apply to it the same high standards of integrity and loyalty which became second nature to them throughout their professional careers.

I will mention [two] of them, the President of my Association, Lord Quickswood; [and] the chairman, Major Grant. . . .

Lord Quickswood, formerly Lord Hugh Cecil, lived in retirement in a large house at Boscombe. He was over 80. I had known him as a boy at Eton when he was Provost. "Known" is an overstatement. I revered him. . . . I [had] looked forward, as Member, to a long association with this great man. But he was ill. . . .

When I saw him, he was usually in bed, needlessly apologetic for his growing infirmities, and amused, I think, to see how the political accidents which had shaped his own career, were repeating themselves in another generation. . . . When I found myself in serious trouble in December 1956, he came at once to my aid with a stinging rebuke for the Association of which he was President: "I have no hesitation whatever in saying that Mr. Nicolson has done quite rightly in thus voting. He was sent to Parliament to be a representative of the whole Commons of the Realm speaking in the name of the whole Commons, and not as a delegate of the particular constituency who had the right to appoint him." It was the last letter he ever wrote. He died a week later. As I stood by his open grave at Hatfield, I knew that I had lost a valuable friend and ally.

The chairman of the Association, Major Grant, had a very different background. He had retired comparatively young after service in the Indian Army, and an ordeal as a prisoner-of-war in Japanese hands. His main interests in retirement were the Hampshire Red Cross and the Conservative Party. When I first knew him, he was chairman of the Highcliffe branch at the eastern extremity of the constituency, and at both my elections it had given me great pleasure to spend the last half hour of polling day in his company, so well had he organized his ward and so infectious was his enthusiasm. Until the moment of my disgrace we were on excellent terms. But after it, he felt that he could not allow a personal friendship to affect his judgement, and our mutual sympathy inevitably declined. He did what he honestly conceived to be his duty. . . .

Before coming to the events of 1956, I must in fairness mention two other occasions when I offended my constituents. These incidents have lately been revived as proof that, apart from capital punishment and Suez, I was already regarded as a renegade.

Six weeks after my election, in March 1952, I made a speech at a luncheon of the Bournemouth Habitation of the Primrose League. According to the report in the local paper, this is what I said:

Too many Conservatives are indulging in a form of hatred against certain members of the other side—notably Mr Bevan. It is not in the tradition of the Conservative Party or the country. In our opinion Mr Bevan is misguided, but he is not wicked. If he became Prime Minister, there is no need for you to fear that he would eliminate whole categories or classes of the population, or plunge us into an alliance with Russia. You can only deal with people like that, not by hating them, but by understanding their point of view. If Conservatives go about saying, "Bevan is a monster," they are only strengthening his hand.

There was a gasp of horror in the audience, for these were the days before Mr Bevan was considered respectable. I am not in the least proud of my speech. I think it was ill-expressed, tactless and jejune. Nevertheless, I do not think that what I said was untrue, or a sufficient basis on which to erect a theory that I am not really a Conservative at all, but a Socialist in disguise.

The second incident occurred about two years later. I was addressing a week-end conference of the Wessex Area Conservatives, and several of my own leading supporters were present. It was a private meeting confined to Conservatives, and my speech was not reported. The theme of it was that both main political parties desired precisely the same ends: they both wanted peace, and they both wanted prosperity: the only quarrel between them, and it was a serious quarrel, was about the means of attaining these ends. These observations sound trite, and they were. But they caused such consternation that I felt obliged to request a special meeting with the chief officers of my Association to justify my conduct. Fortunately, two representatives of Central Office had heard the speech, and in response to an appeal for their judgement, replied that they had found no fault with it; indeed, they had thought it quite stimulating.

I believe that these are the only two incidents of which complaint has been made. Their unorthodoxy is magnified in recollection. In between, stretched months and years of peace in the constituency. In 1953 I married, and bought a house near Christchurch. I felt welcome wherever I went. I enjoyed being the Member. . . .

Then came capital punishment. I have described [elsewhere] that my [abolitionist] attitude on this subject was well known in the constituency immediately before the election, when some protest could have been made, and none was; and how I modified it in response to Major Grant's personal appeal. I think it right that these facts should be remembered now. When it is said that I opposed my constituents' wishes, it might be added that when Parliament was about to make an irrevocable decision, I did what they wished me to do. Whether I was right or wrong to compromise, compromise I did, and I was the first of the Conservative abolitionists to promise complete support for Major Lloyd-George's Homicide Bill. . . .

This was the background of Suez: four years of peace, broken by two minor incidents; an election which was a triumph for the Association; capital punishment, on which I expressed disagreement with a majority of my electors and then compromised at the decisive stage in deference to their opinions; an autumn series of constituency speeches against the use of force to solve the Canal problem; and then catastrophe.

A meeting between myself and the Executive Council to discuss the Middle East had already been planned for late November, but the ultimatum forestalled it. Within twenty-four hours of hearing the Prime Minister's statement in the House, I telephoned to Major Grant, and told him that I could not support the Government for the reasons, among others, which I had explained in my autumn speeches. Though he much regretted my decision, he agreed with me that it would be right to say nothing until the fighting in the Canal Zone was over. I had to make two constituency speeches that week-end. It would be impossible to avoid the topic which was in everybody's mind. I therefore suggested that I should state the Government's case for intervention, without stating my objections to it. Major Grant agreed that this was the best course.

I have never had to make two more difficult speeches. My audiences were bewildered by the ultimatum, and I had to explain it. As I carried on, "The Prime Minister says. . .," "The Government feel. . .," I could sense the atmosphere lightening. I was convincing them by the arguments which I would later have to destroy, and strengthening the attack on myself which I foresaw must follow. "Not many knew, as I knew," Major Grant gallantly said at a later stage, "that in his first two speeches, Mr Nicolson was loyally trying to present the Government's view objectively, suppressing his own objections and misgivings for the moment because our troops were then about to go into action." At the second meeting, I had to contend with one or two Conservatives in the audience who strongly criticized the Government's action, and reminded me of my own autumn speeches. I could only reply, "The Prime Minister would probably answer your question by saying. . ." Though I said nothing to commit myself, I realized that few people who heard me could have imagined that I agreed with the questioner and not with the Prime Minister. . . .

These two speeches were made on November 2nd and 3rd, 1956. On Sunday the 4th, I went to see Major Grant in his house, and handed him a letter explaining why I could not support the Government. I asked him to show it in confidence to any of the leading officers of the Association, but not

for the moment to give it wider circulation. I returned home to listen to Mr Gaitskell's broadcast on television, and heard him appeal to Conservative back-bench Members to desert their leader. I was horrified. I realized that of the ten or twelve million people to whom he was then speaking, I was one of the handful to whom he was addressing his main message. I knew that it would be said (as it was said) that I had responded to his appeal, although I had made my firm decision several days before, and had given formal notice of it to my chairman a few hours earlier. It was the only moment when I felt tempted to withdraw.

On November 6th the Prime Minister announced the cease-fire, and our acceptance of the United Nations Emergency Force. On the 8th there was to be a full debate in the House of Commons, followed by a vote of confidence in the Government. I knew that I must abstain, but I did not wish to do so without first explaining my reasons. The chance of catching the Speaker's eye in the debate was, I knew, slender. Therefore, when the secretary of the United Nations Association rang me up in London on the morning of the 7th to ask if I knew of anyone who would be free to speak to the Bournemouth UNA Branch that evening, I seized the opportunity. I said I would go myself. It was exactly the platform I needed at the very moment when I needed it. My speech would be made in a hall within a mile of my own constituency boundary, in the centre of Bournemouth, where many of my constituents could attend. It would be made to an all-party organization of which Sir Anthony himself was President, and which stood for the international principles to which my own party had so frequently pledged itself. . . .

I made the speech. It was the first public back-bench protest against the Suez policy. "A Government should never put the country in a position where it can be condemned by the rest of the world of duplicity and aggression," I said. "A Member of

Parliament must oppose his own party when he feels that the pledges he has given his electors in its name have been broken. I will not withdraw what I have said under any circumstances—I repeat, under any circumstances whatever." A Brigadier rose to his feet and walked out of the hall. Several speakers of all parties came forward from the audience and condemned or praised what they had heard. I had almost no Conservative support. I returned home, and waited for the storm to burst next day.

When it came, it took two forms. There was the charge of disloyalty, which was the most persistent; and the charge of presumption, that I should dare to set myself up as a greater authority on international relations than the Prime Minister. The latter charge was the more difficult to deal with. Of course there was no statesman in the country, and probably none in the whole world, who had more knowledge of international affairs than Sir Anthony Eden. Against that I could only put my meagre experience as a British delegate to the Council of Europe, and my recent travels in the Middle East and America. . . . But this was a matter on which every person, whether a Minister, a Member, or one of his constituents, had a duty to make up his own mind. The essential facts were known to all. The principles involved were self-evident. There was only one question: if the means which we employed at Port Said were such as to antagonize almost the whole world, should we have embarked on the operation at all? Everybody could now see the results of it. The crisis was already in its post-mortem stage. If our action had been wise, why had it not also been successful? . . .

That I appeared to be siding with the Socialists against my own party made my behaviour doubly inexcusable. Yet the fact that the Labour Party had consistently opposed a policy of force, was among my main motives for opposing it myself. I believed that a nation like our own should only resort to an act of large-scale violence when opinion in favour of it is almost

unanimous. "It should never be forgotten," Sir Frank Medlicott had written to the Prime Minister when he took the same decision as myself, "that in the two great wars, the margin between victory and defeat was perilously narrow, and in my view the margin by which we triumphed was due solely to the nation-wide conviction that we were in the right." I wholly endorsed his words. . . .

During the month which followed the UNA meeting, I made no public attempt to justify my conduct, except by a single letter to the local paper. I was told that a special meeting of the whole Association had been called for December 5th, at which I would have an opportunity to state my case. Meanwhile the Executive Council had met to repudiate my views and pledge their loyalty to the Government. They also drew up a resolution to be debated at the special meeting. It deplored my speech of November 7th on the grounds that it had "caused embarrassment to the Prime Minister and Government, misrepresented the views of the vast majority of his supporters in the constituency, and encouraged and delighted the Opposition." There was an ominous item to be considered at the close of the debate on this resolution:

4. Instruct the Executive Council to take such action as may be deemed necessary.

The meeting at the Selwyn Hall, Boscombe, on December 5th, 1956, was the only occasion, before or since, that I have been given an opportunity to speak to my Association, or any part of it, in my defence. I was refused permission to attend the Executive Council when my conduct was discussed. I was not allowed to visit any of the branch committees when they were framing their own resolutions for submission to the special meeting. I was in quarantine. Thus, when the date of the meeting came, the inner core of the Association had not only reached a verdict, but in their minds had passed sentence, before the accused had been heard at all. My speech was not even a speech from the dock: it was a speech from the condemned cell. It was delivered to an audience of 400 people out of the 8,000 members of the Association, the 28,000 who had voted for me at the previous election, and the 60,000 who composed my total electorate. My fate lay in the hands of less than one per cent of those to whom I was ultimately responsible.

I do not blame the organizers. They had booked the largest hall in the constituency, and it was only to be expected that the most ardent party-workers would come early, some on foot, others in organized coach-loads from the more distant part of the constituency, to fill the few available seats. When I arrived at 7.30 p.m. the police were doing their best to quieten an angry crowd against whom the doors had been shut. As I fought my way through to the side-door, there were cries of "We're all with you, but we can't get in!" and "The meeting's been packed," mingled with some boos and other indications that they were by no means all on my side. . . . I . . . went into the back-room of the hall, where I found the chief officers of the Association and the area agent looking remarkably grim.

The area agent suggested that the whole meeting should be postponed till a later date, when we could hold it in the much larger Town Hall in central Bournemouth. I disagreed. I said that I had been given special leave to miss an important debate in the House, and that not only did I wish to say what I had come to say, but the audience would never allow us to send them away empty-handed. . . .

We climbed the short flight of steps to the platform. There was an immediate outburst of booing, and a few cheers. The proceedings opened with a speech by Major Grant, in which he fairly summarized the course of the dispute until that date. The chairmen or secretaries of the twelve branches then came in turn to the foot of the platform, and read out the resolutions which their committees had passed without consulting the main body of their members. The resolutions were all hostile. Eight of them called for my immediate resignation. . . .

I then spoke for about forty minutes. I ended with the words: "It is for those reasons, with which I believe you will one day all agree, even if some of you do not agree now, that I must decline any invitation to resign my seat." The speech was heard in almost complete silence. Only when I said, "we should have informed the Americans and the Commonwealth, who would have helped us . . . ," was there a stir of incredulity. When I quoted Churchill's magnificent words about parliamentary democracy, I thought for a fleeting moment that I might have the majority with me. But when my wife and I were asked to leave the hall at the end of my speech, I knew that I had lost. Dr E. W. Deane, another previous chairman of the Association, whose support for me never wavered, followed us home an hour later to tell us what had happened in our absence.

A local Conservative Councillor mounted the platform and said: "You have listened to a long and skilful torrent of words. Your attention has been diverted from the issue. Are you going to be represented by a loyal Conservative or not? Do you want Nicolson or Eden? (Cries of "Eden! Eden!") Whom do you want, a Conservative or a piebald politician?" He was followed by another speaker who reminded the audience of my "Socialistic utterances" at the Primrose League, and of a book which my firm had published about Guy Burgess. But it was not all one-sided. Several speakers, including Brigadier Windsor [an ex-chairman of the Association] pleaded for moderation. But clearly the branch resolutions which had been drawn up many days previously, and were read out before I made my speech, had already committed a large part of the audience to vote against me.

A motion was finally put to the meeting in these terms:

This meeting regrets that it has no further confidence in the intention of Mr Nigel Nicolson adequately to represent in Parliament the political views of Bournemouth East and Christchurch

Conservatives, and instructs the Executive Council to take steps to obtain a prospective Conservative Candidate to contest the constituency at the next Parliamentary Election.

It was carried by 298 votes to 92. I was surprised that the minority vote was so large.

I had naturally considered whether I should resign the seat. The Chairman of the party, Mr Oliver Poole, encouraged me not to do so, and no demand for my resignation was ever made to me officially by Major Grant. But I feared at one moment that to insist on my constitutional rights and remain on as Member after a vote of no-confidence had been passed on me, would put me in the position of a sacked housemaid who insists on her week's notice. In much the same circumstances, Stanley Evans, the Labour Member for Wednesbury, who had supported the Suez policy, acceded to his constituency party's demand for his resignation, explaining that "a general without an army, living on borrowed time, seldom wields much influence, and loses all dignity." . . . *The Times* had commented on the Wednesbury case that the attitude of the constituency party "deserves nothing but censure. Mr. Evans is free to act as his conscience bids him, but he should not expect his action to be regarded, now or ever, as an example." This seemed to be the general view of Parliament. I was strongly pressed by fellow-Members not to resign. A principle of some importance was at stake. If a series of resignations followed constituency pressure over Suez, no Members except the most servile could consider themselves safe in future. . . .

The resolution passed at the meeting on December 5th did not call for an immediate selection of a new prospective candidate, and I soon suggested to Major Grant that its implementation should be delayed to give time for Conservatives to reflect, and to enable me to go round the branches and discuss with them what had happened. I told him that I did not dispute that an Association has the constitutional right to disown or expel its Member: I only ques-

tioned whether it was a happy precedent to have done so in the heat of the moment, and because of my disagreement on a single point of policy, on the merits of which there were widespread doubts throughout the country. Only a very small proportion of the Association had taken part in the decision. Lord Quickswood, the President of the Association, and two of its ex-chairmen, had supported me. There had been an outcry in the national press. Several Conservative Members had written letters of protest to the newspapers pointing out the sorry implications of the Bournemouth incident. Many local Conservatives were deeply disturbed. Would it not be better, in the party's interests, before going to the full length of breaking all connection with me, to pause a while? . . .

Major Grant rejected these arguments. The Association was already split, he said. I had split it. Only a new man could restore unity. It was presumptuous of me to suggest that I should be permitted to go round the branches, "to renew your attacks on the Eden Government." The breach was complete. Henceforward no branch would be permitted to invite me to address them; my annual donation to the Association's funds was returned; I could not use the office even to interview constituents; and the allegiance of the whole Association would be transferred from me to the new candidate as soon as he was selected. A selection committee was set up on December 17th, and they soon had some sixty names in front of them.

The attitude of Conservative Central Office and the party leaders was one of non-intervention. Their public comments on the affair were generalized and carefully guarded. But it was clear that the behaviour of my Association contrasted strongly with the party's tradition of tolerance, which at this time was frequently reaffirmed. For instance, Mr Harold Macmillan, in his speech on accepting the leadership of the party on January 22nd, 1957, said: "We do not believe in expelling people. I think that is a good thing, because I, no doubt, would have been a candidate for expulsion many years ago. It is this tolerance which makes us a national party." . . . But neither Mr Oliver Poole, the Chairman of the party, nor Mr Macmillan, thought it right to give my Association any public advice, and Lord Hailsham, when he succeeded to the Chairmanship, took the same view. A constituency Association was autonomous. Unless it breaks one of the party's rules, the party leadership cannot interfere. Mine had broken no rule. It had acted within its undoubted rights, and it had been guided throughout by the area agent, whose role was to see that nothing unconstitutional was done.

Eventually, on February 11th, 1957, Major Grant wrote to the Prime Minister at my suggestion and with the consent of Mr Poole, asking for his views on the matter, and informing him that the Executive were selecting a candidate that very night. This was Mr Macmillan's reply, which was published in the local paper a few days later:

February 12th 1957   10 Downing Street
Dear Major Grant,
    The Chairman of the Party organization has kept me informed of the situation which has developed between the Bournemouth East and Christchurch Conservative Association and the Member of Parliament for the Division, Mr Nigel Nicolson. It is a very long tradition of our Party that the Leader of the Party should not intervene in matters between a Member and his constituents. I am sure the Association in deciding its action will bear in mind the best interests of the Conservative Party, nationally as well as locally.
    I am sending a copy of this letter to Mr Nigel Nicolson, and would have no objection to your publishing your letter and my reply in the Press if you wish to do so.

Signed: Harold Macmillan

I was left to make the most I could of the phrase "the best interests of the Conservative Party, nationally as well as locally." But it was too late. Major James Friend had been selected and proclaimed as the prospective candidate two days before the Prime Minister's letter was even received. . . .

[*Major Friend, having been discovered collaborating with an extreme right-wing organization called the League of Empire Loyalists, retired early in 1959. The Bournemouth East and Christchurch Conservative Association then broke with precedent and held a ballot among its members. Nigel Nicolson failed to be readopted by 3,762 votes to 3,671.*]

Robert E. Dowse

2. MEMBERS AND THE PUBLIC

A citizen with a grievance in Britain can write to his member of Parliament, just as an American writes to his Congressman. In Britain any member of the public can also attend his M.P.'s "surgery." (A doctor's consulting room in Britain is called his surgery.) As Robert E. Dowse discovered, some 80 per cent of all M.P.s hold surgeries regularly in their constituencies. Mr. Dowse argues that such links between M.P.s and the general public are growing in importance.

One of the most widespread folk-myths of British politics is that MPs are, or should be, legislators or the critics of legislators —men and women who either orate on the floor of the House of Commons or fail in their chosen task. The MP who does not speak regularly is, according to the myth, only half a representative, a fine brute vote, a sheep or—the epithets are normally agricultural—a lump of lobby fodder. A popular TV programme . . . pillories 13 MPs who have held their peace, and the liberal press complains that Parliament is "inefficient" because, "hundreds of members are kept hanging around the House for large parts of the day, with little or no chance of being heard in debate."

In part, the assumption that each MP is an underdeveloped Demosthenes, waiting an opportunity to orate and legislate, derives from a 19th century view of liberal politics: full publicity for all political decisions so that an informed public might allocate responsibility in order to punish political vice and reward political virtue. Further, as representatives, however defined, the MPs were expected to represent, and to do so by talking publicly. After all, Parliament is a "talking shop"! Probably these assumptions no longer fit the facts

since most governmental decisions are made on the basis of private negotiations with interested parties. Indeed, the primary assumption of effective pressure group activity in Britain is secrecy; for good or ill Britain is a "responsive" democracy by virtue of secrecy and not of open debate. Further, the development of party discipline and the activities of pressure groups have cut away the area within which public debate is desired or necessary. If a Government comes to an arrangement about policy with the accredited representatives of pressure groups and those affected by a proposed policy, it is hardly likely that it will be unduly swayed by the orations of MPs. It may, however, be responsive to an MP's representations concerning the effect that *detail* has on people's lives. The development of the welfare state, of the positive intervening state, has involved the administration far more deeply and intimately in the day to day life of the country, a circumstance which ensures that the MP will be in constant demand as an intermediary between his constituents and the administration.

How effectively have MPs attempted to fill the role and how much importance do they attach to it? In order to answer at least

From Robert E. Dowse, "M.P.s and the Public" in *New Society* vol. 3. no. 67 (January 9, 1964), pp. 9–10. Reprinted by permission of the author and *New Society*. A fuller version of this article will be found in *Political Studies* vol. XI, no. 3 (October 1963), (Oxford: The Clarendon Press), pp. 333–341.

a part of this question I sent a question-naire to a random sample of 100 MPs of whom 69 answered. Over 80 per cent of the Conservatives and almost 85 per cent of the Labour MPs replied that they held surger-ies regularly, and frequently they were held fortnightly. Obviously the surgery, a pub-licly advertised meeting at which the MP will discuss individually and in private the cases and worries of constituents, is a sig-nificant liaison between MP and constit-uency. The surgery is normally held in the offices of the MP's political party and, in my experience, the atmosphere is often clinical. Impromptu discussions of social ailments and aches abound, cases are com-pared by the attenders in the boredom of waiting amidst the apparatus of political activity — posters, propaganda and brown paint.

It emerged from the survey that surgery, from a public point of view, was more im-portant for the working class than the mid-dle class. Labour MPs as a group are con-sulted far more in surgery by their constituents than are Conservative MPs and they were more likely to stress its im-portance. One Labour MP wrote that "after 17 years as an MP I am fully convinced of the value of surgery," but a more typical Conservative response was "Don't over-stress its importance."

Another significant difference between the two parties emerged in the answers to a question about the two most frequent matters which were raised in surgery; both parties' respondents stressed housing and pensions, typical working class problems. Yet in answering a question concerning the class composition of surgery less than 50 per cent of Conservatives thought their at-tendants were mainly working class and only 7 per cent thought attendance was equal. Almost 90 per cent of Labour MPs, on the contrary, thought their attendants were mainly working class and only 7 per cent thought attendance was equal. Since it was established that constituents in Con-servative seats preferred to write rather than attend surgery, and since the prob-lems brought to both parties' surgeries are mainly those of the working class, it fol-lows that an element of bias had entered into the answers. No doubt Labour MPs are inclined to classify a wide variety of people as working class, and, Labour MPs nor-mally have a higher percentage of working class constituents, but it is apparent that an element of Conservative "class blindness," the ideology of One Nation, also was im-portant.

This hypothesis was strengthened by the answer to a question "Do you think you are consulted more by people who voted for you than against you?" (See table for answers).

	Cons.		Lab.	
	No.	%	No.	%
Yes	9	29.0	19	63.3
No	4	12.9	3	10.0
DK	18	58.1	8	26.7
Total	31	100	30	100

The startling difference between Labour and Conservative answers, despite virtual unanimity in answer to a question on whether or not surgery wins votes, strengthens the One Nation hypothesis. Conservative answers also suggested a greater readiness to dismiss class consid-erations. Remarks such as "I find it very hard to define class," "I am not sure who is middle or working class" were frequent among the Conservative replies.

In answering a question whether or not surgery helped them get the feel of their constituency the MPs were in agreement (65 per cent Labour and 59 per cent Con-servative answered yes). However, Labour replies were usually more strongly couched than were those of Conservatives. Con-servatives often weakly affirmed "only a little" while Labour MPs replied "definite-ly" or "it shows where the shoe pinches." The negative character of Conservative re-plies possibly arose from a tendency to re-gard people with political gripes as atypi-cal of the electorate. Any government party

139

might well feel the same. Since the Labour MPs believed that their surgery attendants were typical of the electorate it might have been expected that they would regard their surgeries as a potential source of irritating questions for use in the Commons.

Labour MPs did, but less frequently than might have been supposed, regard their surgeries as a potential source of grievance to be publicly aired in the Commons, Conservatives emphatically did not. Nearly 45 per cent of Conservatives *never* raised a question in the House arising from surgery while only 14 per cent of Labour MPs never did so. It is probable that the difference is not so much one of temperament or party but rather between pro and anti-Government MPs. Ten per cent of Conservatives had done so more than ten times in the previous two years and 21 per cent of Labour members had done the same. Taking the answers *rarely* (less than 10 times in two years) and *never* together, 86 per cent of Conservatives and 72 per cent of Labour MPs fall into the category.

Clearly, the *public*, the dramatic and oratorical, side of question time is all too frequently overstressed in the textbooks. It may be that much of the significance of question time lies in those questions which are never asked! A question, for most members, is the last desperate bid for a remedy rather than the first and a very large number rarely find it necessary. Many MPs pointed out that a private letter to the appropriate Minister was the most effective way of obtaining redress or help with constituents' problems. Evidently, as one MP explained, they do not "put down a question unless the correspondence (with the Minister) has failed to satisfy." Equally clearly, the probity of MPs in putting redress of grievance before personal publicity cannot be too highly regarded. If MPs do pay considerable count to their constituents, they do not do so for the reason suggested by one eminent authority: that "a few hundred votes" may be important.

This moderation, a willingness to act outside the spotlight of publicity, was the

more impressive in that less than a third of MPs in both parties believe that surgery won them votes. About 42 per cent of Conservative and 47 per cent of Labour MPs thought that their work as intermediaries did not win them votes. Only 29 per cent of the Labour and 27 per cent of the Conservative respondents believed that they were able to win support by taking up a constituents case, but even here there was considerable doubt and it was made evident that vote catching was not an important motive. Replies such as the following were frequent: "not interested," "I regard this as genuine social work," "possibly I lose some from people I am unable to agree with or help." The temptation to win votes by a public show of concern might have been thought overwhelming for those MPs in marginal seats, yet this was not the case. Fifty per cent of the Labour MPs were marginal — less than 5,000 in 1959 — yet only 21 per cent had frequently asked questions: 22 per cent of Conservative MPs are in marginal seats yet only 10 per cent had frequently asked a public question.

The only disturbing answers in the whole of the replies were those in response to a question asking where the surgeries were held. Whether as a result of virtue or poverty, just 28 per cent of Labour MPs held their surgeries on "neutral" premises, such as local government offices, while only 20 per cent of Conservatives did the same. Seventy five per cent of Conservatives held theirs in the local party offices as did 64 per cent of their Labour colleagues. This feature of surgery is undesirable, not only because it militates against the genuinely non-party attitude of most MPs to their surgeries, but also because a potential attender may regard the assistance rendered as placing him in debt to a party. Also, some of those who need help, a Conservative in a Labour seat or a Labour voter in a Conservative seat, may be reluctant to face an "enemy" MP.

As with so much else in British political life, the significance of surgery is buried beneath official reticence and secrecy. It has previously been argued that one of the working secrets of British politics is secrecy; consultation with pressure groups — the very nub of official decision making — depends upon each side observing a decent reticence. One can only deduce from the fact that few pressure groups willingly break the "confessional oath" of secrecy that at least some of their demands are met. So it is with the MP and his political party where the amazing thing is that there are not more revolts. Either MPs are too cowed to revolt or discipline is a two-way matter. Similarly with the MP and his constituents' grievances. Do so few make the grievances public because of the power of the party whip or is it because the privacy of the Minister's ear or "in tray" is effective? Certainly most MPs suggest that it is the latter that keeps them from the floor of the House at question time. To condemn them for failing to speak, to suggest that more opportunities for speaking are required, is surely to ignore the great mass of useful private negotiation in order to focus upon a relatively insignificant public aspect of their work? . . .

Reform, if it is to be effective, can hardly work against the tide of events which has left the British MP as assiduous a fence-mender as the American Congressman. Two major problem areas need to be tackled, one quite simple and the [other] much more intractable. The MP cannot be fully effective as an intermediary — and as a part time social worker — without a great deal more trained assistance. Most MPs are lucky if they have a secretary, and very few indeed have one in the constituency and the House of Commons: at the very least they need a secretary and the advice of a trained social worker. Another minor reform necessary is that the holding of surgeries in party offices should be discontinued and neutral offices placed at the MPs' disposal. A dingy party office with brown political paint and a few partisan tracts scattered around can hardly be the most suitable venue. Far more important than such structural reforms would be recognition by [the] public of the facts of the parliamentary situation. The average MP cannot be judged solely by the number and length of the speeches he makes and the questions he asks. Demosthenes and Burke are both pre-welfare state.

For better or worse the average MP has assumed the role of strategically placed intermediary between constituents and executive. He is in a sense, a minor and part time ombudsman. If the House of Commons cannot be regarded as a source of policy or as a legislature pure and simple, then at least the MP's role as a watchdog of liberty and welfare can be enhanced by making him efficient.

Martin Redmayne and Norman Hunt

3. THE POWER OF THE WHIPS *the mediator*

Few members of any government wield as much potential power as the Chief Whip—and few are so little known to the general public. An atmosphere of secrecy surrounds the office, its occupant, and his activities. No Chief Whip has written a candid volume of memoirs, and there exists almost no academic literature on the subject. The term "whip" itself is mildly sinister. Who are the whips? What are their functions? Dr. Norman Hunt put these and other questions to Martin Redmayne, then the government Chief Whip, in two interviews broadcast by the B.B.C. in December 1963.

NORMAN HUNT: The Government Chief Whip is invariably a man of the utmost discretion, for he is privy to so much confidential information. He shares many of the Prime Minister's innermost thoughts; at the same time he has to know the personal views, strengths and weaknesses of all the government supporters in the House of Commons. At times of crisis . . . the Chief Whip's role is often crucial.

In this conversation the Government Chief Whip, the Rt. Hon. Martin Redmayne, reflects on the . . . nature of his job. I began by asking him which he regards as his more important function—to maintain party discipline or to keep the party leadership fully aware of the views of its own backbenchers.

MARTIN REDMAYNE: Certainly the first function must be the flow of information from the backbenchers to the leadership— that is either to the Prime Minister or to other Ministers, depending on what the subject of any particular comment may be. Discipline really flows from the success with which the first function is performed. You never get discipline unless the backbenchers are happy that the Whips are

performing the function of communication properly.

HUNT: How much is it part of your job to explain the policy of the government to your backbenchers?

REDMAYNE: The explanation of policy is properly done by Ministers. It has always been my habit as Chief Whip to get the Minister concerned to talk to the backbenchers who have a complaint or a criticism, because after all he is the man responsible for policy. My job is to see that the two sides are brought together.

HUNT: How are you organized as a Whip's office to do this job of conveying the views of the backbenchers to the government?

REDMAYNE: I have thirteen Whips plus my deputy, and each of those has, first of all, what we call an area—a geographical area of the country in which there are thirty or forty Conservative members. His business is to keep contact with them, and not merely to keep contact with them but to know them so well that he may in emergency be able to give a judgment as to what their opinion will be without even asking them. Then each Whip is allocated to one or more party committees; he keeps in touch with the chairman and the officers of

From Martin Redmayne interviewed by Norman Hunt, "The Commons in Action" in *The Listener*, vol. LXX, nos. 1812–1813 (London: British Broadcasting Corporation, December 19,26, 1963), pp. 1011–1013, 1056–1057. Reprinted by permission of the authors.

those committees, attends their meetings, and reports to me anything of interest — that is anything that is likely to be the subject of adverse comment. And every Whip in his ordinary round of the House — and they live in the House most of the time when it is sitting — has his own contacts with those who are his friends or those he may dine with, may meet in the smoking room, and so forth. He is always ready to pick up anything which may be useful to the government — and equally useful to the backbenchers, because no party can succeed unless it works as one in matters of opinion.

HUNT: How much notice does the government take of the information which they give you and which you pass on to the government?

REDMAYNE: A great deal. The Chief Whip sits on various government committees. He is always there to make comment when asked by the chairman of the committee, maybe the Prime Minister, maybe other Ministers. Or, if he thinks that Ministers are taking a view which will not be acceptable to the party, then he speaks on his own account. Of course, these things are not always done in committee; as the information flows into my desk, literally hour by hour throughout the day, I frequently write notes to this Minister or that, to say that the party or this member, as the case may be, takes this view or that view, and that in my opinion the policy ought to be amended accordingly; and these things are always taken into account. Obviously my suggestion or advice is not always accepted; but it is always taken into account.

HUNT: How much personal access do you have to the Prime Minister?

REDMAYNE: At any time a Chief Whip can see the Prime Minister, and indeed one of the charming things about Mr Macmillan, as Prime Minister, was that never in the four years in which I served him — and I know this was the same in the case of my predecessor — did he ever show the least sign of annoyance or irritation if I went in with some particular niggling problem,

even though he might be busy with things of far greater importance in a national sense.

HUNT: Is it significant in this respect that one of your bases is No. 12 Downing Street?

REDMAYNE: Yes, I suppose it is; this is traditional. It does mean that I can go to No. 10 unobserved whenever I wish, and this has its advantages.

HUNT: This is because there are intercommunicating doors?

REDMAYNE: There are in fact intercommunicating doors, yes.

HUNT: How often does the Prime Minister ask you how the backbenchers will react to a particular proposal?

REDMAYNE: I see the Prime Minister every day; this is routine. He may ask me many things, or if he doesn't ask me, I may tell him that this or that subject is topical, and this or that will be the backbench reaction to it.

HUNT: But have there really been changes in policy as a result of the representations which you have made?

REDMAYNE: Oh yes, this is constant. I don't think any advantage is served by my giving you examples of it, but you must accept my assurance that there are changes — though not necessarily major changes, because a government ought to try to put across its policy in a complete form which will be acceptable. That is where half my function comes in, to look for the snags in advance.

HUNT: So you are consulted at the early stages of policy formation, to assess the likely views of backbenchers.

REDMAYNE: The word consulted, I think, puts it in too much detail. As Chief Whip I am there the whole time, and my function is to be there and to be on the watch as best I can — in my limited knowledge and wisdom — to see what the snags are and to point them out.

HUNT: And to say whether future lines of policy are likely to be acceptable to the party?

REDMAYNE: Just so.

HUNT: When you have a government with

a large majority as you have at present, does this produce a situation in which the government backbenchers have got more influence on government policy than when the government has only a small majority?

REDMAYNE: Yes, although I would put it in a slightly different way. There is no question at all that when you have a government with a small majority you get a much more automatic loyalty. I of course, for my sins, have been in the Whip's Office since the Conservative Government started in 1951; and in those days we had a majority of 18, and even the most junior Whip could use the argument: "Well, old boy, you mustn't rock the boat." It isn't much use using that argument when you have a majority of 100 because the boat takes a good deal more rocking.

HUNT: So Conservative backbenchers have had more influence on government policy since 1959 than in the years between 1951 and 1959?

REDMAYNE: Provided the government wants to listen to its backbenchers, and in recent years it always has done so. I think it is true to say that the larger the majority the greater the power of the opinion of the backbenchers.

HUNT: Under Mr. Macmillan's leadership as Prime Minister was he particularly amenable to the views of backbenchers?

REDMAYNE: He was a great House of Commons man, and delighted in the contacts which he got in the Commons, both in the House and in the smoking room and so forth. He used to be in often and enjoyed it; you could see, even when he was tired, that he blossomed in the House of Commons and therefore his personal contacts were excellent.

HUNT: So here was a Prime Minister much influenced by backbench opinion?

REDMAYNE: Certainly, but at the same time with a strong sense of his own duty to govern and to lead. . . .

HUNT: Some people think that there is too much emphasis on strict party discipline and party voting in the House of Commons. Would that be your view, Mr. Redmayne?

REDMAYNE: Discipline is a difficult thing to explain. I hate to give away secrets, but I sometimes feel that my powers of discipline are not nearly strong enough for the occasions that arise. The fact is that discipline only arises from goodwill, and goodwill arises from good understanding between the backbenches and the government. You can be sure that if your discipline appears to be good, then your morale is good and your policy is good. If, on the other hand, at times your discipline appears to fall down, the fault — and I am not trying to excuse the Whips or myself in this matter — lies much more with the sort of undercurrents that impair morale than with any active discipline that can be exerted by the Chief Whip.

HUNT: But wouldn't it perhaps add to the prestige of the party if the general public could, more regularly, see members of parliament voting against their own party sometimes, because members of the public do know that the party can't be completely united on every issue, and yet here is the spectacle of M.P.s always voting for their party?

REDMAYNE: Yes I know, "here is the spectacle of M.P.s always voting for their party," but this is far from the truth. There are many occasions on which members refuse to yield to the pressures which I exert on them, inform me that they cannot support us, and therefore abstain. Sometimes they abstain publicly with great show, sitting in their places in the House, and noted by the press; sometimes they just quietly stay away; but their abstention, in the sense that it shows that the government in this particular matter has not got the united support of its party, is significant.

HUNT: But on the average number of divisions in the House in a week, would there be more than a handful of abstentions from your side on any one of them?

REDMAYNE: I don't think there would be any more than a handful of abstentions on any side whatever government there was, but the handful is significant.

HUNT: But in any given week, Mr. Redmayne, on how many divisions in the

House would there be any abstentions at all, as far as your supporters are concerned?

REDMAYNE: I would say that in any week there are occasions on which anything between one to half a dozen members may demonstrate in this way.

HUNT: But what is the good of these abstentions if the general public in fact knows nothing about them?

REDMAYNE: The public, if they choose to find out, if they take sufficient interest in the issues involved and in the actions of their members in regard to those issues, *can* find out the position.

HUNT: But it's a bit difficult to do so?

REDMAYNE: It is difficult; but life doesn't want to be too easy all the time.

HUNT: How much does it depend on the Prime Minister whether there is a rigid amount of party discipline or not?

REDMAYNE: A good deal. When people talk about the Chief Whip's powers, these powers only stem from the Prime Minister. And if you have a situation in which as Chief Whip you want to propose to a Prime Minister that really the services of this or that member ought to be dispensed with, by withdrawing the Whip (although this has been rare all this century), it is the Prime Minister who has the final word.

HUNT: You said earlier that to keep members of parliament in line, one of the arguments you used is "Don't rock the boat," but how far is hope of office one of the main factors that keeps a backbencher in line?

REDMAYNE: I must just correct you. What I said was that under present conditions it is the one argument I can't use, because the majority is so large. It can only be used with very small majorities. I suppose that in an age in which the Conservative Party is much younger than it used to be, and being younger more ambitious, the hope of office is an incentive to give support to the government; but if you look through the enormous turnover of ministerial appointments in these twelve years, you will see that, all in all, the fact that a man may have been from time to time for good reason opposed to the government, or not wholly in

agreement with the government, on this or that policy has certainly not been a bar to office.

HUNT: But you wouldn't appoint a regular rebel to high office?

REDMAYNE. I think a regular rebel, a man who just abstains the whole time because he gets into the habit, is by definition not suitable for office. He can't be. It isn't a sensible attitude.

HUNT: How far are you consulted by the Prime Minister on appointments to ministerial office?

REDMAYNE: It's difficult to answer that but obviously a Chief Whip is probably the person who is best able to describe the character of any particular member, and therefore the Prime Minister, whose sole responsibility it is to appoint Ministers, would obviously consult him.

HUNT: And so a backbencher clearly knows that a good or bad word from you to the Prime Minister about himself could have an important effect on his future career?

REDMAYNE: Yes, I suppose so, but at the same time I hope that my reputation, or that of my predecessors, would not be that we were stupidly obstructive of any man's future, simply because we happen not to have agreed with him at some particular time. It would be a senseless sort of attitude to take.

HUNT: How far is a government threat to dissolve parliament a factor which helps you to maintain party discipline?

REDMAYNE: Members of parliament have a duty to get themselves re-elected and they therefore would have strong opinions about dissolution if they thought it was untimely; therefore, if actions of theirs were inclined to force a dissolution, it might persuade them that those actions should be modified.

HUNT: Or if you were threatening a dissolution, it might change their views?

REDMAYNE: One does not, I think, threaten a dissolution. It's too big a thing. . . .

HUNT: Does the fact that Conservative M.P.s, and perhaps ex-Ministers, can so easily get good jobs in the City — directorships and so on — make them rather less amenable to party discipline than they otherwise might be? Does it make them more independent?

REDMAYNE: Ministers are not particularly well paid—I think frankly they should be paid more. Therefore, apart from the prestige and honour of serving in a government, which are very great, when you get to the dividing point there is no other inducement, and you can say that once they reach that point it may well seem attractive to them to do better for themselves in a material sense. I don't think this weighs very heavily.

HUNT: But a man with substantial business interests outside the House, who is a backbencher—he can be slightly more independent of the Whips, can he, because his need for office is not so great?

REDMAYNE: This is a theory. I must say I don't think it shows itself in the system.

HUNT: One of your most difficult jobs recently I suppose was maintaining the government's majority before the summer recess in the debate on the Profumo affair. What arguments did you use then with your backbenchers and how difficult was your job at that time?

REDMAYNE: It was particularly difficult because of the actual timing of all this. You recollect that Mr. Profumo resigned on Whit Tuesday, and the House came back on the following Monday week. There had been every opportunity for members to take the worst possible view of what was in any case a difficult situation, and therefore when we came back to debate it on that Monday those of us who had this responsibility had to try to get across what were the facts of the case, right or wrong, and to get them accepted. On the whole we succeeded fairly well. I don't mind telling you that I anticipated before that day that the government's majority would be worse than in the event it was, and it was not very good at that.

HUNT: Did you have to make any specific promises or threats to get the majority what it was?

REDMAYNE: There has been a suggestion that there was a bargain—that is what you mean by a promise: there was certainly no such bargain; all that I had to do was to try to see that that vote was treated on its merits, and it was difficult enough to handle the merits of the case without embarking on other arguments outside it.

HUNT: Was the suggestion put about that if the government did not have a substantial majority, it might have to resign?

REDMAYNE: It was not put about, it was obvious. This is the same as the Neville Chamberlain case: that if a Prime Minister found he had not got the full enough support of his party he might have to resign. Just how much that lack of support should be to produce that circumstance is a matter of opinion, and I am not making any expression of opinion on that.

HUNT: How important a factor do you think this was—this knowledge that the government majority must not drop too far—in maintaining the substantial support that Mr. Macmillan managed to get in the division on that debate?

REDMAYNE: I think one must answer that Macmillan was a Prime Minister who was greatly admired. It appeared at first sight that the government was considerably open to criticism over the handling of this Profumo affair, but the great majority of people in the party would have said that this was no occasion to take parliamentary action which would lead possibly to the resignation of the Prime Minister on this account, especially a Prime Minister of such eminent distinction.

HUNT: So that some members of parliament, because they knew an abstention might well bring Mr. Macmillan down on this occasion, did not in fact abstain when really they would have been happiest in fact in abstaining?

REDMAYNE: Obviously I cannot know that that is true, but it could be a factor in men's minds; although I profess to know the party fairly well, I have not got a crystal ball.

HUNT: How far is a large and virile opposition vital for the health of the House of Commons?

REDMAYNE: It is vital for the health of the

House of Commons. Parliament is a battle, and battles are much better fought between active and skilful opponents. If that battle is good and hot and strong, the contenders on both sides tend to be happier.

HUNT: But it would still be true to say, wouldn't it, that the government takes more notice of its own backbenches, and the views of its own backbenches, than it does of the Opposition, however strong and virile the Opposition may be?

REDMAYNE: Politics is a matter of power, and any good government can always gets its way. Paying attention to its own backbenches is part of the technique of ensuring that it will get its way. At the same time Parliament is a reasonable place and one has to depend to a certain extent on the goodwill of the Opposition; therefore you pay attention to the good points which they make. I think more attention is paid to constructive suggestions from the Opposition than the outside public give credit for.

Nigel Birch

4. "LET HIM NEVER COME BACK"

A party leader or Prime Minister who loses the confidence of his followers in Parliament may be able to survive, but his authority will be gravely impaired. Harold Macmillan came under fire from a section of the Conservative Party as early as 1961. Two years later, with the resignation of John Profumo as army minister, his position began to seem untenable. In March 1963 Profumo denied in the House of Commons that there had been anything improper in his relations with Miss Christine Keeler. On June 5, he submitted his resignation, admitting that he had lied. The House of Commons debated the security aspects of the affair two weeks later. Among the speakers was Nigel Birch, a prominent Conservative ex-minister who had been one of Macmillan's chief critics. He was heard in almost total silence.

MR. NIGEL BIRCH (Flint, West): In many organs of the Press and, to a certain extent, during the latter part of the speech of the Leader of the Opposition, there has been a suggestion that the whole moral health of the nation is at stake and is concerned in this debate. I do not believe that that is true. As far as the moral health of the nation can be affected by any human agency, it is affected by prophets and priests and not by politicians. But this certainly has been one of the best field days that the self-righteous have had since Parnell was cited as co-respondent in O'Shea's divorce case. In all these miseries, the fact that so many people have found some genuine happiness is something to which, in all charity, we have no right to object.

I must say that I view the activities of the editor of *The Times* with some distaste. . . . He is a man about whom it could have been predicted from his early youth that he was bound to end up sooner or later on the staff of one of the Astor papers.

Nor do I think that this debate is primarily concerned with the security aspect, although that, of course, is important. It was fully dealt with by my right hon. Friend the Prime Minister and, for my part, I am perfectly prepared to accept every-

From *Parliamentary Debates (Hansard) Fifth Series*, vol. 679 (June 17, 1963), columns 95–99.

147

thing that the Prime Minister said about security. I believe that what he said was right and true and I am not prepared to criticize my right hon. Friend in any way concerning the question of security.

What seems to me to be the real issue is something much simpler and much narrower. The real issue seems to be whether it was right to accept Profumo's personal statement. There are two aspects here. There is, first, the moral aspect of accepting that part of the statement which Profumo himself subsequently denied and there is a second issue of whether the Prime Minister in this case acted with good sense and with competence.

I will deal with these two issues in order. First, there is the question of accepting Profumo's statement. We know a deal more now about Profumo than we did at the time of the statement, but we have all known him pretty well for a number of years in this House. I must say that he never struck me as a man at all like a cloistered monk; and Miss Keeler was a professional prostitute.

We have had a legal disquisition from my right hon. and learned Friend the Member for Chertsey (Sir L. Heald) about the legal etiquette in all this matter, but as someone who does not understand the law, I simply approach it from the basis of what an ordinary person could or would believe. Here one had an active, busy man and a professional prostitute. On his own admission, Profumo had a number of meetings with her, and, if we are to judge by the published statements, she is not a woman who would be intellectually stimulating. Is it really credible that the association had no sexual content? There seems to me to be a certain basic improbability about the proposition that their relationship was purely platonic. What are whores about? Yet Profumo's word was accepted. It was accepted from a colleague. Would that word have been accepted if Profumo had not been a colleague or even if he had been a political opponent? Everyone must, I think, make his own judgment about that.

We were told that special consideration ought to have been given to Profumo because he was a colleague. It is certainly true that a Prime Minister owes to his subordinates all the help, comfort and protection that he can give them. But surely that help, that comfort and that protection must stop short of condoning a lie in a personal statement to this House.

Then we are told, in many organs of the Press and in many speeches, that special weight ought to have been given to Profumo's words because he was a Privy Councillor and a Secretary of State. I am a Privy Councillor and I have been a Secretary of State, but when I sustained the burden of both offices I did not feel that any sea change had taken place in my personality. I remained what I was, what I had always been and what I am today; and I do not believe it reasonable to suppose that any sea change took place in Mr. Profumo's personality.

He was not a man who was ever likely to tell the absolute truth in a tight corner, and at the time the statement was made he was in a very tight corner indeed. There are people — and it is to the credit of our poor, suffering humanity that it is so — who will tell the whole truth about themselves whatever the consequences may be. Of such are saints and martyrs, but most of us are not like that. Most people in a tight corner either prevaricate . . . or, as in this case, they lie.

This lie was accepted. I have meditated very deeply on this, and though I have given some rather tough reasons for not accepting that Profumo's statement was credible, I have after deep consideration come to the conclusion that my right hon. Friend did absolutely genuinely believe it. I will give my reasons now for taking that view, and these reasons concern the competence and the good sense with which the affair was handled.

Profumo on his own admission had been guilty of a very considerable indiscretion, for a Minister at any rate. He was not a particularly successful Minister. He had no great place in this House or in the country. I cannot really see that the Prime Minister was under any obligation whatever to retain his services, nor do I think that getting rid of Mr. Profumo would, in fact, have made the political situation any worse than it then was. On the other hand, to retain him entailed a colossal risk and a colossal gamble. The difficulties and dangers were obvious enough. The Press were in full cry. They were in possession of letters. They were hardly likely to have bought letters unless they had something of interest in them. Miss Keeler was pretty certain to turn up again, and if she did, editors were sure to make use of her literary talent. The dangers were enormous, and yet this colossal gamble was taken, and in this gamble, as it seems to me, the possible gain was negligible and the possible loss devastating.

The conclusion that I draw from that is that the course adopted by my right hon. Friend the Prime Minister could have been adopted only by someone who genuinely and completely believed the statements of Profumo, and therefore, I absolutely acquit my right hon. Friend of any sort of dishonour. On the other hand on the question of competence and good sense I cannot think that the verdict can be favourable.

What is to happen now? I cannot myself see at all that we can go on acting as if nothing had happened. We cannot just have business as usual. I myself feel that the time will come very soon when my right hon. Friend ought to make way for a much younger colleague. I feel that that ought to happen. I certainly will not quote at him the savage words of Cromwell, but perhaps some of the words of Browning might be appropriate in his poem on "The Lost Leader", in which he wrote:

. . let him never come back to us!
There would be doubt, hesitation and pain.
Forced praise on our part—the glimmer of
   twilight,
Never glad confident morning again!

"Never glad confident morning again!"—so I hope that the change will not be too long delayed.

Ahead of us we have a Division. We have the statement of my right hon. and noble Friend Lord Hailsham, in a personal assurance on television, that a Whip is not a summons to vote but a summons to attend. I call the Whips to witness that I at any rate have attended.

[*At the end of the debate 27 Conservatives ostentatiously abstained from supporting the government. Harold Macmillan eventually resigned for health reasons in early October 1963.*]

Sir Frank Markham

5. RESALE PRICE MAINTENANCE

Governments in Britain can, of course, normally count on the votes of their supporters in the House of Commons. It is tacitly understood, however, that a government will not bring forward controversial legislation without first taking at least some informal soundings among backbenchers. As a leading Conservative minister once put it: "You have to let them see the cat before you let it out of the bag." Early in 1964 the government of Sir Alec Douglas-Home startled many on the Conservative side by introducing a bill to abolish resale price maintenance (the practice whereby manufacturers dictated the prices that retailers were to charge for their products). Sir Frank Markham was only one of many Tory M.P.s who protested vehemently in the House of Commons.

MAJOR SIR FRANK MARKHAM (Buckingham): This is one of those rare occasions in the history of our Parliamentary democracy when the Conservative Party is split. It has often been said from the other side of the House that the Tories are stupid but united. We are not as stupid as we look, and occasionally we are not as united as we look.

When there is a division in the Conservative Party, it goes down to very deep roots. In the past, in the divisions that I can remember—for example, on Suez and on the Common Market—deep roots were being disturbed. The same is true of to-day's Bill. Part of the shock to the party derives from a sudden inexplicable change on the part of the Board of Trade as recently as January this year.

Let us look at our own Tory history in this matter of resale price maintenance. At the last election, many of us throughout the land could give pledges to some of our most earnest workers and keenest questioners that the Tory Party would not interfere with resale price maintenance. We could do that on the authority not only of the Lloyd Jacob Report but of speeches in the House of Commons by men of the distinction of my right hon. and learned Friend the Member for Hertfordshire, East (Sir D. Walker-Smith) and my right hon. Friend who is now Minister of Defence. Indeed, several Cabinet Ministers said, not only in the House but in the country during the election campaign of 1959, that a Conservative Government had no intention of altering the existing resale price maintenance.

I was pledged, as were many other hon. Members on this side of the House. Indeed, no hint was given of any change, not even as recently as the Queen's Speech of November, 1963. Not a hint was given that anything was brewing either in the Board of Trade or in the Government or that a change was on the way. Still more recently, the "bible" of the party, the fighting war book, the "Campaign Guide," published only a few weeks ago, devoted only two paragraphs to resale price maintenance, very meek and mild and more or less indicating that it was worth while continuing with it.

From *Parliamentary Debates (Hansard) Fifth Series*, vol. 691 (March 10, 1964), columns 354–358.

Into this stream we suddenly got a decision by the Secretary of State [Mr. Edward Heath] that a Bill would be introduced to abolish resale price maintenance, and this — and I put it down as a charge against him — without any consultation with any of the usual bodies like the 1922 Committee of the Conservative Party in this House. [HON. MEMBERS: "Oh."] This is very important.

If the Government want to change policy, surely the first thing they should do is to approach their own supporters — through the normal channels on this side, and hon. Members opposite of course have their own organisation. If the Secretary of State had done that, if he had come to the 1922 Committee or called a special meeting of the party's Trade and Industry Committee and said, "This is what we propose. What is your opinion and advice?" we should have been glad to have co-operated in the drafting of a Bill.

But there was no choice of that at all, and in consequence the Secretary of State must bear the charge of rocking the Conservative boat pretty badly at a very delicate time. We are described as rebels because we are adhering to policies which have been worked out in the past and have been reaffirmed consistently. We are not rebels. The rebels are on that Front Bench and in the Cabinet. It is they who have changed consistent Conservative policy adopted and approved over the years. . . .

This Bill strikes at the little man. It eases him out because, as the Secretary of State has said, the little man somehow or other is redundant to the Secretary of State's pattern of what the future should be. I stand here not just for the small trader, who is a very necessary part of the British picture. I stand here for the consumer as well. It is the interests of the consumers which are being attacked by the Bill. There will be much less choice of retailer and no possible way in which prices can be reduced. . . .

But that is not my main complaint. I have already made the point that I and my colleagues are not the rebels; the rebels are on the Treasury Front Bench. It is they who have rebelled against good sound policies which have served this nation well, and it is they who are now diverging from good practices into the unknown: a divergence that will sacrifice many little tradesmen. It is they who are changing Conservative policy and it is we who are sticking to the good line that has been tried out so successfully for a generation or so.

My main objection to the Bill has been echoed by hon. Member after hon. Member. One of the interesting things in the debate has been that hon. Members speaking in favour of the Bill, like my hon. Friend the Member for Cirencester and Tewkesbury (Mr. Ridley), have said that although they approve of the Bill they want to change root and branch at least three of the major Clauses. The major Clause in my view is that dealing with the onus of proof.

Time and again, individually and collectively, we have asked the Secretary of State for Industry and Trade to modify this provision. He has refused every time. I and those associated with me find this Clause the biggest stumbling block of all. It has been traditional in Britain that a man or a firm is innocent until proved guilty. The onus of proof Clause lays it down that a firm is assumed to be guilty unless it can prove that it is not acting to the public detriment; and it will cost a firm £25,000 or more to defend itself.

I find that shocking. I know that there is one precedent for it, and I know that the Secretary of State has hung on grimly to this precedent as if it were an angelic lifeline from the depths of hell. But there is no reason why there should be this distortion of our traditional English practices. Unless the Secretary of State or the Chancellor of the Exchequer can assure us that this onus of proof Clause will be amended and that in all these matters of trade, as in other respects, a man or firm will be regarded as innocent until proved guilty, I and my colleagues will divide the House tonight. It may well be that there will only be a dozen or so of us going into the Noes Lobby and only a score abstaining, but we know from talks which we have had in the country and upstairs that the great heart of our party is dead against the Secretary of State on this Measure, and I hope that it will be defeated.

[On the day after Sir Frank Markham spoke, 21 Conservatives voted against the government and another 17 abstained. On a later occasion the government's majority fell to one. The bill, which had been modified considerably in anticipation of a backbench revolt, was further amended in the course of its passage through Parliament.]

Ian Aitken

6. A DISCREET REBELLION

Members of Parliament obey the party whips from a variety of motives. Some seek promotion to ministerial office. Others (mainly Conservative) look forward to being created knights or baronets or even peers. But probably the main single incentive to party discipline is simply the fear of giving aid and comfort to the other side. Government supporters in particular do not wish to embarrass their leaders in public. For this reason, backbench pressures tend to be exerted in private, at party meetings or in deputations to ministers. Ian Aitken, a political reporter for the *Guardian*, provided much the fullest accounts of one rebellion which occurred late in 1964. It began a few days after the Chancellor of the Exchequer, James Callaghan, had introduced a special autumn budget.

November 14, 1964

The first rumblings of dissent over the Chancellor's Budget proposals came to the surface in the Parliamentary Labour Party yesterday. A group of Labour MPs is now pressing the Government to speed the payment of pension increases to old people.

Mr. Richard Kelley (Lab. Don Valley) is one of a team of Labour backbenchers who is urging fellow MPs to write to Miss Margaret Herbison, the Minister of Pensions, insisting that the new pension rates cannot reasonably be delayed until March 29.

This was the date stated by Mr. James Callaghan, the Chancellor, for the start of the new pensions rates when he announced his Budget proposals on Wednesday.

But many Labour MPs now argue that

the delay in paying the increases cannot be justified on the purely technical grounds advanced by Mr. Callaghan. They are convinced that the Civil Service, if faced with a firm and determined order to seek out a method of paying the new rates before Christmas, would do its duty to the Government.

And they fear that the Labour Government and its supporters will be forced by Mr. Callaghan's proposals to defend exactly the same kind of delay as the Conservative Government experienced when it last raised the basic rates of old age pensions.

Meanwhile, many Labour backbenchers take the view that it would be morally indefensible and politically unwise to vote an increase in pay for members of Parliament before the pensioners get their improved benefits. This attitude received a *de facto*

From the *Guardian* (Manchester), Nov. 14–Dec. 3, 1964. Reprinted by permission of the *Guardian*.

endorsement at the last meeting of the Parliamentary Labour Party when MPs loudly cheered a proposal that members should refuse to accept an increase in salary until the pensioners had been given their rise.

Several MPs privately proclaimed their determination to pay back any extra salary they may receive as a result of a vote in the Commons until the pensions' deadline of March 29.

Only one practical idea to help the pensioners has so far been advanced. Mr William Warbey (Lab. Ashfield) has tabled a question which implies that the Chancellor should authorise the pensioners to draw double benefit in every sixth week until March 29.

Arithmetically, this would give the pensioners more or less the same amount they would have received if the new increases had been paid out at once.

Mr Warbey is usually linked with extreme Left-wing policies in foreign affairs. His latest initiative in the field of social services has already found a large number of supporters.

November 18, 1964

Labour MPs who have been conducting a discreet rebellion against the Government's proposal to delay the latest pension increases until the end of March caught the faintest whiff of a possible victory in the Westminster air last night.

All Labour MPs received an unexpected letter from the Party Whips inviting them to attend a special meeting of the Parliamentary Labour Party today when Miss Margaret Herbison, the Minister of Pensions, will address them. The decision to summon the meeting—there was to have been no PLP meeting this Wednesday—is the first official acknowledgment of the very large number of letters of protest about the delay addressed to Ministers in the past week by backbench MPs.

A strikingly high proportion of these letters has come from new members. They,

even more than their experienced colleagues, have been shocked by the Government's ready acceptance of civil service advice suggesting that it is administratively impossible to pay the increases earlier.

Several MPs have canvassed ideas which would enable the Government to pay out sums of money roughly equivalent to the new increases in the interim period before March 29—the date on which the new pension rates are to take effect. These MPs include Mr Richard Kelley, Mr William Warbey, Mr Arthur Lewis, Mr Jack Mendelson, Mr William Hamling, and Mrs Ann Kerr.

Many of these ideas involve some form of bonus which could be paid to pensioners either in instalments or in a lump sum just before Christmas. At least one backbencher is hoping to enlist the support of civil servants who work in the Ministry of Pensions through their trade unions.

But many of the younger and more impatient rebels are frankly unconvinced by the Government's claim that the payment of the actual increases cannot be speeded. They argue that an allout effort in Whitehall on the scale of some of the wartime administrative crash programmes should be mounted in this case.

The new and generous rises for MPs and Ministers, backdated to October 16, which were announced by Mr Harold Wilson this week, have served only to increase the anxiety and sense of urgency on the Government backbenches. Three MPs have already announced publicly that they intend to pay their salary increases up to March 29 to the pensioners in their constituencies.

Many more say privately that they will either do the same or simply refuse to accept the extra salary until the pensioners get their increased benefits.

There is still no firm evidence to suggest that Miss Herbison will announce a change of timing when she meets MPs today. But many MPs who received letters summoning them to the meeting are allowing themselves to hope that Miss Herbison will have good news for them this morning.

November 19, 1964

Labour MPs who attended a heated emergency meeting of the Parliamentary Labour Party yesterday were assured by Miss Margaret Herbison that the Government intends to examine the practical possibility of backdating the increase in the basic old age pension.

The meeting was summoned because of the number of protest letters received by Ministers from backbenchers about the delay in paying the increased benefits to pensioners. . . .

Miss Herbison argued that it was physically impossible for the Government to speed up the payment of the increases. She told her backbench followers that there were more than 200 permutations on the basic pension rate, and that it was administratively impossible for the Civil Service to prepare and print the necessary documents before the end of March. . . .

Miss Herbison's statement was received in stony silence. It was followed by a heated question and answer session in which MPs accepted the Minister's good faith but questioned whether she had given enough attention to the liability of the Civil Service and the wide opportunities offered by alternative methods of paying extra cash to pensioners.

There was also some bitter criticism of the three Labour MPs who have publicly stated that they will pay their own salary increases to the pensioners in their constituencies. A "freshman" MP stood up to protest that these members would have done better to refuse their salary increases privately without turning their action into a public spectacle.

At least one of the three "guilty" MPs excuses himself on the grounds that if their proposal was embarrassing it was intended to be embarrassing. They are convinced that it was an important contribution towards changing the attitude of mind of the Government on the plight of the pensioners.

A deluge of suggestions was offered yesterday to Miss Herbison and a basic theme was that pensioners should not receive worse treatment than MPs. The almost universal demand was that the increases for the pensioners should be backdated and that some kind of immediate bonus should be paid well before Christmas.

Miss Herbison replied, and many MPs were convinced that her tone was markedly more conciliatory than in her first contribution. She assured her tormentors that the practical suggestions she had heard during the meeting would be closely examined by the Government, and with the utmost sympathy.

New MPs were particularly prominent during the question and answer stage of the meeting. Their attitude was that certain promises had been made during the election campaign, and that these promises must now be honoured.

The universal mood among new and old MPs alike was that the needs of the pensioners, who now face another winter of the old pension rates, were too demanding to justify the Government's respect for Whitehall protocol. . . .

Miss Herbison wound up the meeting with a renewed assurance that the Government would look again at the ideas put up by the backbench MPs. She promised that she would come back again next week to a full meeting of the Parliamentary party to give a full account of her re-examination of the problem.

November 20, 1964

A senior member of the Cabinet will join Miss Margaret Herbison when she attends the resumed meeting of the Parliamentary Labour Party next week to report on her researches into possible ways of speeding the payment of the Government's increased pensions rates.

This assurance has been given to Mr Emanuel Shinwell, the newly elected chairman of the PLP, in reply to a firm recommendation from the parliamentary liaison committee. The decision underlines the seriousness with which Ministers are treating the gentlemanly, but determined, rebellion over pensions that has swept the Government back-benches.

The renewed party meeting has been fixed for Tuesday evening, a timing which will make it possible for a member of the Cabinet to be present. Last night, leading back-benchers were already at work in the lobbies preparing the ground for a resumption of the onslaught. Their objective is to polarise the back-bench attack round a selected few proposals, so as to prevent the meeting becoming merely a repeat performance of Wednesday's confused session. They hope to be able to present Miss Herbison with a united demand for action along the lines of a proposal put up by Mr William Warbey (Ashfield).

Mr Warbey wants Miss Herbison to short-circuit the administrative difficulty involved in paying out the new benefits before March 29 by the simple expedient of declaring double benefit payments in three separate three weeks between now and the end of March. . . .

Leading agitators in this effort to rally the Government's critics behind a single demand include Mr John Mendelson (Penistone), Mr William Warbey (Ashfield), Mr Ben Parkin (Paddington North), and Mr Ian Mikardo (Poplar). Their efforts, ironically, have been made more difficult by the sheer numbers of MPs who feel strongly on the issue. Estimates of the size of the rebellion vary from half the Parliamentary Party, to three-quarters. Hardly any other subject is being discussed in the lobbies, and the new members who entered Parliament last month are as active as their seniors.

Many of the rebels were becoming increasingly optimistic yesterday that the Government will, in the end, give way. Ministers, however, are not so optimistic. They are now more anxious than ever to find a way of satisfying the pensioners — not to mention the backbenchers. They insist that the difficulties are more real than their critics appreciate. The question remains open, but it is by no means certain

that a practical solution will be found.

November 25, 1964

A stunned meeting of Labour MPs was told last night by Mr Douglas Houghton, the Minister responsible for co-ordinating social policy, that the renewed sterling crisis [which had arisen a few days before] now rules out any possibility of speeding-up the payment of increased benefits to old age pensioners.

Within minutes of the end of the meeting — and in the face of the most emphatic appeals for unity, solidarity, and secrecy from Mr Emanuel Shinwell the party chairman — a "round robin" was circulating among Labour backbenchers calling on Mr Wilson to receive an urgent deputation to press the case for the pensioners. Late last night 40 MPs had already signed the document, and the figure was expected to rise to more than 50 before the Commons rose.

Mr Shinwell had warned MPs not to talk to reporters when they emerged from the Grand Committee Room after an hour of noisy debate. And it was so effective that few MPs even dared to enter the public lobbies. Instead, they went to earth in the various private rooms at Westminster.

The attitude of the backbench rebels was crystallised by Mr John Mendelson (Penistone), one of the MPs who was collecting signatures to the "round robin," during last night's noisy and sometimes bitter party meeting. He told the dozen or so senior Ministers who attended:

It is improper for the Government to prove its financial respectability to the international bankers and the IMF by denying the means of livelihood to the old-age pensioners.

It was the increasingly firm conviction of many Ministers as well as backbenchers last night, that the Labour Government, faced with renewed pressure on the pound, in spite of the 7 per cent bank rate, is now the victim of direct sabotage by international financiers. MPs were saying freely in the lobbies that "the gnomes of Zurich" were at work again, and that their victims are the old-age pensioners.

Mr Houghton . . . insisted at last night's meeting that the Government still had not found a workable method of paying out the increased pension rates before the existing date of March 29.

But he left MPs with the clear impression that, even if a workable system had been found, there could be no question of going ahead with the payout in the face of the present crisis of confidence in the pound.

In fact, many Ministers and MPs entered the meeting with the conviction that a system actually had been found, and that the Government intended to announce some kind of pre-Christmas bonus for the pensioners. They were shocked to discover that the entire atmosphere had changed since the weekend.

Some MPs were convinced that the Government actually changed its mind yesterday, when the news reached London that the pressure on the pound was beginning again. And a handful of them expressed the view that the Government must have received direct instructions from the IMF to hold up any further expenditure on the social services until Sterling was again on a sound footing.

The backbenchers' round-robin, which was delivered to Mr Wilson last night while the process of collecting signatures was still going on, was the result of a hurriedly summoned meeting in a basement committee room beneath the Commons chamber. . . . Mr Wilson is expected to agree to receive the backbenchers' deputation. But he is not likely to have much encouragement to offer them. Ministers were in a mood last night of severe disillusionment over the latest Sterling crisis, and were talking unhappily of their disappointment in discovering the limited amount of independence a Labour Government has in conducting Britain's domestic affairs under the surveillance of international financiers.

MPs had been promised after last week's meeting of the parliamentary party that at least one member of the Cabinet would

attend last night's resumed meeting. The Government was better than its word. Not only did Mr Houghton appear to make the major speech for the Government, something like half the Cabinet was also present.

November 26, 1964

The Liberals stepped into the Labour Party's pensions revolt last night, with an amendment to the National Insurance Bill calling on the Government to pay the increased pension scales not later than January 1.

The Liberal manoeuvre is certain to cause the maximum possible embarrassment. It is timed to coincide with the apparent collapse of the Labour Party's own backbench revolt over the delay in paying out pension increases. Yesterday Mr Harold Wilson flatly refused to meet a deputation of backbench Labour MPs representing some 50 signatories of a round-robin addressed on Tuesday night to the Prime Minister.

Not long before Mr Wilson's refusal a small group of MPs, who helped to organise the round-robin, met in a downstairs committee room to consider the situation. They appeared to have reached reluctant agreement that it would be politically impossible to carry the revolt to the point of tabling an amendment to the Government's Bill.

The Liberal amendment is well calculated to re-open the entire dispute. If it reaches the point of public debate during the committee stage of the bill—which was being given its second reading in the Commons last night—it will amount to a Liberal challenge to the rebels on the Labour backbenches to stand up and be counted.

The Government's flat refusal to concede an inch on the timing of the pension increases was received with cowed acceptance by the 50 backbench signatories of the round-robin. The grim realities of the sterling crisis have convinced the great majority of MPs that it is impossible to do anything further. . . .

December 3, 1964

The dying spasm of the Labour Party's pensions revolt is expected to take place in public today when the House of Commons debates a Liberal Party amendment to advance the date of the Government's 12s 6d. a week increase in basic retirement pensions from March 29 to January 1.

A group of Labour MPs, who led the behind-the-scenes demand for an earlier increase in pensions, now intend to make their point public from the Government back benches during the committee stage of the National Insurance Bill.

Their decision is certain to shock Right-wing Labour MPs. Many Left-wing MPs who sympathise with the pensions revolt were alarmed last night when they heard that the dispute would be carried into the Chamber of the Commons.

Leaders of the pensions rebellion declared privately that "many" Labour backbenchers intend to speak during the debate. Their basic argument is expected to be that it is not yet too late for the Government to change its mind about the timing of the pensions increases.

Mr John Mendelson and Mr Ian Mikardo are certain to join the debate if they catch the Speaker's eye. But all the evidence last night was that they are counting on the Liberal Party to withdraw its official amendment to the National Insurance Bill, thus relieving them of the embarrassment of entering the division lobbies against the Government.

But their action in bringing the rebellion into the full limelight of a parliamentary debate has not won the support of all the Labour MPs who originally joined in the pensions revolt. A number of backbenchers made it clear last night that they dissociate themselves from the plan and had no intention of forcing the rebellion into the open. They are worried about the consequences of continuing the dispute in private, let alone continuing it in public. And some of them are asking whether the hard core rebels really want to see Mr Wilson continue as Prime Minister.

[*Several Labour members did speak in the debate, and the Liberals did not withdraw their amendment. But it was defeated easily on a voice vote. In the end, the pension increases were not paid till the prearranged date.*]

Suggestions for Reading

British Politics

Any number of textbook expositions of British politics can be referred to. One of the best is Harry Eckstein's in *Patterns of Government* edited by Samuel H. Beer and Adam B. Ulam, second edition (New York: Random House, 1962). No student should overlook Professor Beer's *British Politics in the Collectivist Age*, a thoughtful essay on parties and pressure groups in the British setting (New York: Alfred A. Knopf, 1965).

For a more "behaviorist" interpretation, see Richard Rose, *Politics in England* (Boston: Little, Brown and Company, 1964). Jean Blondel in *Voters, Parties, and Leaders* (Baltimore: Penguin Books, 1963) introduces much new material into a discussion of the social fabric of British politics; he concludes with an analysis of the idea of an "establishment."

Much the fullest general bibliography on British politics is that compiled by Colin Seymour-Ure and included in R. H. S. Crossman's edition of Walter Bagehot, *The English Constitution* (London: C. A. Watts & Co., 1964). Dr. Rose's book also contains a large number of useful references.

Citizens and Electors

Apart from studies of voting behavior, little work has been published on political participation in Britain. For a discussion of popular attitudes towards politics in Britain and other countries, see *The Civic Culture* by Gabriel A. Almond and Sidney Verba (Princeton: Princeton University Press, 1963). Among the many voting behavior studies available, probably the best is R. S. Milne and H. C. Mackenzie, *Straight Fight* (London: Hansard Society, 1964). David Butler and Donald E. Stokes are currently (1966) preparing a nationwide study of voters' attitudes and behavior. Also of interest is John Bonham, *The Middle Class Vote* (London: Faber and Faber, 1954).

Grassroots

The centralization of British politics has led political scientists to neglect the study of local parties. A. H. Birch, *Small-Town Politics* (New York: Oxford University Press, 1959) was until recently the only work in its field. It has now been joined by Frank Bealey, J. Blondel, and W. P. McCann, *Constituency Politics, a Study of Newcastle-under-Lyme*, which is concerned with parties and voters in a middle-size industrial city (London: Faber and Faber, 1965). The major work on candidate selection is Austin Ranney, *Pathways to Parliament* (Madison and Milwaukee: University of Wisconsin Press, 1965).

Attitudes and Ideologies

The literature on party principles and policies in Britain is vast. Professor Beer's book, referred to above, is probably the best introduction. Anyone can profit from browsing in the annual conference reports of the two major parties.

For a full statement of the moderate position in the Labour Party, see C. A. R. Crosland, *The Future of Socialism* (London: Jonathan Cape, 1956). Ralph Miliband's *Parliamentary Socialism* (London: George Allen & Unwin, 1961) is harshly critical of the Labour establishment. Some of the most wayward and stimulating contributions to Labour's perennial controversies are to be found in *Planning for Freedom* by R. H. S. Crossman (London: Hamish Hamilton, 1965).

Conservatives, being less ideologically inclined than socialists, have produced rather less doctrinal literature. Quintin Hogg's *The Conservative Case* (Baltimore: Penguin Books, 1959) has a certain flavor. A number of Conservatives were driven into print by the party's defeat at the hands of Labour in 1964. For the views of a man on the "radical right" (to the extent that there is such a thing in Britain), see *A Nation Not Afraid: the Thinking of Enoch Powell*, ed. John Wood (London: Batsford, 1965).

The fullest exposition of contemporary Liberalism is to be found in Jo Grimond's *The Liberal Challenge* (London: Hollis & Carter, 1963).

Followers and Leaders

The standard work remains R. T. McKenzie's *British Political Parties*, second revised edition (New York: Praeger, 1964). See also I. Bulmer-Thomas, *The Party System in Great Britain* (London: Phoenix House, 1953). Comments on the "McKenzie thesis" are to be found scattered throughout the British press and in almost every general work on British politics. For two different types of criticism, see Saul Rose's article (selection no. 14 above) and Anthony King's review in the *American Political Science Review* for September 1964, vol. LVIII, no. 3. On the Liberals, see Jorgen Scott Rasmussen, *Retrenchment and Revival, A Study of the Contemporary Liberal Party* (Phoenix: University of Arizona Press, 1964).

Elections and Electioneering

Nuffield College, Oxford, sponsors a descriptive account of each British general election as it occurs. The two most recent are D. E. Butler and Richard Rose, *The British General Election of 1959* (New York: St. Martin's Press, 1960), and D. E. Butler and Anthony King, *The British General Election of 1964* (New York: St. Martin's Press, 1965). For a lucid and concise introduction to British electoral politics, see R. L. Leonard's *Guide to the General Election* (London: Pan Books, 1964).

Pressure Politics

A dry but highly competent introduction to the subject is J. D. Stewart, *British Pressure Groups* (New York: Oxford University Press, 1958). S. E. Finer in *Anonymous Empire* (London: Pall Mall, 1958) is more argumentative and outspoken. Among the many excellent case studies of British pressure groups, three by Americans are particularly recommended: H. H. Wilson, *Pressure Group, the Campaign for Commercial Television* (London: Martin Secker & Warburg, 1961); Harry Eckstein, *Pressure Group Politics, the Case of the British Medical Association* (Stanford: Stanford University Press, 1960); and James B. Christoph, *Capital Punishment and British Politics* (London: George Allen & Unwin, 1962).

Members of Parliament

The standard work by a constitutional lawyer is Sir Ivor Jennings, *Parliament*, second edition (New York: Cambridge University Press, 1957). A useful introduction is Roland Young's *The British Parliament* (London: Faber and Faber, 1962). Peter G. Richard's *Honourable Members*, second edition (London, Faber and Faber, 1964) is indispensable but suffers from being based largely on written sources.

The whole of Nigel Nicolson's *People and Parliament* (London: Weidenfeld &

Nicolson, 1958) is worth reading. A pioneering study of M.P.s' attitudes is S. E. Finer, H. B. Berrington, and D. J. Bartholomew, *Backbench Opinion in the House of Commons 1955–59* (New York: Pergamon Press, 1961). Hansard, the official report of parliamentary debates, should of course be dipped into by anyone wanting to become familiar with the manners and customs of the House of Commons.

Memoirs and Biographies

One of the best ways into another country's politics is almost always through the reminiscences and biographies of its politicians. The more interesting recent British examples include: Dudley Smith, *Harold Wilson* (London: Robert Hale, 1964); Lord Kilmuir (Sir David Maxwell-Fyfe), *Political Adventure* (London: Weidenfeld & Nicolson, 1964); Reginald Bevins, *The Greasy Pole* (London: Hodder & Stoughton, 1965); and Hugh Dalton, *Memoirs*, 3 vols., (London: Frederick Muller, 1953, 1957, 1962).

Documentary Appendix

The following four documents embody the main rules governing the Conservative and Labour parties at the national level. The Conservative Party lacks a formal constitution, but its structure is set out informally in an official booklet entitled *The Party Organisation*. The Party's new rules for electing its leader were promulgated in a press release in February 1965. The Labour Party's constitution is still basically that of 1918, although it has frequently been amended. The Parliamentary Labour Party also amends (or even abolishes) its standing orders fairly frequently. Those published here are the most recent and were adopted in 1961. To elect a leader of the Parliamentary Labour Party, successive ballots are held until one candidate secures an absolute majority of the votes cast. On all aspects of British party organisation, see R. T. McKenzie's *British Political Parties*.

CONSERVATIVE PARTY ORGANIZATION

THE PARLIAMENTARY PARTY

The Parliamentary Party is composed of all Members of Parliament who take the Conservative Whip, thereby signifying their acceptance of the policy of the Party as declared by the Leader. The management of the Party in the House of Commons rests with the Chief Whip who is appointed by the Leader of the Party.

There is a regular weekly meeting of the Party in the Conservative Members' Committee which is commonly known as the "1922 Committee." The Chairman is a prominent back bench Member. He is elected by the Committee together with a small Executive Committee. Four members of this Executive Committee sit on the Executive Committee of the National Union, and all Conservative Members of Parliament are members of the Central Council. The 1922 Committee selects each year five of its members to sit on the Advisory Committee on Policy. When the Party is in Opposition, meetings of the

1922 Committee are attended by front and back bench Members alike; when the Party is in office, meetings are attended by back bench Members only but Ministers attend from time to time by invitation.

The Parliamentary Party has a number of committees each of which deals with a specific subject, e.g., Defence, Foreign Affairs, Commonwealth Affairs, Finance, Trade and Industry, Agriculture, etc., and which discuss the forthcoming business of the House. The committees are served by the Conservative Research Department. When the Party is in Opposition, the committees are attended by both front and back bench Members, the Chairman of each committee normally being a front bench Member appointed by the Leader of the Party. In Opposition, the principal officers of all committees meet regularly in the Business Committee to advise the Leader of the Party on matters affecting the conduct of Parliamentary business. When

From Conservative and Unionist Central Office: *The Party Organisation* (revised August 1964), chapters 2, 3, 4, 5 and 6. Certain minor deletions have been made.

the Party is in office, membership of the committees is confined to back bench Members, who elect their own Chairmen. The appropriate Ministers attend from time to time by arrangement. In office, Parliamentary business is a matter for the Cabinet.

Conservative Peers in receipt of the Party Whip who desire to be members of the Central Council of the National Union have to make application annually. One Peer is appointed to sit on the Executive Committee, and two to sit on the Advisory Committee on Policy.

THE NATIONAL UNION

The National Union of Conservative and Unionist Associations, usually known as "The National Union," is the federation to which are affiliated constituency associations and central associations of boroughs with two or more constituency associations throughout England, Wales and Northern Ireland. It is established on a representative and democratic basis, and by a chain of constituency, area and national councils and conferences is enabled to bring all sections of the organisation into direct touch with the Leader of the Party.

The functions of the National Union are:

(1) To promote the formation and development of a Conservative and Unionist Association in every constituency in England, Wales and Northern Ireland, and to foster thought and effort in furtherance of the principles and aims of the Party.

(2) To form a centre of united action, and to act as a link between the Leader and all organisations of the Party in England, Wales and Northern Ireland.

(3) To maintain close relationship with the Conservative and Unionist Central Office.

(4) To work in close co-operation with the Scottish Unionist Association and the Ulster Unionist Council.

PARTY CONFERENCE

The Annual Party Conference is organised by the National Union. It is held at various important centres in England and Wales, and consists of members of the Central

Council and two additional representatives of each constituency association, together with certificated agents.

The Conference reviews the work of the year as submitted in a report presented by the Executive Committee.

Motions on matters of organisation and policy are submitted in the names of the Executive Committee, General Purposes Committee, National Advisory Committees of the Executive Committee, Area Councils, constituency associations and central associations of boroughs with two or more constituency associations. The decisions arrived at are conveyed to the Leader of the Party.

CENTRAL COUNCIL

The governing body of the National Union is the Central Council, which includes:

The Leader of the Party and other principal officers and officials of the Party.

Five representatives from each constituency association, with representation from central associations of boroughs with two or more constituency associations, and from Provincial Area councils and their advisory committees.

Members of the Houses of Parliament in receipt of the Party Whip; prospective candidates (approved by the Standing Advisory Committee on Candidates and officially selected by a constituency association).

The Scottish Unionist Association and the Ulster Unionist Council are also entitled to representation.

The Central Council is constituted annually, and elects a President, a Chairman and three Vice-Chairmen of the National Union.

The Central Council meets in London, and at each meeting considers a report from the Executive Committee. It also considers such motions as have been submitted by area councils, constituency associations and central associations of boroughs with two or more constituency associations and the decisions arrived at are conveyed to the Leader of the Party.

The Central Council has power to make such amendments to the rules of the National Union as may be found necessary.

EXECUTIVE COMMITTEE

The Executive Committee is constituted annually and includes:

The Leader of the Party and the principal officers and officials of the Party.

Six representatives from each Area Council, namely, the Area Chairman, the Area Treasurer, the Chairman of the Area Women's Advisory Committee, a Young Conservative, a Trade Unionist, and one elected representative. The Areas containing more than 30 constituencies have additional representation.

The Scottish Unionist Association and the Ulster Unionist Council are also entitled to representation.

The Committee elects its own Chairman by ballot, and appoints an Honorary Secretary and Secretary of the National Union.

Meetings of the Executive Committee are usually held every other month. Matters of general political and party importance are dealt with.

The Committee exercises the powers of approval and the withdrawal of such approval in relation to membership of the National Union and gives decisions upon or takes such steps as it shall think fit to bring about a settlement of any dispute or difference submitted by the Executive Council of a Constituency Association (being a Member of the National Union) after the officers of the appropriate Provincial Area shall have failed to bring about a settlement acceptable to all parties to the dispute or difference.

Schemes and proposals by the Central Office for the furtherance and welfare of the Party are placed before the Committee for its consideration.

The Committee has power to set up such Advisory Committees as it considers necessary.

GENERAL PURPOSES COMMITTEE

The General Purposes Committee is constituted annually and includes: the principal officers and officials of the Party; the Chairman of each Area Council; twelve members (3 men, 3 women, 3 Young Conservatives and 3 Trade Unionists), elected by the Executive Committee.

The Chairman of the Executive Committee is Chairman of the Committee.

The Committee meets monthly and has authority to perform all ordinary and emergency acts on behalf of the National Union except those reserved to the Executive Committee.

It considers the reports of the National Advisory Committees, and resolutions passed by Area Councils, and by Central and Constituency Associations.

Its other duties are to prepare the agenda for the Annual Party Conference and for Central Council meetings, and to consider and report on any matter referred to it.

WOMEN'S NATIONAL ADVISORY COMMITTEE

This is an Advisory Committee of the Executive Committee, and its functions are to advise the Executive Committee on all questions affecting the organisation of women supporters of the Party, and the subjects in which they are especially interested. Under its auspices a Women's Conference and Mass Meeting are held annually in London, which are attended by representatives of affiliated constituency associations in England and Wales and by representatives from Scotland and Northern Ireland.

The Committee also forms a link between the centre and the Area Women's Advisory Committees.

YOUNG CONSERVATIVE AND UNIONIST NATIONAL ADVISORY COMMITTEE

The Young Conservative National Advisory Committee promotes and co-ordinates political activity among young Conservatives and advises the Executive Committee about the affairs which affect them.

TRADE UNIONISTS' NATIONAL ADVISORY COMMITTEE

The Trade Unionists' National Advisory Committee advises the Executive Committee on matters relating to Trade Unionism and industrial problems generally.

ADVISORY COMMITTEE ON LOCAL GOVERNMENT

The Advisory Committee on Local Government advises the Executive Committee on local government problems and on new and impending legislation.

NATIONAL ADVISORY COMMITTEE ON POLITICAL EDUCATION

The National Advisory Committee on Political Education consists of the Chairmen of the Area Education Committees and nominees of the Executive Committee, with power to co-opt. It maintains liaison between the National Union and the political education movement of the Party.

ADVISORY COMMITTEE ON PUBLICITY AND SPEAKERS

This is a committee appointed by the Executive Committee, whose meetings are attended by representatives of the departments concerned. It is a means of bringing up for discussion constructive suggestions and criticisms for improving the helpfulness of the work of these departments in Central Office.

OTHER ADVISORY COMMITTEES

In addition, the following committees have been approved as advisory committees of the Executive Committee:

National Advisory Committee of the Conservative and Unionist Teachers' Association.

National Advisory Committee of the Federation of University Conservative and Unionist Associations (Undergraduates).

The National Advisory Committee of the Conservative and Unionist Teachers' Association advises the Executive Committee on problems relating to education and the teaching profession and coordinates the activities of Area Advisory Committees.

The National Advisory Committee of the Federation of University Conservative and Unionist Associations (Undergraduates) fosters the development of Conservative and Unionist Associations among University students and co-ordinates their activities.

OTHER CENTRAL COMMITTEES AND BOARDS

In addition to the Committees described in the previous Chapter there are six other Central Committees or Boards which occupy an important place within the framework of the Party Organisation. They are (1) the Advisory Committee on Policy; (2) the Consultative Committee on Party Finance; (3) the Central Board of Finance; (4) the Standing Advisory Committee on Parliamentary Candidates; (5) the Examination Board; and (6) the Superannuation Fund.

THE ADVISORY COMMITTEE ON POLICY

The Advisory Committee on Policy consists of a Chairman and Deputy Chairman, appointed by the Leader of the Party, and of 15 others, seven to consist of Members of both Houses of Parliament (five selected by the Conservative Members Committee and two selected by Conservative Peers) and eight selected by the Executive Committee of the National Union from its own members, one of these eight to be a Young Conservative.

The Committee has power to co-opt up to 4 members and to appoint Sub-Committees. The Conservative Research Department places all its resources at the Committee's disposal.

The Committee is responsible to the Leader of the Party.

THE CONSULTATIVE COMMITTEE
ON PARTY FINANCE

This Committee consists of the Treasurer of each Area (with the respective Chairman as alternate) one representative (with an alternate) of the Executive Committee of the Conservative and Unionist Members' Committee, one representative of the Conservative and Unionist Peers, the Chairman of the Executive Committee of the National Union, the Chairman of the Party Organisation and the Treasurers of the Party, with power to co-opt not more than three persons.

The Chairman of the Party Organisation is ex-officio Chairman and the Treasurers are deputy Chairmen of the Committee.

The function of the Committee is to receive information and to assist the Treasurers of the Party by giving advice and information.

THE CENTRAL BOARD OF FINANCE

In order to meet post-war needs, a Central Board of Finance was set up to raise money for the funds of the Party.

This Board is responsible to the Chairman of the Party organisation and carries out its work throughout England and Wales by means of representatives in each of the Provincial Areas. The task of these representatives is to raise for the Party money which would not normally be obtained by or go to the constituencies. They work in co-operation with Area and Constituency officials.

The Board now consists of the Party Treasurers, the Area Treasurers (with the respective Area Chairmen as alternates) and up to a maximum of five co-opted members. The Board has power to elect its own Chairman from the whole body of members.

THE STANDING ADVISORY COMMITTEE
ON CANDIDATES

This Committee was set up by the Central Council of the National Union in 1935. Its purpose is to assess on broadest grounds the suitability of men and women who wish to become approved Candidates for Parliament. A list of approved Candidates, together with brief biographies, is sent on request to constituency associations which are selecting a prospective Candidate. When one of these approved Candidates is subsequently adopted by a constituency association, he or she becomes an official Conservative prospective Candidate.

The Committee consists of the following: The Chairman of the Central Council of the National Union, the Chairman of the Executive Committee of the National Union, the Chairman of the Women's National Advisory Committee, the Chairman of the Young Conservative National Advisory Committee, the Chairman of the Trade Unionists' National Advisory Committee, the Chairman of the Party Organisation, the Chief Whip of the Party in the House of Commons and the Honorary Secretary of the National Union. . . .

THE CENTRAL OFFICE

The Conservative and Unionist Central Office is the headquarters of the Party Organisation. It is charged by the Leader of the Party with the responsibility of seeing that the organisation throughout the country is efficient, making known the policy of the Party, and conveying to him from time to time the feeling in the constituencies. It works in close co-operation with the National Union, with which there is a constant interchange of information.

The rôle of the Central Office is to guide, inspire and co-ordinate the work of the Party throughout the country, to advise and assist constituency associations and area councils and to provide such services as can best be organised centrally.

The officers of Central Office who are appointed by the Leader of the Party are:

The Chairman;
The Deputy Chairman;
The Vice-Chairman;
The Hon. Treasurers.

The Deputy Chairman and Vice-Chairmen assist the Chairman generally in interviews and supervision of the various Party activities and one of them is responsible for all questions of Parliamentary candidature.

The Honorary Treasurers are responsible for the finances of the Party.

The General Director is the principal official in charge of the Central Office, responsible to the Chairman for the general organisation of the Party.

CENTRAL OFFICE
DEPARTMENTAL ORGANISATION

The principal spheres of activity of the Central Office and its officials may be grouped under the following headings:

Constituency Organisation and Finance

The Organisation Department, controlled by the Chief Organisation Officer, gives advice on all matters appertaining to constituency Organisation, and the closest contact is maintained, through the Central Office Agents, with constituency officers and agents.

Advice is available for constituency officials on raising money and improving the financial position in a constituency.

Arrangements are made for the training of men and women to be constituency agents and of women organisers, and assistance is given to them in securing posts with constituency associations.

The Organisation Department also gives advice on registration and election law in connection with both Parliamentary and Local Government elections.

The department is responsible for the production of the Organisation series of booklets, for the Parliamentary Election Manual, and for the Guide to Local Government Elections.

Publicity and Propaganda

A group of departments controlled by the Chief Publicity Officer is responsible for all aspects of the Party's publicity, Press and public relations, and (with certain exceptions) for Party literature.

It is responsible for co-ordinating publicity campaigns on a national scale, making use of the Press, radio, television, films, posters, public meetings, and special literature. It also provides a complete service of articles, cartoons, etc., for constituency magazines and biographical information and photographs of Conservative personalities.

The Radio and Television Department is equipped with a studio for training broadcasters on sound radio and television. Recording machines are available for the rehearsal and timing of scripts.

These services are at the disposal of constituency organisations in connection with any of these activities, and Area Publicity Officers responsible to the Chief Publicity Officer have been appointed to assist in this work.

The Press Department maintains close relations with national, provincial and local newspapers, technical and other periodicals and the Empire and overseas Press. It issues the texts of speeches made by members of the Party both in the Houses of Parliament and in the country and frequent Press communiqués about all aspects of the Party's work.

The Production Department prepares and

produces a literature service consisting both of regular periodicals and of a great variety of posters and pamphlets both of topical and of long-term interest.

Speakers

Conservative members in both Houses of Parliament find it convenient to leave their speaking engagements in the hands of the Speakers' Department. Lecturers for political education purposes and voluntary and paid speakers for propaganda meetings are obtained by application through the Central Office Agents. The Information for Speakers' Service provides a regular supply of literature of special use for speakers. Tutors are available to conduct the training of speakers to supplement the Central, Area and Constituency Panels, and to instruct in chairmanship and business procedure. Speaking Competitions are held, culminating in a National Competition. A special week-end course for speakers is also held each year at Swinton.

Industrial Problems

The Industrial Department keeps a close watch on political developments in the Trade Unions and Co-operative Societies. It devotes special attention to the organisation of Councils of Trade Unionists and to industrial and social problems as they affect the wage-earner.

Local Government

This department assists Associations and Conservative members of local councils on all questions connected with local government.

It co-ordinates Party activities in connection with local government elections.

Young Conservative Organisation

Advice is given on the formation and development of branches of the Young Conservative Organisation in constituencies.

Young Conservative organisers are available to assist Associations. Application for their services should be made to the Central Office Agent concerned.

Young Britons Organisation

Advice can be obtained on the formation and development of Young Britons Branches in the constituencies.

Conservative and Unionist Teachers' Association; Federation of University Conservative and Unionist Associations

This department deals with the organisation of Conservative Teachers and Conservative Graduates and Undergraduates at the various Universities and Colleges in the country.

THE CONSERVATIVE POLITICAL CENTRE

The Conservative Political Centre is the headquarters of the political education movement of the Party. Its aims are: to encourage people to think about and to discuss politics; to develop understanding of topical and long-term issues; to secure a wider and deeper knowledge of Conservative principles; and to stimulate and give currency to new ideas within the Party.

The C.P.C. organises national functions such as the Annual Summer School, the C.P.C. meetings held during the Party Conference and the Central Council meeting, and special briefing conferences and meetings. An outstanding feature of its work is the Two Way Movement of Ideas between the Centre and informal discussion groups throughout the country. Two-Way Topics and Ten Minute Topics are published each month and the reports of discussion groups are collated and presented to the Chairman of the Party and members of the Government concerned with the subject of the Topic.

C.P.C. publications include discussion booklets on topical subjects, objective research studies on important political problems and contributions to the formulation of new thought and policy.

The C.P.C. membership scheme provides the means whereby those wishing to keep abreast of political developments receive C.P.C. publications and news of C.P.C. meetings and activities.

The Political Education officers are the representatives of the C.P.C. in the Areas. . . .

CONSERVATIVE RESEARCH DEPARTMENT

The Conservative Research Department in its present form is the result of the amalgamation in 1948 of the then existing Research Department, the Parliamentary Secretariat, and the Library and Information Department of the Conservative Central Office. Although, strictly speaking, it is not a Department of the Central Office, it comes within the framework of Party Headquarters.

It is presided over by a Chairman who is appointed by the Leader of the Party and is responsible to him. The chief executive is the Director, who also acts as Secretary to the Advisory Committee on Policy with which the Department works in close association.

The Department contains Research, Economic, Home Affairs, Foreign, Commonwealth and Defence Sections. It is also responsible for the Party's Reference Library and for a Press Cuttings Section.

The functions of the Department may be described as follows:

(a) To undertake long-term research and to assist in the formulation of Party policy.

(b) To provide official secretaries for the Parliamentary Committees of the Party and to prepare briefs on issues coming before Parliament.

(c) To provide Members, Candidates, speakers and all Party workers with information and guidance on current political affairs.

(d) To assist all departments of the Central Office with factual information. . . .

PROCEDURE FOR THE SELECTION OF THE LEADER OF THE CONSERVATIVE AND UNIONIST PARTY

1. There shall be a ballot of the Party in the House of Commons.

2. The Chairman of the 1922 Committee will be responsible for the conduct of the ballot and will settle all matters in relation thereto.

NOMINATIONS AND PREPARATION OF THE BALLOT

3. Candidates will be proposed and seconded in writing. The Chairman of the 1922 Committee and a body of scrutineers designated by him will be available to receive nominations. Each candidate will indicate on the nomination paper that he is prepared to accept nomination, and no candidate will accept more than one nomination. The names of the proposer and seconder will not be published and will remain confidential to the scrutineers. Nominations will close twenty-four hours before the first and second ballots. Valid nominations will be published.

4. The scrutineers will prepare a ballot paper listing the names of the candidates and give a copy to each voter at a meeting

---

Promulgated by the Leader of the Conservative and Unionist Party, Sir Alec Douglas-Home, on February 25, 1965.

called by the Chairman of the 1922 Committee for the purpose of balloting and consisting of all Members of the House of Commons in receipt of the Conservative and National Liberal Whips.

FIRST BALLOT

5. For the first ballot each voter will indicate one choice from the candidates listed, and hand the ballot paper to the scrutineers who will count the votes.

6. If as a result of this ballot one candidate *both (i)* receives an overall majority *and (ii)* receives 15 per cent more of the votes cast than any other candidate, he will be elected.

7. The scrutineers will announce the number of votes received by each candidate, and if no candidate satisfies these conditions a second ballot will be held.

SECOND BALLOT

8. The second ballot will be held not less than two days and not more than four days after the first ballot, excluding Saturdays and Sundays. Nominations made for the first ballot will be void and new nominations, under the same procedure as for the first ballot, will be submitted for the original candidates if required and for any other candidate.

9. The voting procedure for the second ballot will be the same as for the first, save that paragraph 6 above shall not apply.

If as a result of this second ballot one candidate receives an overall majority he will be elected.

THIRD BALLOT

10. If no candidate receives an overall majority, the three candidates receiving the highest number of votes at the second ballot will be placed on a ballot paper for a third and final ballot.

11. For the final ballot each voter must indicate two preferences amongst the three candidates by placing the figure "1" opposite the name of his preferred candidate and the figure "2" opposite the name of his second choice.

12. The scrutineers will proceed to add the number of first preference votes received by each candidate, eliminate the candidate with the lowest number of first preference votes and redistribute the votes of those giving him as their first preference amongst the two remaining candidates in accordance with their second preference. The result of this final count will be an overall majority for one candidate, and he will be elected.

PARTY MEETING

13. The candidate thus elected by the Commons Party will be presented for election as Party Leader to the Party Meeting constituted as at present.

CONSTITUTION AND STANDING ORDERS OF THE LABOUR PARTY

CLAUSE I — NAME

The Labour Party.

CLAUSE II — MEMBERSHIP

(1) There shall be two classes of members, namely:

(a) Affiliated Members.

(b) Individual Members.

(2) Affiliated Members shall consist of:

(*a*) Trade Unions affiliated to the Trades Union Congress or recognised by the General Council of the Trades Union Congress as *bona fide* Trade Unions.

(*b*) Co-operative Societies.

(*c*) Socialist Societies.

(*d*) Professional Organisations which, in

As amended by the Annual Conference in Brighton, 1962.

the opinion of the National Executive Committee, have interests consistent with those of other affiliated organisations.

(e) Constituency Labour Parties and Central Labour Parties in Divided Boroughs.

(f) County or Area Federations of Constituency Labour Parties, hereinafter referred to as Federations.

(3) Political organisations not affiliated to or associated under a National Agreement with the Party on January 1, 1946, having their own Programme, Principles and Policy for distinctive and separate propaganda, or prossessing Branches in the Constituencies or engaged in the promotion of Parliamentary or Local Government Candidatures, or owing allegiance to any political organisation situated abroad, shall be ineligible for affiliation to the Party.

(4) Individual Members shall be persons of not less than fifteen years of age who subscribe to the conditions of membership, provided they are not members of Political Parties or organisations ancillary or subsidiary thereto declared by the Annual Conference of the Labour Party (hereinafter referred to as "the Party") or by the National Executive Committee in pursuance of Conference decisions to be ineligible for affiliation to the Party.

(5) British citizens temporarily resident abroad may become Individual Members, or retain such membership of the Party, by enrolment with the Head Office provided they accept the conditions of membership in Clause III.

CLAUSE III — CONDITIONS OF MEMBERSHIP

(1) Each affiliated organisation must:

(a) Accept the Programme, Principles, and Policy of the Party.

(b) Agree to conform to the Constitution and Standing Orders of the Party.

(c) Submit its Political Rules to the National Executive Committee.

(2) Each Constituency Labour Party, Central Labour Party, and Federation must, in addition to the conditions mentioned in Section 1 of this Clause, adopt the Rules laid down by the Party Conference.

(3) Each Individual Member must

(a) Accept and conform to the Constitution, Programme, Principles and Policy of the Party.

(b) If eligible, be a member of a Trade Union affiliated to the Trades Union Congress or recognised by the General Council of the Trades Union Congress as a *bona fide* Trade Union.

(c) Unless temporarily resident abroad, be a member of a Constituency Labour Party, either (i) where he or she resides, or (ii) where he or she is registered as a Parliamentary or Local Government elector.

CLAUSE IV — PARTY OBJECTS

National

(1) To organise and maintain in Parliament and in the country a Political Labour Party.

(2) To co-operate with the General Council of the Trades Union Congress, or other Kindred Organisations, in joint political or other action in harmony with the Party Constitution and Standing Orders.

(3) To give effect as far as may be practicable to the principles from time to time approved by the Party Conference.

(4) To secure for the workers by hand or by brain the full fruits of their industry and the most equitable distribution thereof that may be possible upon the basis of the common ownership of the means of production, distribution, and exchange, and the best obtainable system of popular administration and control of each industry or service.

(5) Generally to promote the Political, Social and Economic Emancipation of the People, and more particularly of those who depend directly upon their own exertions by hand or by brain for the means of life.

Inter-Commonwealth

(6) To co-operate with the Labour and Socialist organisations in the Commonwealth Overseas with a view to promoting the purposes of the Party, and to take com-

mon action for the promotion of a higher standard of social and economic life for the working population of the respective countries.

International

(7) To co-operate with the Labour and Socialist organisations in other countries and to support the United Nations Organisation and its various agencies and other international organisations for the promotion of peace, the adjustment and settlement of international disputes by conciliation or judicial arbitration, the establishment and defence of human rights, and the improvement of the social and economic standards and conditions of work of the people of the world.

CLAUSE V — PARTY PROGRAMME

(1) The Party Conference shall decide from time to time what specific proposals of legislative, financial or administrative reform shall be included in the Party Programme.

No proposal shall be included in the Party Programme unless it has been adopted by the Party Conference by a majority of not less than two-thirds of the votes recorded on a card vote.

(2) The National Executive Committee and the Parliamentary Committee of the Parliamentary Labour Party shall decide which items from the Party Programme shall be included in the Manifesto which shall be issued by the National Executive Committee prior to every General Election. The Joint Meeting of the two Committees shall also define the attitude of the Party to the principal issues raised by the Election which are not covered by the Manifesto.

CLAUSE VI — THE PARTY CONFERENCE

(1) The work of the Party shall be under the direction and control of the Party Conference, which shall itself be subject to the Constitution and Standing Orders of the Party. The Party Conference shall meet regularly once in every year and also at such other times as it may be convened by the National Executive Committee.

(2) The Party Conference shall be constituted as follows:

(*a*) Delegates duly appointed by each affiliated Trade Union or other organisations to the number of one delegate for each 5,000 members or part thereof on whom affiliation fees and by-election insurance premiums were paid for the year ending December 31 preceding the Conference.

(*b*) Delegates duly appointed by Constituency Labour Parties (or Trades Councils acting as such) to the number of one delegate for each 5,000 individual members or part thereof on whom affiliation fees and by-election insurance premiums were paid for the year ending December 31 preceding the Conference; where the individual and affiliated women's membership exceeds 2,500 an additional woman delegate may be appointed; where the membership of Young Socialist Branches within a constituency is 200 or more an additional Young Socialist delegate may be appointed.

(*c*) Delegates duly appointed by Central Labour Parties or Trades Councils acting as such in Divided Boroughs not exceeding one for each Central Labour Party provided the affiliation fees and by-election insurance premiums have been paid for the year ending December 31 preceding the Conference.

(*d*) Delegates duly appointed by Federations not exceeding one for each Federation provided the affiliation fees have been paid for the year ending December 31 preceding the Conference.

(*e*) *Ex-officio* Members of the Party Conference as follows:

(*i*) Members of the National Executive Committee.

(*ii*) Members of the Parliamentary Labour Party.

(*iii*) Parliamentary Labour Candidates whose candidatures have been duly endorsed by the National Executive Committee.

(*iv*) The Secretary of the Party.

Ex-officio Members shall have no voting power.

(*f*) Any special Party Conference shall be called on the same basis of representation as that upon which the last Annual Party Conference was convened.

(3) In the event of a duly appointed delegate being elected as Treasurer or as a member of the National Executive Committee, the Affiliated Organisation responsible for his or her appointment as a delegate may claim authority at subsequent Party Conferences during his or her period of Office, to appoint a delegate additional to the number applicable to it under paras. (*a*), (*b*) and (*c*) of Section 2 of this Clause, provided the delegate elected as Treasurer or as a member of the National Executive Committee:

(*i*) Remains qualified to be appointed as a delegate under Clause VII; and

(*ii*) Continues to be duly appointed as a delegate by the Affiliated Organisation claiming authority to appoint an additional delegate within the provisions of this Section.

CLAUSE VII — APPOINTMENT OF DELEGATES TO THE PARTY CONFERENCE

(1) Every Delegate must be an individual member of the Labour Party as described in Clause II, Section 4.

(2) Delegates must be *bona fide* members or paid permanent officials of the organisation appointing them, except in the case of Members of the Parliamentary Labour Party or duly-endorsed Parliamentary Labour Candidates appointed to represent Constituencies in accordance with Section 4 of this Clause.

(3) Delegates appointed by Federations or Central Labour Parties must be resident within the area of the organisation concerned or be registered therein as Parliamentary or Local Government electors.

(4) Members of the Parliamentary Labour Party and duly-endorsed Parliamentary Labour Candidates may be appointed as Delegates by Constituency Labour Parties

responsible for their candidatures; otherwise, Delegates appointed by Constituency Labour Parties must be resident in the Constituency appointing them, or registered as Parliamentary or Local Government electors therein.

(5) No person shall act as a Delegate for more than one organisation.

(6) No person shall act as a Delegate who does not pay the political levy of his or her Trade Union.

(7) Members of Parliament not members of the Parliamentary Labour Party are ineligible to act as Delegates.

(8) The following are also ineligible to act as Delegates:

(*a*) Persons acting as candidates or supporting candidates in opposition to duly-endorsed Labour Candidates.

(*b*) Persons who are members of political parties or organisations ancillary or subsidiary thereto declared by the Annual Party Conference or by the National Executive Committee in pursuance of the Conference decisions to be ineligible for affiliation to the Labour Party.

CLAUSE VIII — THE NATIONAL EXECUTIVE COMMITTEE

(1) There shall be a National Executive Committee of the Party consisting of 25 members and a Treasurer, elected by the Party Conference at its regular Annual Meeting in such proportion and under such conditions as may be set out in the Standing Orders for the time being in force. The Leader and Deputy Leader of the Parliamentary Labour Party shall be *ex-officio* members of the National Executive Committee. The National Executive Committee shall, subject to the control and directions of the Party Conference, be the Administrative Authority of the Party.

(2) The duties and powers of the National Executive Committee shall include the following:

(*a*) To ensure the establishment of, and to keep in active operation, a Constituency Labour Party in every Constituency, a

Central Labour Party in every Divided Borough, and a Federation in every suitable area, in accordance with the Rules laid down by the Party Conference for the purpose.

(*b*) To enforce the Constitution, Standing Orders, and Rules of the Party and to take any action it deems necessary for such purpose, whether by way of disaffiliation of an organisation or expulsion of an individual, or otherwise. Any such action shall be reported to the next Annual Conference of the Party.

(*c*) To confer with the Parliamentary Labour Party at the opening of each Parliamentary Session, and at any other time when it or the Parliamentary Party may desire a conference on any matters relating to the work and progress of the Party.

(*d*) To see that all its Officers and members conform to the Constitution, Rules and Standing Orders of the Party.

(*e*) To present to the Annual Party Conference a Report covering the work and progress of the Party during its period of office, together with a Financial Statement and Accounts duly audited. The Report, Financial Statement and Accounts shall be sent to affiliated organisations at least two clear weeks before the opening of the Annual Party Conference.

(*f*) To propose to the Annual Party Conference such amendments to the Constitution, Rules and Standing Orders as may be deemed desirable and to submit to the Annual Party Conference or to any Special Party Conference, called in accordance with the Standing Orders, such resolutions and declarations affecting the Programme, Principles and Policy of the Party as in its view may be necessitated by political circumstances.

(*g*) To organise and maintain such fund or funds as may be thought necessary for any or all of the objects for which the Party exists, including a fund to finance Parliamentary by-elections and a fund established for the purpose of insuring against the forfeiture of Returning Officers' Deposits at every Parliamentary General Election.

(*h*) To secure advances from time to time or to raise loans, either on mortgage or otherwise and on such terms as it may deem expedient; to employ any part of the funds at its disposal in the purchase of any freehold or leasehold building or site and/or in the building, leasing, holding or rental of any premises and in the fitting-up and maintenance thereof; and to invest any moneys not immediately required in such securities as it may deem proper and to realise or to vary such investments from time to time and to appoint Trustees and/or form a Society, Association, Company or Companies in accordance with the provisions of the Friendly Societies Acts or the Companies Acts for any or all of the above purposes and to define the powers of such Trustees, Society, Association, Company or Companies and the manner in which such powers shall be exercised.

(*i*) To sanction, where local circumstances render it necessary, modifications in the rules laid down by the Annual Party Conference for the various classes of Party Organisations in the Constituencies and Regions, provided that such modifications comply with the spirit and intention of the Annual Party Conference and do not alter the objects, basis or conditions of affiliated and individual membership, vary the procedure for the selection of Parliamentary Candidates (except as provided in the rules) or effect a change in the relationship of Central Labour Parties or Constituency Labour Parties with the Labour Party.

(3) The decision of the National Executive Committee, subject to any modification by the Party Conference, as to the meaning and effect of any Rule or any part of this Constitution and Standing Orders, shall be final.

(4) The National Executive Committee shall have power to adjudicate in disputes that may arise between affiliated and other Party organisations, and in disputes which occur within the Party's Regional, Federation, or Constituency machinery, and its

decisions shall be binding on all organisations concerned.

CLAUSE IX — PARLIAMENTARY CANDIDATURES

(1) The National Executive Committee shall co-operate with the Constituency Labour Party for each Constituency in selecting a Labour Candidate for any Parliamentary Election.

(2) The selection of Labour Candidates for Parliamentary Elections shall be made in accordance with the procedure laid down by the Annual Party Conference in the Rules which apply to Constituency and Central Labour Parties.

(3) The selection of Labour Candidates for Parliamentary Elections shall not be regarded as completed until the name of the person selected has been placed before a meeting of the National Executive Committee, and his or her selection has been duly endorsed.

(4) No Parliamentary candidature shall be endorsed until the National Executive Committee has received an undertaking by one of its affiliated organisations (or is otherwise satisfied) that the election expenses of the Candidate are guaranteed.

(5) Labour Candidates for Parliamentary Elections duly endorsed by the National Executive Committee shall appear before the electors under the designation of "Labour Candidate" only. At any Parliamentary General Election they shall include in their Election Addresses and give prominence in their campaigns to the issues for that Election as defined by the National Executive Committee in its Manifesto.

(6) At a Parliamentary By-Election a duly-endorsed Labour Candidate shall submit his or her Election Address to the National Executive Committee for approval. The National Executive Committee, whenever it considers it necessary shall give advice and guidance on any special issue to be raised, or in the conduct of the Campaign during such By-Election.

(7) No person may be selected as a Parliamentary Labour Candidate by a Constituency Labour Party, and no Candidate may be endorsed by the National Executive Committee, if the person concerned:

(a) is not an Individual Member of the Party and, if eligible, is not a member of a Trade Union affiliated to the Trades Union Congress or recognised by the General Council of the Trades Union Congress as a *bona fide* Trade Union; or

(b) is a member of a Political Party or organisation ancillary or subsidiary thereto declared by the Annual Party Conference or by the National Executive Committee in pursuance of Conference decisions to be ineligible for affiliation to the Labour Party; or

(c) does not accept and conform to the Constitution, Programme, Principles, and Policy of the Party; or

(d) does not undertake to accept and act in harmony with the Standing Orders of the Parliamentary Labour Party.

(8) Any Candidate who, after election, fails to accept or act in harmony with the Standing Orders of the Parliamentary Labour Party shall be considered to have violated the terms of this Constitution.

CLAUSE X — AFFILIATION AND MEMBERSHIP FEES

(1) Each affiliated organisation (other than Federations, Constituency and Central Labour Parties) shall pay an affiliation fee of 1s. per member per annum to the Party.

(2) Each Constituency Labour Party shall pay an affiliation fee of 1s. per annum on each individual member attached to the Party directly or indirectly through its local Labour Parties, Polling District Committees, Ward Committees, and Women's Sections, subject to a minimum payment of £50 per annum.

(3) Each Central Labour Party shall pay an affiliation fee at the rate of £5 per annum for each Constituency Labour Party within the Divided Borough.

(4) Each county Federation shall pay affiliation fees in accordance with the following scale: —

		Per annum
Federations of 2, 3, or 4 Constituency or C.L.P.		£1 10s.
" 5 or 6 " "		£2 5s.
" " 7, 8 or 9 " "		£3
" " 10, 11, 12 or 13 " "		£4 10s.
" of over 13		£6 15s.

(5) Each Individual Member of the Party shall pay a minimum membership fee of 6d. monthly to the Party to which he or she is attached in the manner laid down in Constituency and Local Labour Party Rules except Old Age Pensioners who have retired from work and they shall be allowed Individual Membership of the Party on the minimum payment of 1s. per annum. These contributions shall be entered on membership cards supplied by the National Executive Committee to Constituency Parties at 1s. per card, which sum shall include the affiliation fee payable by such organisation to the Party in respect of such members.

CLAUSE XI — PARTY CONFERENCE ARRANGEMENTS COMMITTEE

(1) There shall be appointed in accordance with the Standing Orders at each Annual Party Conference a Party Conference Arrangements Committee of Five Delegates for the Annual Party Conference in the year succeeding its appointment, or for any Party Conference called during the intervening period. A member of the Head Office staff shall act as Secretary to the Committee.

(2) The duties of the Party Conference Arrangements Committee shall be:

(a) To arrange the order of the Party Conference Agenda.

(b) To act as a Standing Orders Committee.

(c) To appoint Scrutineers and Tellers for the Annual Party Conference from amongst the Delegates whose names have been received at the Head Office of the Party two clear weeks prior to the opening of the Conference and submit them for approval to the Conference. In the case of a Special Party Conference called under Clause VI, the National Executive Committee may appoint a date prior to which such names must be received.

CLAUSE XII — AUDITORS

There shall be appointed in accordance with the Standing Orders at each Annual Party Conference two delegates to act as Auditors of the Party Accounts to be submitted at the Annual Party Conference next succeeding that at which they are appointed.

CLAUSE XIII — ALTERATION TO CONSTITUTION AND RULES

The existing Constitution and Rules or any part thereof, may be amended, rescinded, altered or additions made thereto, by Resolution, carried on a card vote at an Annual Party Conference (in manner provided in the Standing Orders appended hereto) held in every third year following the year 1956, unless the National Executive Committee advises that amendments shall be specially considered at any Annual Party Conference. Notice of Resolutions embodying any such proposals must be sent in writing to the Secretary at the Offices of the Party as provided in Standing Orders.

CLAUSE XIV — STANDING ORDERS

The Standing Orders of the Party Conference shall be considered for all purposes as if they form part of this Constitution and shall have effect accordingly. New Standing Orders may be made when required, or the existing Standing Orders amended, rescinded, or altered by Resolution in the same manner as provided for alterations in the Constitution itself.

STANDING ORDERS

STANDING ORDER 1.
ANNUAL PARTY CONFERENCE

(1) The National Executive Committee shall convene the Annual Party Conference during October in each year, in accordance with the conditions laid down in the Constitution and these Standing Orders. It may also convene Special Sessions of the Party Conference when it deems necessary.

(2) When a Party Conference is called at short notice, the Secretaries of affiliated organisations shall, on receiving the summons, instantly take steps to secure representation of their organisations, in accordance with the Constitution and these Standing Orders.

(3) Any Session of the Party Conference summoned with less than ten days' notice shall confine its business strictly to that relating to the emergency giving rise to the Special Session.

(4) A delegation fee of £2 per Delegate shall be payable by affiliated organisations sending Delegates to the Party Conference. *Ex-officio* members of the Party Conference in attendance shall pay a fee of £2. Such fees must be paid to the Secretary of the Party before credentials are issued.

(5) To secure the publication for circulation to affiliated organisations of an Official List of Delegates attending the Annual Party Conference, the names and addresses of Delegates appointed by affiliated organisations must be sent to the Secretary not later than three clear weeks before the opening of the Annual Party Conference. In the case of a Special Conference called under Clause VI, the National Executive Committee may appoint a date prior to which such names and addresses shall be sent to the Secretary.

(6) The National Executive Committee shall make arrangements each year for the pooling of railway fares in respect of delegations appointed by Federations, Central Labour Parties, and Constituency Labour Parties.

STANDING ORDER 2. AGENDA

(1) Notice of Resolutions for the Annual Party Conference, not exceeding one resolution on one subject from any one affiliated organisation shall be sent in writing to the Secretary at the offices of the Party not later than twelve clear weeks before the opening of the Conference, for inclusion in the first Agenda, which shall be forthwith issued to the affiliated organisations. At any Annual Conference at which Amendments to the Constitution are to be considered each affiliated organisation may submit one Resolution in addition to a Resolution proposing to amend the Constitution. In the case of a Special Conference called under Clause VI, the National Executive Committee may appoint a date prior to which such notices shall be sent to the Secretary.

(2) Resolutions will be accepted only from those affiliated organisations which have paid affiliation fees in accordance with Clause VI, Section 2, paragraphs (*a*), (*b*), (*c*), (*d*), of the Constitution and Standing Orders and by-election insurance premiums for the preceding year, not later than twelve clear weeks before the opening of the Conference.

(3) Notice of amendments to the Resolutions in the First Agenda, not exceeding one amendment on one subject from any one affiliated organisation (consequential amendments to a main amendment shall not be counted), and nominations for the National Executive Committee, Treasurer, Auditors, and Party Conference Arrangements Committee, shall be forwarded in writing to the Secretary not later than six clear weeks before the opening of the Conference for inclusion in the Final Agenda of the Conference. In the case of a Special Conference called under Clause VI, the National Executive Committee may appoint a date prior to which such notices shall be forwarded to the Secretary.

(4) Amendments will be accepted only from those affiliated organisations which have paid affiliation fees in accordance with Clause VI, Section 2, paragraphs (*a*), (*b*), (*c*), (*d*), of the Constitution and Standing Orders and by-election insurance premiums for the preceding year, not later than six clear weeks before the opening of the Conference.

(5) No business which does not arise out of the Resolutions on the Agenda shall be considered by the Party Conference, unless recommended by the National Executive Committee or the Party Conference Arrangements Committee.

(6) When the Annual Party Conference has, by Resolution, made a declaration of a general Policy or Principle, no Resolution or Motion concerning such Policy or Principle shall appear on the Agenda for a period of three years from the time such declaration was made, except such Resolutions or Motions as are, in the opinion of the National Executive Committee, of immediate importance.

STANDING ORDER 3. VOTING

Voting at the Annual Party Conference shall be by cards on the following bases:

(*a*) National and Constituency Organisations: One voting card for each 1,000 members or part thereof on whom affiliation fees were paid for the year ending December 31 preceding the Conference.

(*b*) Federations and Central Labour Parties: One voting card each.

Voting at any Special Party Conference shall be on the same bases as those upon which voting took place at the preceding Annual Party Conference.

STANDING ORDER 4. ELECTION OF THE NATIONAL EXECUTIVE COMMITTEE

(1) For the purpose of nomination and election the National Executive Committee shall be divided into four Divisions:

Division 1 shall consist of twelve members, to be nominated by Trade Unions from among their duly appointed delegates, and elected by their delegations at the Annual Party Conference.

Division II shall consist of one member, to be nominated by Socialist, Co-operative, and Professional Organisations from among their duly appointed delegates, and elected by their delegations at the Annual Party Conference.

Division III shall consist of seven members, to be nominated by Federations, Constituency Labour Parties and Central Labour Parties, from among their duly appointed delegates, and elected by their delegations at the Annual Party Conference. A Constituency Labour Party may nominate its Member of Parliament, or duly endorsed Candidate attending the Conference as an *ex-officio* member.

Division IV shall consist of five women members, to be nominated by any affiliated organisation, and elected by the Annual Party Conference as a whole. A Constituency Labour Party may nominate its woman Member of Parliament or duly endorsed woman Candidate attending as an *ex-officio* member of Conference.

(2) The election for each Division shall be made by means of ballot vote on the card bases as provided in these Standing Orders.

(3) Nominations for the National Executive Committee shall be made in accordance with the following conditions:

(*a*) Except in the case of Members of Parliament and duly-endorsed Candidates representing Constituency Labour Parties, nominees must be *bona fide* paying members of the organisations submitting their nominations.

(*b*) Except where a Constituency Labour Party desires to nominate its Member of Parliament or its duly endorsed Candidate, the nominees of Federations, Constituency Labour Parties, and Central Labour Parties must either reside in or be registered as Parliamentary or Local Government Electors in the area of the Federation or Party submitting the nomination.

(*c*) Only persons appointed to attend the

Annual Party Conference as Delegates or, in the case of Division III and Division IV, Members of Parliament or duly-endorsed Candidates attending as *ex-officio* members of Conference shall be eligible for nomination for a seat on the National Executive Committee. Nominees who do not attend the Annual Party Conference shall be deemed to have withdrawn their nominations, unless they send to the Secretary, on or before the day on which the Conference opens, an explanation in writing of their absence, satisfactory to the Party Conference Arrangements Committee.

(*d*) Members of the General Council of the Trades Union Congress are not eligible for nomination to the National Executive Committee.

(*e*) Before sending in nominations affiliated organisations must secure the consent in writing of their nominees. Unless such consent is obtained and is attached to the nomination paper, nominations will be rendered null and void.

(*f*) Each affiliated organisation may make one nomination from among its duly appointed delegates, for its appropriate Division of the National Executive Committee. In the case of Division III a Constituency Labour Party may nominate its Member of Parliament or duly-endorsed Candidate attending as an *ex-officio* member of Conference. Where an affiliated organisation pays fees on 500,000 members or more it may make one additional nomination (either man or woman) for such Division.

(*g*) Each affiliated organisation may make one nomination for Division IV of the National Executive Committee.

(4) Any vacancy which occurs amongst members of the National Executive Committee between Annual Party Conferences shall be filled by that Committee by co-opting the highest unsuccessful nominee in the Division concerned, as shown in the results of the Election for the National Executive Committee at the Annual Party Conference immediately preceding the vacancy.

STANDING ORDER 5.
ELECTION OF OFFICERS

(1) The National Executive Committee shall elect its own Chairman and Vice-Chairman at its first meeting each year.

(2) The Treasurer shall be nominated and elected separately by the Annual Party Conference. Every affiliated organisation may nominate a person for Treasurer who is a duly-appointed Delegate to the Annual Party Conference, or a Member of Parliament or a duly-endorsed Candidate, attending Conference as an *ex-officio* member.

(3) The Secretary shall be elected by the Annual Party Conference, on the recommendation of the National Executive Committee, and be *ex officio* a member of the Conference. He shall devote his whole time to the work of the Party and shall not be eligible as a Candidate for or a Member of Parliament. He shall remain in office so long as his work gives satisfaction to the National Executive Committee and Party Conference. Should a vacancy in the office occur between two Annual Party Conferences the National Executive Committee shall have full power to fill the vacancy, subject to the approval of the Annual Party Conference next following.

(4) Every affiliated organisation may nominate one duly-appointed Delegate, or a Member of Parliament or duly-endorsed Candidate attending Conference as an *ex-officio* member, for a seat on the PartyConference Arrangements Committee, who, if elected, must be a Delegate to, or an *ex-officio* member of, any Party Conference held during his or her period of office. In the event of a member of the Party Conference Arrangements Committee being unable to fulfil his or her duties, the Delegate or *ex-officio* member, who received the highest number of votes amongst those not elected shall be called upon, but should the voting list be exhausted the affiliated organisation to which the elected Delegate, or *ex-officio* member, belonged shall nominate a substitute.

(5) Every affiliated organisation may

nominate one duly-appointed Delegate, or a Member of Parliament or duly-endorsed Candidate attending Conference as an *ex-officio* member, to act as Auditor. In the event of an Auditor being unable to perform the duties, the same procedure shall be followed as in the case of the Party Conference Arrangements Committee.

STANDING ORDER 6.
RESTRICTION OF NOMINATIONS

No Delegate shall be eligible for nomination to more than one position to be filled by election at any Annual Party Conference. In the event of any Delegate being nominated for more than one such position, the Delegate shall be requested to select the position for which he or she desires to remain nominated. After the selection has been made the Delegate's name shall be omitted from the nominations for all other positions. Should no selection of position be made not later than six clear weeks before the opening of the Conference, all nominations made on behalf of the Delegate shall become null and void.

STANDING ORDERS OF THE PARLIAMENTARY LABOUR PARTY

1. If the Party is to be an effective force politically, its activities must be co-ordinated and collective decisions taken. The privilege of membership of the Parliamentary Labour Party involves the acceptance of these decisions.

2. The Party recognises the right of Members to abstain from voting in the House on matters of deeply-held personal conscientious conviction, but this does not entitle Members to cast votes contrary to a decision of the Party Meeting.

3. It is the duty of the Parliamentary Committee to bring before the Party Meeting cases of serious or persistent failure by Members to act in harmony with the Parliamentary Labour Party, including a bad record of attendance in the Division Lobbies.

4. The Parliamentary Party has the right to withdraw the Whip on account of things said or done by Members of the Party in the House. The Member or Members concerned shall have the right to be heard at the Party Meeting before the Whip is withdrawn.

5. The National Executive Committee shall be informed of any decision to withdraw the Whip.

6. In appropriate cases the Parliamentary Party may recommend to the Party Meeting that the Member or Members concerned shall be reported to the National Executive Committee. The Member or Members concerned shall have the right to be heard by the Parliamentary Committee and by the Parliamentary Party.

7. For the purpose of securing concerted action in the House, Members shall consult the Officers of the Parliamentary Party before tabling any Motion, Amendment or Prayer. The tabling of such Motion, Amendment or Prayer shall be delayed for one sitting day should the Officers so request. Where the Officers are unable to give approval to the tabling of any Motion, Amendment or Prayer, this must be made known by the sponsor or sponsors to such other Members as may be approached in seeking support of the Notice of Motion.

8. Minutes of meetings of the Parliamentary Labour Party shall be kept and shall be available for inspection on application to the Secretary of the Parliamentary Labour Party.

9. These Standing Orders may be amended, rescinded, added to, suspended, or reinstated for such period and under such conditions as may be determined, after due notice, by a duly-constituted meeting of the Parliamentary Labour Party.

As adopted at a meeting of the Parliamentary Labour Party on December 13, 1961. From *Report of the Sixty-First Annual Conference of the Labour Party*, Brighton, 1962 (London, The Labour Party, 1963), p. 85.

STUDIES IN HISTORY AND POLITICS

A New Series of Readings
AMERICAN HISTORY · EUROPEAN HISTORY
AMERICAN POLITICS · COMPARATIVE POLITICS

Each volume combines four elements:

1. THEMATIC ORGANIZATION
   tracing the complete development of a major topic

2. PRIMARY MATERIALS
   enabling students to read and analyze source materials and essential documents

3. INTERPRETIVE ESSAYS
   acquainting students with fresh, provocative interpretations by leading specialists

4. EDITORIAL NARRATIVE
   introducing parts and selections, and providing continuity as the topic is developed